PEDIGREE OF

FLY
GYP
KIEN
VI
IMP
EVE
KY
POL
PEPPER
MIDGE
JACK
FOL
BABBLING BINKS
TUT TUT
CH BIFFIN OF BEAUFIN
LITTLE JANE
CH. FARNDON RED DOG
TINITT
TINY TIM OF BIFFIN
PINCHUS
NEACHLEY SOVEREIGN
MIDGE OF BOXTED
BINGO OF BOXTED
CH. MISS MANETTE P.E. MARCH 1934

JANE (I)
TRUMPINGTON TOWSER
JANE (II)
KIEN
GYP
CARR
SUSAN
TINY TIM OF BIFFIN
KNIPTON STRUMPY
COLONSAY ATTABOY
COLONSAY MOLLY
BARKIS P.E.
TATTY CORAM P.E.
RED PEPPER P.E. 14.11.34
QUARTZHILL SNIFF
TINY TIM OF BIFFIN
KNIPTON STUMPY
COLONSAY ATTABOY
COLONSAY MOLLY
CH. BIFFIN OF BEAUFIN
LITTLE JANE

JILL
CH BIFFIN OF BEAUFIN MAY 1932
LITTLE JANE
KNIPTON RUSTY P.E.
COLONSAY GLOOM CHASER 23.4.40
COLONSAY BLINK
ROGUE RIDERHOOD P.E.
QUARTZHILL SNEEZE P.E.
KNIPTON RUSTY P.E. 3.3.38
COLONSAY BLINK

DAWN OF CYNVAL
...STON ROGUE 29.2.36
...TANNER OF ...VENEY VALLEY
VALLEY
CONGHAM PENNY (IE)
LONGHAM WIGGIE
COLONSAY GLOOM CHASER
COLONSAY HUDSON
COLONSAY BIRD SEED
CH BIFFIN OF BEAUFIN

ELFE
COLONSAY DIMO
COLONSAY FLAMING ON
COLONSAY TINY TIM OF BIFFIN
KINMOUNT PIP
TINY TIM OF BIFFIN
LITTLE JANE

PIP
PID NOWNIK
KINMOUNT PIP
CH BIFFIN OF BEAUFIN
LITTLE JANE
KINMOUNT JACK
KINMOUNT DUMPTY
KIEN
GYP
CARR
SUSAN
KIEN
GYP

KINMOUNT JACK
KIEN
GYP
CARR
KIEN
GYP
SAM BROWNE NEACHLEY TOFFEE
AIRMANS SAM BROWNE
AIRMANS STORM
KY
POL
PEPPER
MIDGE
JACK
POL
TUT TUT
BABBLING BINKS
POL
KY
PEPPER
MIDGE
HORSTED M...
POL

CARR
SUSAN
TOODLUMS
TOO FRESH
HORSTED MICK
NIP
CH BIFFIN OF BEAUFIN
LITTLE JANE
HORSTED MICK
FLAME
CH. FARNDON RED DOG
JUDY
BABBLING BINKS
TEASEL OF BOXTED
BABBLING BINKS
TEASEL OF BOXTED P.E.
SMUDGE
PEGGOTTY
BURHILL SHADOW
BUNTY
KIEN
GYP
KIEN
GYP
SMUDGE
PEGGOTTY
CH BIFFIN OF BEAUFIN
NEACHLEY BRACKEN
CH FARNDON RED DOG
CHERRY PECKSNIFF 7.4.35
CH BIFFIN OF BEAUFIN
LITTLE JANE
CH. FARNDON RED DOG
TINITT
TINY TIM OF BIFFIN
PINCHUS
NEACHLEY SOVEREIGN
MIDGE OF BOXTED
KIEN
GYP
CARR
SUSAN
KIEN
GYP
AIRMANS STORM

HORSTED MICK
NEACHLEY RU...
TOODLUMS
TOO FRESH
SMUDGE
PEGGOTTY
KIEN
GYP
CARR
SUSAN
TOODLUMS
TOO FRESH
HORSTED MIC...
NIP
CH BIFFIN OF BE...
LITTLE JAN...
HORSTED MICK
FLAME
CH. FARNDON RED
JUDY
BABBLING BINKS
TEASEL OF BOXTED
KY
POL
PEPPER
MIDGE

BABBLING BINKS
TUT TUT
KY
POL
PEPPER
MIDGE
TOBIT
NEACHLEY TOFFEE
HORSTED MICK
TEMPEST
MUSTARD
PEN
KY
MUSTARD
JOSE
RUFUS
MIDGE
HORSTED
NEACHL...

The Norfolk Terrier

Figure 1:
Pioneer Norfolk Terrier breeder Marion Sheila Scott Macfie with her winning Colonsay Dalmations and Terriers. On her doorstep at Hobjoins in Stenying, Sussex, 1955. The terriers are Ch. Junior, Hop Out, Dyraaba Candy, Malum, Flip, Limbo, Maleesh, and Land Girl. *Photo Spencer Lane.*

The Norfolk Terrier

Joan R. Read

Nat R. LaMar, Editor

First Edition, 1989

This book was prepared for publication by
RIEnterprises, Livermore, California
Graphic Designer, Kristen Salcedo

FRONT COVER : Castle Point Norfolks
BACK COVER: Ratting in Oyster Bay
INSIDE COVERS: Pedigree courtesy of Eileen Needham

Library of Congress Cataloging in Publication Data
Read, Joan R.
    The Norfolk Terrier
    Includes index.
    1. Dogs   2. Terriers   I. Title
        636.7
    Summary: History, breeding, training, and showing
                of Norfolk Terriers.
ISBN 0-9623261-0-0

First Edition

DEDICATION

To Norfolk Terriers everywhere—past, present, and future—and to the friendships they have forged throughout the world.

FOREWORD

The aim of this book is to share a collection of Norfolk data, photographs, drawings, and thoughts with others who love the breed. Recognizing the need for specific Norfolk Terrier information, fellow Norfolk owner Nat La-Mar volunteered his professional expertise as editor in 1986. More than a routine assignment, the book's organization from outline to completion reflects Nat's tenacity, involvement, and inestimable assistance with its three year production.

We both feel most fortunate that Marianne Foote accepted the challenge of designing, publishing, and distributing this book. Those who read these pages will soon realize the scope of other volunteers whose names appear in text or photography. A special thanks goes to Tom Horner for letting us share some of his thoughts on structure, breeding, and showing; to Sally Anne Thompson and Constance S. Larrabee for their photographs and historic material; to Renee Sporre Willis for her conformation drawings; and to George Bragaw, consultant. Special manuscript aid was received from Sheila Foran, Eileen Murphy, Linda Plummer, Mickey Presnikoff, Susan Stedman and Melanie Wallwork. I regret any oversights in the corps of contributors, kennel reports and captions and trust they will be forgiven.

Most of all I salute my daughter Bee whose artwork, time, care, and love of our dogs made my efforts a reality.

Joan Redmond Read, Collector, Author

CONTENTS

Figure 2:
First American champion, Merry of Beaufin, sired by Ch. Biffin of Beaufin, the first English champion. *Painting by Edwin Megargee.*

				Mustard
			Ky	Bustle
		Kien		Ky
			Pol	Pen
	SIRE: Ch. Biffin of Beaufin			Mustard
			Pepper	Jose
		Gyp		Unkown
			Midge	Unkown
CH. MERRY OF BEAUFIN, August 1935				Pepper
			Crumpet	Dorcas
		Babbling Binks		Norrie
			Jumble	Wich
	DAM: Susan			Jack
			Norrie	Nettle
		Tut Tut		Jack
			Wich	Nell

WHY NORFOLK?

A wise breeder once said: "Norwich say, 'Look, what I've done,' while Norfolk think, 'What shall I do?' "

Although Norfolk and Norwich Terriers share the same ancestry, there has been little interbreeding of ear types since ring competition resumed after World War II. Despite their similar Standards, 40 years and more of selective breeding have subtly differentiated the shape and character of the Norfolk from the Norwich since 1932, when Norwich Terriers received breed recognition in England. Even then, most of the pendant (drop ear or D.E.) and erect ear (prick ear or P.E.) devotees were divided into separate camps. This rift deepened after the War, with the determined Miss Marion Sheila Scott Macfie leading the charge for the drop ear cause. Convinced the more prevalent drop ears were the original breed, "Mac" did not like seeing them defeated in the show ring.

During the 1930s, six Norwich Terriers became champions—three of each ear type. Yet the decade following the War found the prick ears winning most of the honors in both England and America. This caused further tension, as the breed clubs in both countries were dominated by drop ear enthusiasts. At that time the prick ear winners led in showmanship, eyes, bites, and presentation, although it was generally conceded the drop ears excelled in coats, toplines, and movement.

Pedigrees reveal that drop ears have a broader base through a variety of lines back to Ch. Biffin of Beaufin, while the prick ear gene pool appears more limited. Informing a canine columnist about the breed's origins in 1936, the first English Norwich Terrier Club secretary wrote:

There is what might be called a different branch but with the same root bred in the Midlands. These are

9

Figure 3:
Print from *Studies
of Animals in Four
Crayons by Charles
R. Havell, 1876.*

longer on the leg having less weight for size, usually with dropped ears and without the true Norwich coat and foxy, keen expression so typical of the dogs bred in Norfolk.

Two decades later Leo Wilson, a noted judge, observed:

If it were merely a matter of ear carriage there would be no difficulty, but the variations of type between the two varieties is most marked.

In America the terrier authority William Ross Proctor

suggested separate classes for each ear type in 1962; and this division was used in American Club sponsored shows and matches until 1979.

Though the breed Standards were changed twice in the U.K. and six times in the United States before separation, this tinkering failed to produce an equalizing effect among show winners. In the end it was Miss M.S.S. Macfie's perseverance that finally achieved Norfolk recognition. After repeated refusals to divide Norwich Terriers into two varieties, the English Kennel Club agreed to separate breed names and Standards. On October 4, 1964, an emergency meeting of the Norwich Terrier Club was held for the "creation of the Norfolk Terrier." A club was then formed, and Miss Macfie was elected its first lifetime president.

That year F. Warner Hill wrote:

> In 1932 The Kennel Club recognized . . . the Norwich Terrier including . . . the type we now call Norfolk as an integral part. Naming of breeds by town, county or area has long been maintained. The Norwich has a prick ear, foxy face, and rather short body on general working terrier lines. The Norfolk, a drop ear, squarish muzzle and longer body. Why should they be split over such a simple thing as ear carriage? Actually, there have always been two breeds, perhaps the original mistake was classifying them as one.

Fifteen years after separation of Norwich and Norfolk in England, the American Kennel Club finally recognized the Norfolk Terrier and transferred all Norwich Terrier drop ears to the new breed stud book. Unlike England, where each breed has its own active parent club, a series of artful maneuvers here allowed the Norwich and Norfolk Terrier Club in America to cling tenaciously to both breeds. (This misguided precedent was later used to continue both Wire and Smooth Fox Terriers under one parent club after these were split into two breeds by the American Kennel Club in 1986.)

In 1979 the American Norfolk Terrier Association (ANTA) was formed exclusively for Norfolk breeders and fanciers, reaching its members through its own quarterly publication, *ANTIC (American Norfolk Terrier Information Circular)*. Today ANTA schedules grooming and Obedience clinics, provides educational tapes, holds matches and sporting competitions, and rewards Norfolk breeders' achievements. With separate membership from the parent club in half the states and six foreign countries, the universal appeal of this group is enthusiastically recognized. The purpose of ANTA is to recognize, develop, and promote the unique characteristics of the Norfolk Terrier and to put aside forever that misguided old saw: "The only difference between the breeds is ears."

Vive la Différence!

Ear carriage is not the only breed difference between the Norfolk and the Norwich. Norfolk have small eye rims, while Norwich appear to wear mascara. Norfolk have more generous feet, better rear angulation in stifle and hock, and tend to have flatter muscles on shoulders and hindquarters. In outline, though similar to the Norfolk, the Norwich is broader, usually shorter in neck and coupling, and lower to the ground. In general, Norfolk are angular, Norwich more round. Norfolk go through more changes while growing and are generally slower to mature, but are precocious leg lifters.

Norfolk are more apt to suffer from jealousy than Norwich, and they frequently become hunting or racing addicts with great powers of concentration. Norwich adapt more easily to urban life, preferring the company of humans over other dogs. Norfolk are more "back to nature," easier to breed, and more independent. Norfolk tails quiver; Norwich tails wag. Norfolk can have high, squeaky barks, overbites that correct, and early tooth loss—all rare in Norwich. In the show ring a Norwich defies you to put him down, while a Norfolk says, "Please put me up!"

Figure 4:
Int. Nordic Ch. Guestlings Catch A Star by Ch. Nanfan Category x Ch. Redriff Rambling Rose.
Photo Susann Bjorkfall.

Figure 5:
Castle Point Styx.
Photo Dickson Green.

Figure 6:
Ch. Chidley Dandelion.
Photo © Sally Ann Thompson.

Figure 7:
**Historical print,
circa 1850.**

1

HISTORICAL PERSPECTIVE: ENGLAND

EARLY TERRIERS

Terriers have been known in England since the Norman Conquest. The English writer Sir Joycelyn Lucas, in **Hunt and Working Terriers,** points out that two small dogs, apparently terriers, are depicted in the Bayeux Tapestry running with the hounds in King Harold's hawking party. Dame Juliana Berners in the fifteenth century includes "terroures" in her catalogue of sporting dogs. In the sixteenth century Dr. Caius mentions terriers for their value in running to ground fox and badger.

By the last half of the seventeenth century terriers had evolved into what could be considered two distinct types: straight-limbed and shaggy-coated; and crooked-legged, generally with smooth coats. By the late nineteenth century terriers used for fox hunting are described as predominantly either wire-haired and white with spots and long legs, or black and tan with smooth coats and short-legged. By then, many an English or Irish squire and huntsman living on estates where there were foxes to be caught or otters to be killed would nurture a particular strain of terrier, developing a type that was kept pure. This, of course, contributed to the wide variety of terrier breeds that subsequently came into being.

Many of today's well-known terriers were virtually unknown as recently as a hundred years ago. Among these are the Irish, Scottish, West Highland, Cairn, Sealyham, and Border. Yorkshire Terriers, originally a broken-coated ratting breed, fared somewhat better in recognition. They were brought to Yorkshire by Scottish weavers in the mid-1800s and were first shown in England in 1861. But just as well-known "modern" terriers grew in number and popularity, so some older varieties, once valued for their working qualities, either continued in obscurity or vanished. No longer found are some of the tough little "hard-bitten earth dogs" once bred in Suffolk, Norfolk, or Shropshire. Gone, too, are the sandy-colored terriers of Lancashire and Cheshire that closely resembled the modern Irish Terrier.

Fortunately, through careful selection under astute modern breeders, many of those inherent qualities that so distinguished the original strains have been preserved and even intensified in some modern breeds.

NORWICH ORIGINS IN ENGLAND

Cantab Terriers: Charles "Doggy" Lawrence

In the 1880s owning a small ratting terrier became a fad among undergraduates at Cambridge University. Dog dealers of this period are described as scruffily dressed individuals who led small curs about the streets on large ropes. Of one, R. C. Lehmann wrote: "Everybody knew him, nobody believed him yet his margin of profit must have been considerable, but his dinginess never altered nor did his general disreputability decrease."

The most famous dog man of the day was Charles "Doggy" Lawrence of nearby Chesterton, who bred terriers, horses, and game fowl. Said to use small Irish, Yorkshire, and native East Anglian red terriers ("gypsy dogs"), Lawrence developed his so-called Cantabs as student companions and ratters. These small terriers were able to survive on meager fare and offered good sport in the local pits behind many country public houses.

There are various conjectures regarding the ingredients of the Cantab strain. According to one theory small red terriers accompanied Irish gypsies, who were said to spend part of each year in or around Norfolk. An observer described these short-legged terriers as "devils to poach."

Joy Taylor of the Nanfan prefix believes Ballybrick Terriers may have been used in the breed's development. This strain of working fox bolters was bred by a

Colonel Vaughn, an elderly relative of Joy Taylor's father who lived in County Wicklow. The Colonel kept his own pack of hounds, and his terriers were described as very small and red, with drop ears and crooked legs. Colonel Vaughn never parted with a bitch, but after his death his terriers went to relatives, including one near Chesterton.

Trumpington Terriers: E. Jodrell Hopkins

Upon graduation from Cambridge in 1899, E. Jodrell Hopkins remained in the town to open a livery stable on Trumpington Street. Following Charles "Doggy" Lawrence's example, Hopkins also kept stable terriers, and eventually his particular strain was dubbed "Trumpington." These dogs became popular in Norwich and Leicestershire before Hopkins moved to Newmarket.

Jodrell Hopkins originally crossed a dark brindle Aberdeen-type Scottish Terrier bitch he inherited from a South African war recruit with a longer, red, harsh-coated Cantab Terrier. This produced the dominant

Figure 8: The Trumpington Terrier Jack from Doggy Lawrence's stock.

red, rough-coated dog, Rags, and a darker small bitch, Nell, whom Hopkins kept. Rags, a prick ear, went to J. E. Cooke, master of the Norwich staghounds, who owned a crop-eared black terrier bitch from Ireland. Cooke bred Rags to a wide variety of sporting terriers, and all the puppies were red.

While a branch of Trumpingtons was developing in the Norwich area, Hopkins purchased Jack, a cropped, sandy, bandy-legged sire, who produced amenable red or grizzle ratters from Nell and her dam. (The dam, said to be "death on poultry," was passed on to another home.)

In Market Harborough, John Henry Stokes was an early admirer of Trumpingtons and also kept stable ratters. Stokes was a reputable horse dealer who hired out mounts for foreign fox hunters and also developed steeplechasers.

Another early owner of Trumpingtons was the local feed man, W. E. West, whose love of working terriers for more than 30 years was rewarded when his first bench champion, Farndon Red Dog, a registered Norwich of Trumpington-Jones ancestry, gained both his fox-bolting badge (MFH certificate) and a Crufts CC in 1937.

Figure 9:
Trumpington
Dorcas.

Norwich Terriers:
Frank "Roughrider" Jones

Frank Jones, tall, strong, and personable, came from County Wicklow, Ireland, with a pair of "fiery red-coated mites" and a reputation as "a great horseman over country." Jones later gained fame schooling "green" horses with the Fernie, Pytchley, and Quorn foxhound packs in Leicestershire, thus earning the title "Roughrider." His first position, however, was as whip to the Norwich staghounds in 1901. He was 25 when he went to work for the pack's master, J. E. Cooke, and was said to be "the best horseman in Norfolk who spoke his mind and ruled his field."

Although it was once held that Frank Jones's original pair of terriers were of the Glen of Imaal breed, it now seems more likely they were miniature Irish Terriers or a local strain of cottagers' watchdogs. The Glen of Imaals were described as a larger, soft-coated breed on short legs, more like a 35-pound Sealyham (three times a Norfolk's weight), with wheaten or blue soft coats, aggressive ways, and rose ears.

Certainly Frank Jones, "the perfect horseman," unwittingly played a major part in the development of Norwich Terriers both in England and America. It was his proximity to Trumpingtons that provided his start in dog breeding. Later his renown as a horse breaker gave his stable ratters their lasting exposure.

When Jones arrived at J. E. Cooke's Brooke Lodge, Rags, the Trumpington owned by Jodrell Hopkins, was already a popular sire. Besides being mated to his owner's Irish bitch, Rags was used on locally owned terriers belonging to Cole, Cooke's stud groom; R. J. Read, the Horstead miller; and Lewis "Podge" Low, the son of a popular Norwich veterinarian. The famous artist A. E. Munnings describes the elder Low as a hospitable "father" whose hearth was always open to horsemen. Podge's popular red (and occasionally black and tan) puppies were pets among the local horsemen.

In time J. E. Cooke proved an overly demanding employer to Frank Jones, and the gregarious Whip soon tired of his master's tongue. In those days horses and hounds went by train to and from meets, and accommodating farmhouses provided an important part of the day's sport:

Figure 10:
Lewis "Podge"
Low and the
terrier type he
established.

On another occasion at a Meet we were inside a hospitable farmhouse. Decanters of port, sherry and other glittering cheerful-looking bottles and concoctions stood in close assembly with the cold eatables on shining tables; all were busy—talking, sipping—eating; Jones, looking spruce in his scarlet, talking to a group. Suddenly the Master came up and said to him, 'Get out to the stables and horses, where your place is,' and Jones went. Said Jones, later, as we galloped, 'Sure, and it is a great man, and maybe he is right—but one day when he cusses me, I'll get off my horse, let him go, fling my red coat on the ground and walk off.'

Jones made good his word and moved to J. H. Stokes's in Market Harborough for the remainder of his long life. He took credit for naming the Norwich breed, for when asked what he called his pack of little terriers, having just left Norwich, he called them after that town. In the United States these dogs were called "Jones Terriers" after the Roughrider.

From the time Frank Jones moved to Market Harborough, he often brought in terrier litters, first by Rags, to supply the demand for his ratters. He liked his puppies small, keen, prick-eared, and whole-colored: red or black and tan, without white marks on their heads, limbs, or back. World War I greatly depleted Jones's supply of dogs, although he continued breeding. (Once he tried docking and cropping a litter of Border Terriers, but the results proved disappointing.)

By 1930 there was a nucleus of Norwich Terrier owners attempting to gain Kennel Club recognition for the breed. Jones detested this idea and so referred overseas clients to hunt-terrier breeders in Ireland to discourage the movement. When Roughrider Jones attended a show in 1956, he pronounced the breed changed. His own dogs had been not much bigger than Yorkshire Terriers, and he did not care for the "improvements." His happiest memories were horse-related, and included schooling the Duke of Windsor over fences, "lifting a pint" with the artist Sir Alfred Munnings, and caring for Lady Zia Werner's Brown Jack, the greatest "chaser of them all."

Figure 11:
Frank Jones and
his terriers from
An Artist's Life
by Sir Alfred
Munnings.

BREED RECOGNITION

By 1932, through the efforts of the Cairn fancier Mrs. D. Normandy-Rodwell, a loyal but diverse group of 13 Norwich Terrier owners formed the first Norwich Terrier Club. From the beginning there were difficulties, due particularly to individual preferences for color and ears. Ear cropping had been outlawed by the Kennel Club in 1898, but Doggy Lawrence, E. J. Hopkins, and Roughrider Jones continued to crop some of their unregistered, Norwich-related terrier breeds, claiming this was done not for appearance, but to prevent ears from being torn. Practical motives notwithstanding, it seems more likely that ear cropping was an attempt to bridge diversities in ear shape, carriage, and size that both Norwich and Norfolk inherit to this day. In August 1932 the Kennel Club chairman, Mr. A. Croxton Smith, noted that "ear carriage will probably offer more difficulties, for both erect and pendant ears are appearing." Another breeder, Colonel Gell, concurred that "in this vascillating ear regulation, the Norwich Terrier Club is laying up for itself, trouble in the future."

The first Norwich Terrier Club president, and one of its founders, R. J. "Jack" Read of Hapton Hall, Norwich, held as his ideal his own red prick-eared Norwich, the famous Horstead Mick. The latter was the product of various crossbreedings begun with a Rags bitch bought by Read from Podge Low and including a blue Bedlington, a miniature brindle Staffordshire Bull Terrier, and "Alysham," a red terrier named for the market town where he had been found. Jack Read proved a difficult and outspoken Club president who refused to include black and tan and drop-eared Norwich in the draft of the first breed standard. Similarly Mrs. Normandy-Rodwell, the Club's first secretary, felt these terriers should be exclusively "brilliant orange" in color, and furthermore believed only prick ears should be recognized. Read, however, conceded that although he would put down a black and tan, no Norwich should be put down for having "white on its chest."

R. J. Read resigned as Norwich Terrier Club president when the first breed standard was approved in 1935, because in spite of his opposition it included both the black and tan color and pendant ears. His prick ear, Horstead Mick, was the only Norwich Read ever exhibited. His wife, however, continued with terriers and exhibited her Horstead drop ears locally until

Figure 12: Believed to be one of Podge Low's terriers, 1912.

Figure 13: Horstead Mick.

World War II. In time, nevertheless, Horstead Mick proved a progenitor of Norfolk as well as Norwich, and in 1937 his granddaughter, Tinker Bell, became the first champion drop-eared bitch.

DROP EAR NORWICH: THE FOUNDING CHAMPIONS

Ch. Biffin of Beaufin

From the time he was at Cambridge in the late 1880s, Colonel C. Richard Hoare was never without a terrier. Colonel and Mrs. Hoare lived in London, but their dogs killed over 40 rabbits in Scotland during one summer's vacation. One of the Colonel's pets even aided his efforts to destroy old moorhens' nests by swimming out and sitting on them until they sank, while another of their dogs learned to point grouse. Mrs. Hoare claimed her dogs could run all day with horses and were wonderful in London traffic.

Hoare's first terriers had come from Charles "Doggy" Lawrence, who was very elderly when Hoare returned to Cambridge in 1905 in search of another dog. Referred through E. Jodrell Hopkins, Hoare located a puppy in Norwich, bred by Podge Low. The heritage of this dog is unknown. What is known is that young Low had saved a Dandie Dinmont–Fox Terrier mix brought to his veterinarian father to be put down. He named this bat-eared, leggy white dog Ninety and bred her to Jack Cooke's prepotent sire, Rags, thus starting a substrain of Trumpington Terriers which, judging from photos, were both red and black and tan with dropped ears. From this beginning Colonel Hoare developed a line of small, red Norwich that led to the breed's first champion, Biffin of Beaufin, whelped in 1932. Behind Biffin were other Jones-bred dogs owned by a Mrs. Moyses in Cornwall and a Mrs. Beington of Lincolnshire, as well as Midge, Biffin's mysterious, or unregistered, granddam.

Biffin won his championship in 1935, only three years after breed recognition. Like many famous forerunners, he was the subject of controversy. This was due mainly to the carriage of his ears, which no matter how they may appear in various photographs, were neither perfectly dropped nor perfectly erect. This ambiguity notwithstanding, Norwich drop ear breeders from the beginning claimed Biffin as their own; and Mrs. Evelyn Mainwaring, Biffin's enthusiastic exhibitor, preferring drop ears, used weights to train his ears down. As influential as Biffin was in drop ear lineage, his litter sister, Peggoty, a prick ear, was of equal importance in the ancestry of all champion Norwich of today.

Biffin of Beaufin's many prizes included Best of Breed at Crufts in 1933, and at the Kensington Canine Association's Championship Show in April 1934. He is described as "good headed with dark eyes, pronounced stop and hard, wiry, close-lying coat of rich red. He was short-backed, and heavy boned [but] lacked rear angulation." His two most influential sons were Miss M. S. S. Macfie's drop ear, Tiny Tim of Biffin, and a Mr. West's prick ear, Red Pepper. At the death of his owner, Mrs. Evelyn Mainwaring, Biffin of Beaufin joined the Neachley Kennel of Mrs. A. E. Gell.

Figure 14: Ch. Biffin of Beaufin.

Tobit and Ch. Tinker Bell

Mrs. Guy Blewitt, a founding member of the Norwich Terrier Club from Colchester, owned a wonderful stud, Tobit, bred by a local gardener named Ross. This game and typey dog, who earned an MFH certificate for badger, had a hard, rich coat and straight, strong bones, and weighed 12 pounds. Tobit's pedigree was short, since Midge, his dam, was of unknown lineage and Rufus, his sire, by Pepper x Bustle, was from what was referred to simply as "Trumpington stock."

At home Tobit's constant companion was Neachley Toffee, a bitch who came to the Blewitts from Mrs. A. E. Gell, whose working show dogs often attended the Albrighton Hunt meets, "ready to play their part should 'Charles James' elect to take refuge underground." Toffee, by Horstead Mick, was described as a "quick, small, game, and hard red prick ear." Toffee's dam, Neachley Rusty, was the Neachley Kennel matron, "a short com-

Figure 15:
(Left) **Tobit.**

Figure 16:
(Right) **Ch. Tinker Bell.**

pact little bitch with a dense, harsh, fox red coat, dead game and willing to tackle anything at any time." Her ears were semidropped, though most of this kennel's stock was prick-eared.

In 1933 Mrs. Blewitt bred the drop-eared champion, Tinker Bell, whelped that July by Tobit x Neachley Toffee in their first litter. One of Tinker Bell's distinctions is that she figures prominently in the ancestry of both Ch. Waveney Valley Alder and Ch. Gotoground Widgeon Bunny through their respective dams. Besides Tinker Bell, Tobit and Toffee produced: Trump of Boxted in 1937, Josephine Spencer's first American stud; Tinker of Boxted, a black and tan; Airman's Sam Brown; and many other drop-eared ambassadors. Mrs. Blewitt reported that Toffee would never settle down for whelping until Tobit was beside her; but it was Tobit and his daughter Tinker Bell who, by Mrs. Blewitt's account, were most famous as a ratting pair:

> We used to do a lot of ratting, especially at threshing time. Tobit was mad keen, he always climbed up the ladder onto the stack. On one occasion he and Tinker Bell killed 80 big River Rats in one bean stack with the help of two pups.

Ch. Airman's Brown Smudge

A third drop ear Norwich champion made up prior to World War II was Airman's Brown Smudge, bred by Mrs. D. Normandy-Rodwell, the Norwich Terrier Club's founding secretary. Mrs. Rodwell, who originally recognized as the only "true" Norwich those with red ("brilliant orange") coats and prick ears, broadened her earlier views to produce this winner. By breeding Airman's Brown Betty (a CC winner herself), a drop-eared red daughter of Tobit's, to a black and tan prick ear, Smudge, Mrs. Rodwell proved her change of heart regarding color and ear carriage. Her own 1934 advertisement confirms this new tendency towards drop ears:

> This kennel [Airman's] is famous for having dogs of perfect ear carriage whether dropped or prick, though the latter have pride of place.

The prominence of Ch. Airman's Brown Smudge in Norfolk history must be shared with his already mentioned sire, Smudge, bred and co-owned by Mrs. Algernon Cox and Mrs. Phyllis Fagan of Windsor. The latter's first Norwich had come from Jones-bred dogs in 1912, while Mrs. Cox's introduction to the breed had occurred much earlier through her husband's Cantab connections. Mrs. Fagan's foundation dam was Brownie, an extraordinary little bitch. Brownie was the product of a breeding between Sir Robin and Lady Juliet Duff's red dog, Schnapps, a London-based, Jones-bred terrier, and another Jones-bred bitch, Flossie, who belonged to a Captain Belville. According to reliable anecdote, Schnapps was allowed to travel to Windsor for his union with Flossie, and he evidently enjoyed his visit so much that after being returned to Brook Street, London, he was missed the next day and found at Paddington Station looking for the next train back to Windsor! At any rate,

Figure 17: (Left) Ch. Airman's Brown Smudge.

Figure 18: (Right) Smudge.

Brownie, the product of the Schnapps/Flossie breeding was also a distant descendant of Jack Cooke's prepotent Rags, and she ultimately proved a winning ratter and a great little gun dog. Reputedly she would point pheasant and partridge, and would always find wounded or dead birds and retrieve them. Mrs. Algernon Cox reported that with Brownie as their cornerstone dam, and through carefully controlled breedings to a limited number of "true-bred" sires, the black and tan and red lines that she and Mrs. Fagan cultivated were maintained "pure," with no extraneous outcrossings over the course of 20 years.

The Cox/Fagan criteria for ears and color were clearly stated in various *Our Dog* columns of 1936 by Mrs. Cox, who declared that "the black and tan colour is as natural to the breed as the red" and "in our opinion, the original ear was probably a drop-ear (such as Wirehaired Terriers) . . . and we, personally, much prefer a neat drop-ear to the large erect ear. . . ."

NORWICH DROP EAR:
THE NORFOLK CORNERSTONES

Colonsay 1933-1965

Over the course of 30 dedicated years Marion Sheila Scott Macfie led Norwich drop ears from obscurity to their separate and distinct identity as Norfolk Terriers. Her first efforts to promote the breed through its ratting abilities possibly proved its lifeline. During World War II she placed her Colonsay stock on the vast working farms of East Anglia and exported at least two pairs of her Norwich, selected by Percy Roberts for his American clients.

Figure 19:
Tiny Tim of
Beaufin, 1938.

After the War, the Macfie Colonsays went to every show that their owner attended along with her winning team of Dalmatians. Competing in variety classes, the Colonsay drop ear Norwich slowly became known in the canine world and new breeders were to be found increasingly among their admirers.

Sheila Macfie had been reared by her widowed father, a competitive horseman for whom she was hostess-housekeeper. Being a Macfie

and the last of her clan was a position she willingly accepted. She wore the family tartan proudly, disdaining those who sported any plaid without the lineage to back it up. Her father had early instilled in her a love of animals, and she had already been a successful exhibitor of ponies before turning to dogs.

Norwich Terriers D.E. entered Sheila Macfie's life in 1933, when five-month-old Tiny Tim of Beaufin joined the Dalmations at Colonsay. Sheila—"Mac" to her friends —was convinced from her first association with the breed that they must be small, red, hard-coated, and carry their ears down. When black and tans appeared in litters at Colonsay they were given the kennel prefix but never retained for breeding, as this recessive color was believed by Miss Macfie to be linked to full, soft, and

Figure 20: Miss Marion Sheila Macfie with her last two champions, Colonsay Orderley Dog and Banston Belinda, WELKS, 1964. *Photo © Constance S. Larrabee.*

fluffy coats. Colonsay dogs were uniquely named (e.g., "Put A Sock In It"; "Ak Dum"; "Nose Well Down") for characters and expressions from a World War I humor book.

Sheila Macfie inaugurated the first breed handbook on Norwich in 1953. She always supported the Club newsletter and constantly provoked various breeders with her disparaging remarks about prick ears and show presentation. She judged the American Norwich Terrier Club Specialty in 1955 with a record entry of 63 exhibits, which went unbroken for many years. Putting up prick ears, including a black and tan Winners Dog, surprised all the drop ear exhibitors. The Macfie journal succinctly stated the bitches were better than the dogs, that the prick ears dominated the Specialty, but that she had vis-

Figure 21:
**Colonsay terriers:
(L to r) Dixy
(5/10/44); Gibby
(4/2/51); We Three
(7/30/48).**

ited kennels with pleasing drop ears. Mac had few doubts about her duties to the breed, and in 1957 she fought for drop ear ring equality because the majority of Challenge Certificates were being won by prick ear Norwich. Losing this first Kennel Club encounter only fueled her cause, which ended seven years later with complete breed separation and drop ear Norwich renamed Norfolk Terriers.

In 1960 Sheila Macfie wrote this about Colonsay We Three, whelped in 1943:

> He is the foundation of all the present drop ears. He was the nicest natured dog, kept to heel without

being taught, a wonderful ratter.

Mac loved small, cheerful dogs, hated short-docked tails and soft coats, but could tolerate a light eye. ("They can see as well as black ones."). She owned a wonderful winning pair of Norfolk in 1965, the year she died.

Marion Sheila Scott Macfie's Colonsays were a game strain of ratters, and they provided Kedron, Port Fortune, Partree, and Bethway kennels with exceptionally dominant drop ears from the late thirties throughout the early fifties. In England, Waveney Valley, Ragus, Hunston, Robincott, Ravenswing, and Ickworth all credit the Colonsay prefix with their start in the breed.

Waveney Valley 1942 – 1959

Ashmans Hall in Beccles was the home of the successful Suffolk farmer Victor Page, who with his wife, Daisy, honed his drop ear Norwich into a tireless working pack. Page achieved remarkable show awards with his proven workers. Ch. Waveney Valley Alder (1952) and his sire, Elel Spruce, are considered by many the progenitors of today's Norfolk Terriers.

The Pages were introduced to Norwich by owning a working bitch from Miss M. S. S. Macfie's Colonsay Kennels during the early days of World War II; and Colon-

Figure 22: A Waveney Valley team with breeder/owner Victor Page. (L to r) Ch. Waveney Valley Alder; Ch. Waveney Valley Gypsy; Waveney Valley Billy Graham; and Ch. Waveney Valley Joy.

say Cady (1945) was Victor Page's first male working terrier. Page renamed Cady "Ditcher I" for apparent reasons, and about 10 years later Ditcher's granddaughter, Waveney Valley Joy, became Page's first champion. Soon the Waveney Valley dogs were gaining high recognition in the ring and as a stud force. They were among the very few drop ears to win top honors during the years they were shown. In 1955 Alder was the first drop ear to win a Crufts CC, and Ripple was the last Waveney Valley to win a CC, in 1959, in Chester. Although they hardly overlapped with Waveney Valley, it was the Gotogrounds who then took over and multiplied Victor Page's ring successes.

Figure 23:
Elel Spruce, on left, and his Waveney Valley descendants with owner Victor Page.

Noted for their harsh coats and hunting abilities, the Waveney Valley dogs excelled as readily in the field as in the show ring. (The proof that these were true working terriers is apparent from the photograph in the *1958 Dog World Annual*.) In a letter written to Marjorie Bunting of the Ragus Kennels shortly after his wife's death, Victor Page had particular praise for two of his great favorites, Ditcher I, an inveterate and adept ratter, and a bitch, Longtail (named for her undocked status). About the latter he wrote:

> And moles! She was a dab hand at tipping them out when they were tunneling just under the grass.

This brief but strikingly worded description somehow seems to sum up the humor and affection Page always felt for all his Waveney Valley charges.

Ragus 1943 -

The Ragus prefix has been a dominant force in Norfolk and Norwich breeding for almost four decades. It is of singular importance that even before breed separation this kennel had succeeded with both prick ear and drop ear Norwich. In the country of world-noted dog breeders, with no means to support experimental production, the 1974 Breeders of the Year award was won by Ragus. Marjorie Bunting and her daughter Leslie's record 23 Challenge Certificates were awarded to seven Norfolk, seven Norwich, and two Border Terriers.

In describing the now-familiar appeal of Norfolk and Norwich, Marjorie Bunting delineates their most outstanding inherent traits and qualities:

> What was it that so attracted us to these little red dogs? Well basically I suppose it was their character, their tough, sturdy independence, their ability to work out a sticky situation and find the answer for themselves; their great love of people, they more than any other breed I have ever had to do with, can make you feel important and loved. They are great flatterers. They are a very sporting little dog which was important to my father, as to him a terrier was no good unless it could at least catch a rat. Although . . . they are first class ratters they can also have surprisingly soft mouths for a terrier and I have known many Norwich and Norfolks who would retrieve game. Thirdly, for me, they were a challenge as show dogs when shows restarted after the War. A rough little dog, the Cinderella of the terrier group at that time, it was a challenge indeed to show them in variety competition. . . . But show them we did and slowly learnt better handling and presentation until today a good variety win with a Norfolk is no longer unheard of.

The Ragus Kennels started in 1943 when Congham Binder came into Marjorie Bunting's family. This drop ear son of Colonsay War Scar had a prick ear-bred dam by Rogue Riderhood x Quartzhill Sneeze. For his mate Marjorie acquired Shandygaff, a daughter of Colonsay Bimp out of another dam of mixed ear carriage. Through their daughter, Ragus Sweet Sue, this drop ear line carrying the black and tan gene was established — a pioneering event in popularizing black and tans. In 1949 after her mother, Mrs. G. B. Marks, joined Marjorie, more drop ear breeding was done, and this stock was successfully used by others.

In America Ragus Jimmy Joe gained his title and

Figure 24:
**Ragus litter of
seven by Red
Duster of Red-
lawn x Eatonrise
Poppy includes
Ragus Penny
Wise, on right.**

pedigree prominence with a brace of black-eyed champion sons, Bethway's Pound and Bethway's Pence. Soon Ragus Brandysnap arrived in Connecticut in whelp to her kennelmate, Ragus Solomon Grundy, and produced the influential Bethway dam, Ch. Cricket. In New Jersey, Solomon Grundy's son, Eng. Imp. Gotoground Foxhunter, sired three Wendover champions among his numerous sporting offspring, while his only English son, Ch. Gotoground Widgeon Bunny, set new records for the breed there.

In 1960, due to illness the Ragus drop ear contingent was severely reduced. Four years later, when drop ear Norwich became Norfolks, only one drop ear bitch remained. However, as the Norfolk show ring beckoned, three wise additions from Edburton, Withalder, and Nanfan plus patient line breeding brought renewed Ragus show successes. Ragus Sir Bear (1969) became the first black and tan CC winner and went on to sire three champions. Then, in 1971 the first black and tan Norfolk champion, Ragus Whipcord, was whelped. During his long and prolific lifetime this dominant sire wielded broad breed influence, winning the annual Club stud dog trophy 5 times and siring a record 16 champions. Whipcord's first, and probably best, mate was a Ch. Ickworth Ready daughter, Ch. Ragus Brown Sugar. Among their prestigious offspring were: Michael Crawley's dominant sire, Ch. Ragus Browned Off, and his sister Eng. Am. Ch. Ragus Brown Smudge; Eng., Ger. and World Ch. Ragus Bellario; and Eng. and Dutch Ch. Ragus Brown Herb. Other champion bitches from the Ragus Whipcord/Ragus Brown Sugar union were Bitter Orange and Brown Cider, who transmitted their lineage to outstanding offspring at home and abroad. Likewise, the first black and tan Norfolk champion bitch was also a Ragus, and Marjorie Bunting can be justly proud of five generations of bitch champions that have carried on this winning tradition. More recently Ch. Ragus Blacksmith (1982) has proved his abilities as a sire, and so the line of dominant Ragus breeding stock, dog and bitch, continues. As this was written, Ragus Boy Blue is the youngest Norfolk to have won 10 CCs before being eligible for the title of champion at 12 months of age — a new breed record!

Today Ragus continues its illustrious winnings as a family enterprise. Marjorie Bunting's mother, Mrs. G. B. Marks, first made exhibiting possible. Then her husband, Hugh, with his great grooming skills, gave early Ragus exhibits a winning edge. Today Marjorie's artistic daughter, Leslie, continues their dominating partnership in the ring with her tireless work and skillful handling. This extended family also includes Leslie's husband, Michael Crawley, who is adept at writing, and whose successful Elve Kennels provide the Ragus prefix with friendly ring competition.

Marjorie Bunting has bred and exhibited many more Norfolk champions than can be recorded here. But beyond her breeding successes, her generosity in sharing information and research adds to her distinguished place in Norfolk history. The publication in 1983 of her book, **Norwich Terrier**, provides a definitive reference source. Her efforts for the 1982 Norfolk Golden Jubilee Handbook were no less significant. Finally, her continuing contributions to periodicals, newsletters, and judging critiques complete the testimony of her invaluable presence

Figure 25: (L to r) **Ch. Ragus Brown Sugar** by Ickworth Ready x Ch. Ragus Bewitched; Ragus Bijou by Ragus Brass Tacks x Ragus Brown Bonnet; Ch. Ragus Blackberry by Ragus Bitterman x Ch. Ragus Bitter Orange; Ch. Ragus Bow Bells by Ch. Ragus Whipcord x Ch. Ragus Bourbon of Crackshill. *Photo Michael Crawley.*

Figure 26:
Marjorie Bunt-
ing's daughter,
Leslie, holding
CC winner Ch.
Ragus Blue Jay,
dam of Ch. Ragus
Boy Blue.

and knowledge for Norfolk breeders and owners everywhere.

Hunston 1948 – 1974

The Southwicks lived on the Norfolk coast, where the hearth of their home was always welcome to friends and puppies against a bracing wind from the sea. The Hunston prefix produced many wonderful pets, two important stud dogs, and an influential litter of four, including an outstanding champion bitch.

Kay Southwick's love of dogs started in 1914 with a 14-pound Irish-type terrier from Cambridge belonging to her father (ironically remembered as a man who usually scorned terriers). "Paddy" proved the most versatile of companions: "remarkably intelligent and never noisy." Kay's own first dog was a Greyhound, and in the early twenties she became the first female trainer to receive a coursing license. Later Kay's Fox Terriers won prizes at Crufts, and one she bred became an international champion before Kay switched to Norfolk.

On Kay Southwick's first visit to the Colonsay Kennels its owner, Miss M. S. S. Macfie, refused to let her buy the small, wire-climbing black and tan bitch that attracted Kay's fancy. Disliking Norfolks of this color, Miss Macfie stated they were an undesirable throwback and responsible for "those horrid coats," presumed to mean the recessive "fluffies" or "hairy bears," as they were called.

The founding Hunston dam, Colonsay Dizzy, was small, red, and harsh-coated; her son, Hunston Herald, and his daughter, Heralda, proved to be typey producers, with winning descendants today. Heralda's most successful litter was a quartet sired by Ch. Waveney Valley Alder, three of whom gained notoriety:

1. Hunston Hedge Warbler produced Nanfan Hayseed, who was owned by Joy Taylor and was dam of Ch. Nanfan Heckle and five other champions.

2. Ch. Hunston Hedge Betty went to Esmée
   O'Hanlon to become her top-winning bitch
   and dam of two more producing dams: (a)
   Gotoground Cuckoo, whose daughter started
   the Nanfan "C" line as well as winning Ickworth and Bluemarking offspring; and (b)
   Gotoground Diana, granddam of Ch. Ickworth Ready.
3. Hunston Highflier was imported by Katherine
   Thayer to improve American stock. He was
   badly scarred battling a woodchuck and was a
   blasé showman. He produced Ch. Bethway's
   Tony, one of that kennel's most influential
   sires, with winning descendants in present
   competition and several Obedience degree
   winners, including River Bend Tory UD.

Despite Sheila Macfie's stern warnings, Kay Southwick always loved black and tans; and by chance she became a pioneer breeder of that color after taking in a
young puppy for an ailing friend in 1950. Upon lifting
the lid of the pup's traveling box Kay's husband ex-
claimed, "Holy Smoke, whatever is this?" In time this
black and tan became an influential stud; and although
at first a number of wooly coats turned up, by 1968 this
trait was no longer apparent.

Kay's proudest moment came when she won a First
with a homebred, black-backed bitch under Miss Macfie.
When pressed about her decision, Mac replied simply,
"She was the best there." Though una-
ble to attend many shows, Kay's unique
20-year influence on the breed was evi-
denced in 1971 when 8 of the 10 Challenge Certificate holders for that year
carried Hunston blood. In a letter to
Mary Baird (Castle Point) that same
year, Kay mentions an "unintended" litter of "very much Hunston breeding,"
adding, "Wish I was 57 instead of 75. I
would keep the lot until old enough to
assess!"

Two pieces of advice always followed at Hunston bear repeating: (1)
"Never keep more Norfolks than you

Figure 27:
Kay Southwick.

Figure 28:
Colonsay Dizzy (Co-
lonsay We Three x
Colonsay Cag) with
her daughter, Hunston
Hustle, 1949.

can give your personal attention and know intimately, as
they need to be real family dogs if they are to reach their
best"; and (2) "Never strip a Norfolk or subject its coat to
the treatment you might give a Wire Fox Terrier. Breed
the correct hard coat and tidy loose hairs with finger and
thumb."

Kirkby 1948 - 1980

Born to dogs, being the daughter of the Rev. Rosslyn
Bruce, the famous breeder and world authority on
Smooth Fox Terriers, Rhalou Kirkby Peace was an exhibitor, judge, and breeder of Manchesters, Skyes, and
Smooth Fox Terriers as well as Norfolks. Rhalou's inter-
ests included horses, birds, and horticulture; but her
family, her husband, "K," 6 sons, and 18 grandchildren
always came first.

As early as 1943 Rhalou Kirkby Peace bred a Norwich litter by Jericho Toffee from a drop-eared bitch,
Wychdale Nutria. The result, a creditable prick ear, Nutcracker, was shown and subsequently sired several drop
ear Norwich, among them a drop-eared bitch and Kirkby Nutmeg, who won at first as a drop ear but whose
ears came prick by the following Crufts. In the late forties Rhalou Kirkby Peace and Kay Southwick exchanged
stock from the prefixes Wymondley, Rednor, and Colonsay.

Kirkby Ready was whelped in the late forties and

was an early favorite of Kay's and Rhalou's. Years later another Ready became the famous Ch. Ickworth Ready. He was sired by Kirkby Freddy and purchased by Alice Hazeldine in 1968, having been hand-raised since birth. Alice kept his call name but used her own prefix to avoid confusion, since the original Ready was his direct ancestor. Rhalou's Kirkby Freddy also sired another champion son, Ch. Colonsay Red Tabs. Freddy was advertised at stud as a sire of champions and killer of rats. His kennelmate, Carrots, was advertised only as a killer of rats ("No champions yet.").

Rhalou Kirkby Peace contributed to the breed column of a canine weekly, kept elaborate pedigree records, and her pen-and-ink drawings benefited the breed Club at its Crufts stand. In both a 1969 *Dog World* forum conducted by Tom Horner and in her column, Mrs. Kirkby Peace made the following observations: (1) "squirrel" tails are undesirable in any terrier; (2) docking methods affect tail carriage; (3) a correct coat is easy to maintain, probably needs tidying, but soft coats need removal "all at one time"; (4) Norfolks are slower to develop showmanship than Norwich but easier to live with; (5) the high-pitched bark peculiar to certain lines offers a challenge for breeders to correct.

Figure 29: *Norfolk Moving* by Rhalou Kirkby Peace.

Although gratifying that the daughter of such a noted breeding theorist produced what many agree was the blueprint for the Norfolk standard in Ch. Ickworth Ready, this ultimately may have been more by accident than by plan, as the latter's pedigree reveals.

Gotoground 1953 - 1965

One rainy afternoon in 1953, Esmée O'Hanlon closed her West Runton pony school and, in answer to an East Anglian newspaper advertisement, went with her two young daughters to select an eight-week-old drop ear Norwich puppy. Esmée's first contact with the breed had been 20 years earlier on the steps of the Norwich

Agricultural Hall. Returning from a local dog show, she had begged her father for one of the newly recognized Norwich Terriers shown by Mrs. "Horstead" Read, but owning nine dogs already, he wisely refused.

Esmée's 20-year wait proved worthwhile, as her first drop ear Norwich, Ragus Merry Maid, developed into a special foundation dam. "Brownie," as she was called, was a daughter of Ch. Waveney Valley Alder, and her dam was Congham Merry Moth, whom a Mrs. Lane on breeding terms from the Ragus Kennels. Brownie, at her first championship show in May 1954, though beautifully groomed and presented, drew disparaging comments from fellow exhibitors due to her ample proportions. Undaunted, Esmée realized her beloved entry was too large but was "quite sure she would breed the goods." Brownie's first mate, Ch. Colonsay Junior, alternately displayed affection and gameness by digging madly for rats. The result of this courtship was the first home-bred Gotoground champion, Red Sprite.

Figure 30:
Esmée O'Hanlon at WELKS, 1964, with a brace of puppies.
Photo © Constance S. Larrabee.

Another dog, the first champion owned by Esmée O'Hanlon, had been purchased as a puppy from Victor Page. Ch. Waveney Valley Aldersister, or "Boko," arrived soon after Brownie. Boko was "a fussy little monkey, very possessive," and won her owner's first Crufts CC in 1955 after being spoon-fed for conditioning. She went on to win seven CCs and was the dam of dual CC winner Gotoground Moley. Two other wise acquisitions by Gotoground were the stud dog, Ragus Solomon Grundy, and the Ch. Alder daughter from Kay Southwick, Ch. Hunston Hedge Betty, winner of 10 CCs and dam of the famous producers Gotoground Cuckoo and Gotoground Diana.

Pride of the place was held by the incomparable Gotoground Widgeon Bunny. Mistakenly registered by the Kennel Club with both first- and second-name choices, he proved nearly invincible in the ring and a "super sire" among studs. The result of the breeding of Merry Maid (Brownie) to her grandson, Ch. Widgeon Bunny, was a blend of Ragus, Congham, and Waveney Valley blood.

At a time when drop ear Norwich were struggling for ring recognition, Esmée O'Hanlon, using her experience with other terrier breeds, proved her expertise as a breeder and exhibitor. As Marjorie Bunting of the Ragus prefix states:

Figure 31: (Left) Jonquil O'Hanlon with Ch. Gotoground True Blue; (center) Ch. Gotoground Vixen and others, 1965.

> In the short period of nine years Mrs. O'Hanlon won 49 CCs and made six champions, all against prick-ear competition. Prior to her joining the ranks of drop-ear exhibitors, the drops had had a bad time at the hands of the prick-ears and many drop-ear exhibitors themselves had little faith in their ability to best their rivals. Mrs. O'Hanlon literally swept into the show ring and put all that behind us and had complete faith in the ability of her dogs to beat all comers, even the dreaded Whinlatters! The drop-ear flag rose higher and higher until in 1959 for the first time they won an equal number of CCs with the prick-ears and the following year they beat them by winning 16 of the 28 CCs awarded. This is an achievement which no other exhibitor will be able to do for this breed now that we have separation, but I have always felt that it was the wins by the Gotogrounds which kept the drop-ear heart beating and gave them enough energy to press for and finally achieve their independence.

After reaching the top with Gotoground Widgeon Bunny, Esmée O'Hanlon felt no other dog could give her the same thrilling moments and so retired from the ring as a competitor to share her knowledge with others as a judge.

Nanfan 1953 -

Chance played a bit part in Nanfan history, and I

Figure 32:
Ch. Nanfan Heckle by Nanfan Nimble x Nanfan Hayseed.
Photo © Sally Anne Thompson.

came into Norfolks by accident. My children when small put an end to my love affair with Sealyhams and I decided to devote their growing years to a breed I had known since childhood—although not as Norfolks, or even Norwich. Later in the early '50s an aunt acquired a daughter of Colonsay Flip out of Colonsay Full Con, bred by Fred Anstey, and presented her to me to enlarge my kennel as she had proved too neurotic to live with her assortment of house dogs, and she felt she would settle better in a truly rural home. She had started life rather strangely for a terrier with the Ross on Wye otter pack and resumed her sporting life with great dash and vigor, founding a line of gallant working terriers with a fascination for water. So casual and transitory was my early interest in the breed that I registered a separate prefix, feeling that it would only be a short term commitment, certainly not one to be taken seriously and not important enough to share a prefix with the Sealyhams, the Pekes, and the ponies. The prefix was plucked one Christmas day from a sixteenth-century tomb in the village church of a notorious local family, the Nanfans. It carried a coat of arms of a wolf with prick ears on one quarter with a lion with drop ears on the other. It seemed suitable in the days before separation, and unlikely to be confused with the prefix of my more important projects.

Corrie (she was born in Coronation year) was bred in due course to Elel Spruce, then owned by Victor Page, who shared my interest in working terriers, and my early litters were bred with working qualities very much in mind. Together we discussed the advice of the late Sylvester Lloyd, "to keep a few at home barking to bring the workers in at night." It rarely worked for me and it was often necessary to go out after dark with a spade, a shovel and a storm lantern to dig out the laggards who were either too keen or too plump to come home.

Returning from a visit to Beccles in the 1950s, I found a deep red bitch in a street market in Suffolk and bought her out of compassion for 5 pounds, discovering later that she was a granddaughter of Red Wraith with Red Scarlett and Privett Meg doubled up twice in her pedigree, similar breeding to Corrie. The influence of these two in my early lines established the deep red coats which are still peculiar to the Nanfans. Such was the degree of chance in my first excursions into the breed.

Encouraged by Victor Page, I started to show my drop ear Norwich, as I still do, to prove to myself at least that working dogs do have a place in the show ring. Breed type, soundness, and temperament have always been important to me, but I have in recent years added ring presence to my list of priorities, if of lesser importance. Breeding programs are not casual, they are planned ahead and taken very seriously, my showing not at all, and certainly not to be taken seriously, but to be cast like pearls upon the water, to be greatly enjoyed as icing on top of a very fulfilling cake.

© Joy Taylor, 1986.

Figure 33: Joy Taylor with her future champion Eng. Am. Ch. Nanfan Sandpiper.

Figure 34: Gilean White with Vicbrita Tussy Mussy in her arms.

Vicbrita 1955 -

Gilean White's Vicbrita prefix has its roots in the winning Maltese bred by her mother, and in a young drop ear Norwich patient of her veterinary father. As a toddler Gilean so coveted this terrier puppy, which had been left to board, that her parents capitulated, acquired the puppy, and Norfolks gained another stalwart admirer.

The first home-bred Norfolk (Norwich D.E.), Rosrach Mazurka, was whelped in 1955 and remained a beloved pet for many years. The start of the Vicbrita line, however, was Nanfan Nutmeg, a dual Challenge

Figure 35:
Ch. Salad Burnet of Vicbrita, 1973, by Ch. Nanfan Nobleman x Ch. Vicbrita Costmary (center), **with his son, Ch. Heathjul Christmas Cracker** (right) **and a Maltese from the Vicbrita Kennel.**
Photo © Sally Anne Thompson.

Certificate winner by Goto-ground Mouser x Ch. Nan-fan Nimbus. Nutmeg pro-duced a 1967 champion daughter, Vicbrita Cost-mary, who, bred back to her sire, in turn produced Ch. Vicbrita Curry. Two years later Costmary, this time bred to Ch. Nanfan Nobleman, produced Ch. Salad Burnet of Vicbrita. "Tango," as he was called, was a handsome "gentle-man" dog with a horde of admirers.

At home and abroad Gilean White has had a contin-uing and positive influence on Norfolk. Much of the breed's present popularity is due to the combined efforts of this active Club officer and competent judge along with her fellow breeder, Mary Ferguson of the Haycroft prefix. These two creative dog lovers with myriad inter-ests initiated the Crufts breed display stand. With hand-crafted Norfolk treasures produced by Club members and a photographic history mounted by Sally Anne Thompson Willbie, this exceptional booth now has a worldwide clientele.

Wymbur 1957 - 1969

The Wymbur Kennels of Mrs. R. L. "Molly" Richard-son in Attleborough, Norfolk, developed a strong bitch line out of Hunston and Waveney Valley stock. Follow-ing breed separation, the bitch Wymbur Mandy Lou be-came the first Norfolk champion at Crufts in 1965.

Long active in Club affairs as a secretary and then president, Molly Richardson, a tactful office holder, ac-quired Ch. Nanfan Halleluia, a red, who joined her black and tan stud, Wymbur Peter, in 1964. Halleluia sired Candy Peel, the last champion of the Wymbur prefix, in 1969. However, Wymbur ancestry has also figured prominently in the John H. Beelers' New Garden found-ing stock in Greensboro, North Carolina.

Withalder 1958 - 1974

Norman Bradshaw and Reg Finney's Withalder Dalmatian prefix entered the Norwich world in the late 1950s before breed separation. By 1960 these boarding-kennel owners, friends of Miss M.S.S. Macfie, had undertaken the secretarial duties of the Norwich Terrier Club and had acquired both prick ear and drop ear foundation stock. As Norwich Terrier Club secretary, Major Bradshaw succeeded in gaining Kennel Club recognition for Norfolk in 1964. He was secretary/treasurer of the newly formed Norfolk Terrier Club from 1964 until 1971, when he was elected Club president, a position he held until 1974.

Figure 36:
Ch. Wymbur Miss Moppet by Waveney Valley Alder x Waveney Valley High Hopes.

The setting up of the new Norfolk Terrier Club and the divisions of the Club trophies were due entirely to Norman Bradshaw's capable administration. In addition, he was largely responsible for the publication of the first Norfolk Terrier Club Handbook in 1968. Major Bradshaw and Mr. Finney's first Norfolk champion bitch, Withalder We Wingding (by Moortop Markie x Hunston Halfpint), was whelped in 1965, as was her brother, We Winjam. Subsequently exports went abroad, and both partners became judges before finally retiring to Nottingham to maintain their excellent boarding kennels.

Leddington 1960 -

Leddington is a prefix familiar to American and Australian exhibitors through the winning offspring of Leddington Captain Cook (1970). Introduced to the breed through her work with the Nanfans, Diane Blanford has both owned and bred some exceptionally influential dogs. Nanfan Nimble, sire of the great Nanfan Heckle, was the first Blanford drop ear Norwich, in 1962. The record-producing brood bitch, Gotoground Cuckoo, lived at Leddington during her years of retirement. In 1971 at the age of 10 Cuckoo was bred to Ch. Nanfan Thistle and produced one last whelp, Ch. Cinnamon of Nanfan, the first of Joy Taylor's notable "C" line. There are still Norfolks at Led-

Figure 37:
A Withalder Norfolk Terrier.

dington, a prefix of sparing use but of worldwide influence on breed type.

Figure 38:
May Marshall
with a Norfolk.

Figure 39:
Swedish Ch. Ravenswing Flush
Royal by
Nanfan Halleluia
x Ravenswing
Favonian.

Ravenswing 1963 -

In 1963, after many devoted years of assistance to Miss M. S. S. Macfie, "Auntie May" McHale left Colonsay Kennels, where she was manager, to marry another dog lover, W. S. Marshall. At that time May owned a daughter of Ch. Colonsay Orderley Dog, whom she bred once to get her own founding dam, Favonian. Under the Marshall family prefix, Ravenswing, Favonian produced several Challenge Certificate-winning bitches.

Sired by Ch. Nanfan Halleluia, Ravenswing Flush Royal, the first Ravenswing winner, won her Challenge Certificate at only 6 1/2 months; her littermate, Flippant, won 2 CCs; and her full sister, Fay Royal, gained her championship. CC winner and Swedish Ch. Ravenswing Fantasia, by Kirkby Freddy x Favonian, produced May Marshall's useful stud and CC winner, Ravenswing Fleet Leader, in 1974. Leader sired Edwina Hart's Ch. Timberfalling Red Cedar, the dam of future champions, and Montelimar Ravenswing Flotilla, a cornerstone for the T. R. Needhams' Titaniums.

Despite difficulties of active participation, May Marshall maintains a keen interest in the breed. She has served as Club president and judges Norfolk both at home and abroad.

Ickworth 1965 - 1981

Alice Hazeldine was a remarkably successful breeder, exhibitor, Club member, and judge. She was revered and respected by the entire Norfolk community at home and abroad, for the influence of the Ickworth prefix was far flung.

Introduced to Norfolks when they were still called "drop ear Norwich," Alice Hazeldine first handled her friend Sheila Macfie's dogs in the early sixties, when she often drove the ailing Mac to shows. No

newcomer to dogs, Alice had bred her first Wire Fox Terrier litter in 1927, gained firsthand experience with Irish Terriers and Airedales, and learned grooming from the legendary professional terrier man, Arthur Cartledge. During World War II her war work took Alice Hazeldine all over England as a milk tester on farms, but she eventually returned to dogs, and then to Norfolk, when in 1965 she inherited the Colonsays from Miss Macfie.

Although the desire to own the breed's record Challenge Certificate winner had been denied Miss Macfie in her lifetime, shortly after her death Ch. Colonsay Orderley Dog, shown by Alice Hazeldine, accomplished this goal. When Orderley Dog retired after winning the Club Championship Show in 1967, he had 19 Certificates. Although other Colonsay and Ickworth hopefuls had their share of ring successes, when Ickworth Ready made his winning debut at Bath in 1968, breed history was made again. Ready, a singleton whelp, was admired by Alice Hazeldine as a weanling, and his breeder, Rhalou Kirkby Peace, parted with Ready knowing he would have the opportunity to reach his full potential in Alice's capable hands. His achievements in Breed and Group competition were matched by his ability as a sire, and assured the Ickworth prefix a prime place in breed history in a handful of years.

The tall and gracious Alice Hazeldine started producing her own Ickworth winners, proving her level head and devotion to her adopted breed. Her generous grooming advice at shows improved the looks of her competition, and her hospitality and steady conviction gave focus to the breed club's aims. Her export stock proved highly influential in Sweden, Germany, and the United States, where her bridge with Badgewood strongly influenced the latter's successes.

Figure 40:
Alice Hazeldine
with Ickworth
Bacardi by
Ickworth Penny-
wise x Ragus
Bristol Cream.

Figure 41:
Ch. Ickworth
Ready by Kirkby
Freddy x Kirkby
Tresarden Curvet.

Alice Hazeldine's views about the general Norfolk makeup were astute and based on long experience and shrewd observation:

1. TEMPERAMENT: "Temperament in my dogs has always been a strong point . . . I'd never give away temperament for show points. A dog isn't any good as a pet, as well as a show animal, if the temperament is bad."

2. COATS: "I never stripped. I gave them a daily grooming and a hair or two was taken out here and there. My idea is if you keep going over the coat, it's rather like a lawn, you keep it short and dense. You can't prepare a dog for the show ring in a fortnight or so, it's regular attention that counts."

3. EARS: "Well . . . I'll be perfectly honest. That, I presume, is a throwback for generations isn't it. . . . I think also one of the things the breed has lost is the rounded tip."

4. FRONTS: "The front depends upon the shoulder placement. If you have too short a neck, you get an upright shoulder and therefore it affects the movement."

5. EYES: "They should be small, dark and varminty . . . that's the true terrier eye."

6. HEALTH/BREEDING: "I've not had any difficulties producing puppies and never had to have a caesarian."

Figure 42:
(Left) **Babbling Binks, 1925, is an oft repeated ancestor of the early Colonsays, and grandsire of the first American Champion.**
Photo © Sally Ann Thompson.

Figure 43:
(Right) **Ch. Waveney Valley Gypsy, 1954, granddam of Ch. Colonsay Orderley Dog, a prominant influence in the Ickworth "P" line.**

Despite the tragic adversity she suffered of losing, within days of one another, the sister with whom she lived and her beloved Ickworth Ready at age four, Alice Hazeldine carried on alone for another few years until 1981. In her retirement she kept Ickworth Bacardi, whom she considered the embodiment of her aims.

Norfolk Terriers were
originally bred as rat-
ters and stable dogs,
small enough and
game enough to enter
the den of a fox and
bolt the quarry.

2

AMERICAN BEGINNINGS

JONES TO NORFOLK

Willum Jones 1914 - 1928

In 1914 while buying a hunter in Market Harborough, the Philadelphia sportsman, Robert Strawbridge, paid Frank "Roughrider" Jones 10 shillings and sixpence for "Willum," a terrier puppy of exceptional character and conformation. Both the sire and dam of this short-legged, cropped-eared pup were docked and cropped for "safety," being certified as fox bolters with strong Irish Terrier ties.

Willum was a remarkable advertisement for his breeder; and his popular owner, Strawbridge, was never without this charming companion. Soon horse lovers from Vermont to South Carolina found other terrier breeds to cross with the dynamic Willum. Though dominant and prolific, no one ever managed to duplicate this 12-pound, ever-game, go-to-grounder.

Figure 44: Willum Jones, the first import of record, 1914. *"They were not known at that time as any special breed."*—R.E. Strawbridge. From a painting by George F. Morris.

Said to be a "Norfolk Terrier" by J. Watson Webb, master of the Shelburne, Vermont, foxhounds, Willum is described as being the first of Jones's exports to the United States, though not yet of a recognized breed. Willum was red in color and had short legs and a foxlike head. His body was thickset and much smaller than a Sealyham's. Webb used him to develop the Shelburne strain of small fox bolters after other imports proved too large for local dens. Whereas the larger English terriers had the scope and skill to work in earths reclaimed from English badger setts, they proved impractical for the New England terrain.

In the "Roaring Twenties" the reverse snobbism of owning an unregistered Jones Terrier was rife among the "horsey set." Many more of Jones's small red, or black and tan terriers in various shapes and coats now crossed the Atlantic. Their price rose first to 5 pounds, then on to 50, and those without prick ears were now cropped "to smarten appearances" and give them all a similar look.

Though Willum Jones died at age 14 defending his home from marauding strays, he twice gave his name to the breed in America: first, as "Jones Terriers," a name that still finds favor among those who ride to hounds; and second, as Norfolk Terriers, the breed Willum was said to belong to 50 years before it was officially recognized.

The Larrabee "Links" 1926 - 1986

Since 1950 Constance Stuart Larrabee has held a unique position in the development of Norfolk Terriers. From working Jones Terriers, as Norfolk and Norwich were first called, to scores of Norwich winners, she has recorded the breed's progress through the photographer's lens and with the writer's pen.

Settling on a historic Maryland farm after their romantic courtship and marriage, Constance and Sterling Larrabee, MFH, were accompanied by Sterling's Jones Terrier pet, the forerunner of today's King's Prevention champions. Sterling Larrabee, Master of the Old Dominion Hounds, first encountered the breed when the Millbrook, New York, master of foxhounds, Louis Reynal, brought a pair of his Jones imports and a pack of beagles to Virginia on a hunting vacation in 1923. These game little bolters were immediately embraced by the Warrenton sporting set, and in 1926 Colonel Larrabee was able to acquire a Jones bitch for himself. Mink Mouth, as she was called, and her descendants were kept to exterminate barn rats and farm woodchuck. Occasionally a terrier was packed into the leather mailbag and carried by a mounted groom to bolt hunted fox.

Sterling Larrabee was a passionate fox hunter with a

keen eye for a horse. He was respected both as a competitor and a judge. At the beginning of World War II this patriotic American officer was again serving his country as an attaché in South Africa, where he met a young war correspondent, Constance Stuart. As an only child of British immigrants to South Africa, Constance had studied photography in Munich in 1936-1937. She had established her own successful studio in Pretoria before she was 20 and became the only woman correspondent with the South African troops in 1939. She witnessed the Desert War, the invasion of Italy, was in London for the Blitz, and in Paris for its liberation. Constance Stuart Larrabee's war photographs and those of native Africans have been exhibited extensively in galleries, museums, and at universities internationally.

Figure 45:
Constance Stuart Larrabee with Robin, her pet Norwich.
Photo J. Tyler Campbell.

During their quarter of a century together, the Larrabees were a dynamic couple who entertained friends from all over the world. The ever-courtly Colonel was an opinionated charmer who, with the irrepressible and creative Constance, offered stimulating companionship to their vast acquaintanceship at their farm. King's Prevention was named for the pre-Revolutionary force that impeded smuggling on Chesapeake Bay. The Larrabees' acres were almost surrounded by water, and the skies overhead were frequently darkened by flights of geese. At the time Constance and Sterling moved into their 1781 farmhouse there were both unregistered Jones (i.e., Norwich) Terriers and registered ones in the vicinity. The breed had gained American Kennel Club approval in 1936 when Gordon Massey of

Figure 46:
(Right) **Constance Larrabee captured Norfolk character with her photographs.**

Figure 47:
(Right) **1975 NTC Match judge Harry Peters with Sara Dombroski.**

Figure 48:
(Far right) **Anne Winston's model of her first champion Mt. Paul Anderson and his son Hades.**

Figure 49:
(Far right) **Sylvia Warren.**

Figure 50:
(Right) **Visiting English judge Ferelith Hamilton at a 1971 match.**

Figure 51:
(Far right) **1978 NNTC president Ellen Lee Kennelly with Masie's Demi-John and Nanfan Nutshell.**

Photos © Constance S. Larrabee.

Figure 52:
(Top left) **Jones puppies, 1950.**

Figure 53:
(Top right) **Norfolk puppies"Chesapeake" and "Cotswold."**

Figure 54:
(Above left) **Ch. King's Prevention Ahoy.**

Figure 55:
(Above right) **King's Prevention. Jolly Roger.**

Figure 56:
(Left) **Gordon Massey, Josephine C. Spencer, and Col. Sterling L. Larrabee.**
Photos © Constance S. Larrabee

Trappe, Maryland, imported his first, a drop ear, Wither-slack Sport, bred by Lady Maureen Stanley. The Larra-bees became firm friends of the Masseys, and Constance once described "G" on a visit to the Choptank River farm, descending the stairs, an avalanche of small red terriers following in his wake. The tall and handsome Gordon Massey was characterized by one female admir-er as "the kind of man a girl would follow barefoot 'round the world."

It did not take long for Constance Larrabee to be-come intrigued with the Norwich breed, for its diversity and scope held a new challenge for this gifted photogra-pher. Within a few years her darkroom also became a "dogroom," and the kennel prefix "King's Prevention" was appropriately adopted. Noting the need for infor-mation among the growing number of Norwich fanciers, Constance soon channeled her energies into a prize-winning newsletter which, in 1967, "whelped" the com-prehensive and extensively illustrated breed book, **Norwich Terriers U.S.A.** By now champion after prick-ear champion was being spawned at King's Prevention, which provided foundation stock for breeders from coast to coast and kept the nursery pens at home fully occupied.

The void left by the death of Sterling Larrabee in 1974 proved difficult for Constance to reconcile. Her dogs were a comfort, and her creative energies and tal-ents found recognition and reward through the Arts Council at nearby George Washington College in Ches-tertown, Maryland. At first these dual interests—dogs and photography—were equal. On an autumn vacation in England in 1975, which included a visit to Joy Taylor (Nanfan) at Standhill Cottage in Worcester, a new direc-tion was taken. Nanfan Corricle, better known as "Joy," soon joined the pack at King's Prevention, and with this bitch Constance began her brief but successful adventure of breeding "drop ear Norwich," as American Norfolks were still called. Corricle's ring successes were enjoyed, but the famous King's Prevention prefix was to come to the forefront of the Norfolk world predominantly through Corricle's offspring

James E. and Anne Rogers Clark received Ahoy by Ch. Wendover Torrent from Corricle's first litter. After other litters, both Corricle and her daughter by Scandinavian and Am. Ch. Hubbestaad Wee Johan expanded Deborah Pritchard's Glenelg base in Virginia. Corricle's other daughter, King's Prevention Belinda, by Eng. Ch. Ickworth Peter's Pence, before "masquerading" as a Norwich, produced King's Prevention Jolly Roger, the premier black and tan stud for the Clark's Surrey Kennels.

Although the scope of her dog activities has now been curtailed, the King's Prevention flag still flies over Constance Larrabee's land, and the firm Norfolk base that she bequeathed to the Surreys has also unquestionably produced important beginnings for the kennels Norvik and Rightly So. Constance's successful 1982 book, **Celebration on the Chesapeake**, acclaimed Maryland's 300th anniversary, and in September of 1986 she received an honorary doctorate from one of our country's oldest colleges, George Washington, this coming simultaneously with an exhibit, also in Chestertown, of her photographs illustrating the writings of the famous South African novelist, Alan Paton.

During the 30 years in which Constance Stuart Larrabee was active with Jones, Norwich, and Norfolk Terriers she created a unique chronicle both in pictures and in writing, recording not only the development of these dogs but also of the persons "behind" the dogs. Many of the photographs in this book represent Constance Larrabee's story of a breed, a breed with Larrabee "links" to Norwich and Norfolk in this country throughout more than 60 years.

Gordon Massey, Breeder 1936 - 1966

Witherslack Sport was two years old when he became the first Norwich Terrier registered with the American Kennel Club. His owner, Gordon Massey of Trappe, Maryland, had waited a year for Lady Maureen Stanley to part with this harsh-coated, red dog with large drop ears and equally generous feet. "Sport" so appealed to his new owner that more imports soon followed, including Airman's Brown Betty, Airman's Brown Eyes, and the English show winner,

Figure 57: English import Witherslack Sport, first Norwich Terrier registered in the AKC Stud Book.

Figure 58:
Puppies from
different litters
of the Gordon
Massey kennels.
Note the kennel
attire.

Airman's Sam Browne, whose photograph illustrated the breed in many contemporary publications. Although Massey preferred drop ear Norwich, Airman's Sam Browne was used on both ear types, first in England and then here, where he sired the first prick ear dog champion in 1939.

While Gordon Massey had no interest in exhibiting, he and American Kennel Club secretary Henry Bixby were thoroughly interested in breeding better Norwich that conformed to the Standard. "G" liked his Norwich small. He felt 12 pounds was ideal, and all his dogs were weighed regularly. His kennel records were precise, the pack of his amenable house dogs was countless, and when he cared for puppies a kennel coat and spats were considered necessities.

Percy Roberts 1891 - 1977

As an agent, handler, and judge, Percy Roberts brought artistry, knowledge, and respect to that far-from-kingly sport, the dog show. He generously shared his views and observations, especially on type, temperament, and character. Ever courtly and explicit with amateur exhibitors, he took delight, by subtle ring demands, in disciplining a careless or overanxious handler. The attention of his audience was always concentrated on the judge and dogs, for Percy never lost control of his arena. In his handling days, he once replied to a friend who had wished him good luck, "I don't need luck. I need good judging."

All American Norwich and Norfolk Terriers are indebted to the role Percy Roberts played in the breed's establishment. On Percy's annual visits to Britain prior to World War II, he studied Norwich at the shows he attended. He particularly liked Biffin of Beaufin, the first English champion; and although he found type in this "new" breed very unsettled, he preferred drop ear to prick ear Norwich. By 1937 he was bringing over pairs of drop ear Norwich for his New England clientele—Edith

McCausland in Massachusetts and Mrs. Arthur Anderson in Bedford Hills, New York, among others. He was responsible for Jean Hinkle's wise purchase of Colonsay All Kiff, who made her Port Fortune Kennel the first in America to house a black and tan. In 1940 Kiff became the first drop ear male champion, and remained the only black-backed male drop ear to attain an AKC title until Elve Black Shadow's championship in 1985.

Figure 59:
Percy Roberts
judging an early
match.

Dapper and seemingly ageless, Percy Roberts had an interest in Norwich which never flagged. He was the breed's mentor, who also judged the Club Specialty as soon as he was awarded his AKC license—an assignment he repeated a few years later by popular demand. His remarkable memory for dogs and his keen recognition of related stock delighted most serious breeders, who regarded points won under him worth double the value of those gained under others.

Pinch 1936 - 1948

In 1935 Henry Bixby, then secretary of the American Kennel Club, read an article about a newly recognized English breed—the Norwich Terrier—and commissioned the well-known agent and handler Percy Roberts to bring him a Norwich bitch in whelp from England. Instead Roberts returned from his annual visit to England with a pair of drop ear puppies from Mrs. E. Mainwaring; the outgoing bitch puppy was Merry of Beaufin, and the more diffident dog puppy was Mark of Beaufin.

Figure 60:
(L to r) Cherry of
Boxted, Pepper
Pinch, and Pinch
O'Ginger.

Merry proved to be an exceptional Norwich ambassador. In 1939 she became the first breed champion, and her descendants are still at the forefront today. Before gaining her title as the first Norwich champion in the United States, Merry of Beaufin had litters by Gordon Massey's Witherslack

Figure 61:
Josephine
Spencer, NTC
president, and
Henry Bixby,
AKC secretary,
1947.

Sport, the first of the breed to be registered here, and by Port Fortune The Ace. Merry of Beaufin's Pinch line descends, through George Pinch (1947) and Ch. Tuff (1943), to Badgewood; Bethways; Castle Point; Chidley; and Mt. Paul.

Moreover, it remained the good fortune of the breed that Henry Bixby's dedication to drop ear Norwich never wavered. Post-World War II changes in American Kennel Club rules prompted Bixby along with other AKC officers to retire from show competition. Nevertheless, his early breed columns and advice on activating the breed Club in 1947 formed a blueprint for good management and breed sportsmanship. The quality of his match judging for the Club and the soundness of his opinions continued to be of value, as did his assistance in providing other competent and interested judges for Club-sponsored events.

Partree 1938 - 1951

Figure 62:
Ch. Cobbler of
Boxted, a dominant
sire and winner of
the first Club
Specialty Show.

It was at a 1938 point-to-point in England that Josephine Spencer selected a black and tan Norwich Terrier puppy from the "boot" of Mollie Barnett's car. The future president of the Norwich Terrier Club chose "Muffin" as a family pet. Before departing for the United States, Josephine also acquired another Norwich—a dog—from Mrs. Guy Blewitt. The latter, Trump of Boxted, sired by Tobit MFH, out of Neachley Toffee, was a younger brother to the breed's first drop ear champion bitch, Tinker Bell.

Josephine Spencer's English pair, Muffin and Trump, served as the Partree foundation. Although several Partree litters were whelped from American-bred dams, it was the arrival of the English import Cobbler of Boxted that put Partree on top. Cobbler greatly influenced drop ear Norwich in America.

Even before Cobbler's arrival the need for greater organization was evident among early breeders. An earlier breed club had failed to gain recognition. As a result the Norwich Terrier Club was formed in 1947 at an historic first meeting in the old Mechanics Hall in Boston's Back Bay section. This meeting, which saw Josephine Spencer unanimously elected president, was held at the Eastern Dog Show, which in those days always followed Westminster and was regarded as a breeders' showcase.

The team of Josephine Spencer as president and Katherine Thayer as secretary of the Norwich Terrier Club was both innovative and exemplary. A breed-history flier was published, owners were visited, informative columns appeared in magazines, and judges were provided with breed information. The Club held many match shows, and foreign breeders were sought out for advice. Annual trophies were awarded, and above all, every member of the group had a voice in all actions and decisions. Just as the Club started to achieve its aims, Josephine Spencer's tragic death in 1951 left her family and friends devastated. Doing double duty, Katherine Thayer carried on with limited support until Alden S. Blodget was elected Club president in 1955.

Figure 63: Ch. Partree Sparkle, 1948, by Ch. Cobbler of Boxted x Partree Chance, later became foundation dam for Castle Point.

Fortunately for drop ear Norwich, the breeding accomplishments at Partree were not lost. Mary S. Baird at Castle Point in New Jersey founded her kennel on Ch. Partree Sparkle, who combined the best of the Boxted and Colonsay bloodlines.

Kedron 1938 - 1951

Edith McCausland was the first active breeder of drop ear Norwich in Massachusetts. Her founding import was selected by Percy Roberts after winning a CC in England. Angel's Whisper of Colonsay had long, straight legs, well-dropped ears, and competed in the Group ring as well as in Obedience to give the breed exposure.

Although no Kedrons gained titles, a Kedron dam produced two champions for River Bend, and Barbara Fournier's first drop ear was Kedron Cobbler's Biscuit,

Figure 64:
Ch. Angel's
Whisper of
Colonsay, CC -
winning import,
1938, and
granddam of
champions.

Figure 65:
Kedron stock,
1949.

dam of Ch. Brigham Young, Bethway Kennel's founding sire. It was through Edith McCausland's fellow members of the Ladies' Dog Club and Josephine Gould that the breed blossomed in Massachusetts and dedicated judges were developed.

The last of the Kedrons went to Josie Gould of Milton, Massachusetts, a great friend of Miss M. S. S. Macfie's, who wished to emigrate to England— a desire never fulfilled. Josie lived in a charming Georgian house, where the feeding dishes were her best china and the Sheraton sofa served as a dog bed. With an unerring eye for type and soundness, she brought some of England's most promising drop ears to live on Brush Hill Road: Ch. Colonsay Flap, Ch. Colonsay Harkers, and Ch. Waveney Valley Honey. Unfortunately, in returning from the Worcester show, Flap escaped from a car window and was killed. This traumatic occurrence ended Josie Gould's future breeding plans. However, all her dogs lived long and happy lives with their kindly and withdrawn owner.

Port Fortune 1939 - 1962

Like several other members of the all-breed Ladies' Dog Club, Jean Hinkle was first attracted to drop ear Norwich through Edith McCausland's Angel's Whisper of Colonsay. In 1939 Jean commissioned Percy Roberts to select her foundation pair of Norwich from England at Miss M. S. S. Macfie's Colonsay Kennels. These first two denizens of Port Fortune were the compact black and tan dog, Ch. Colonsay All Kiff (from the expression British soldiers used in India, meaning "just right") and his little sister, Colonsay Allcando, who arrived in whelp to Tobit, a founding breed sire. The bitch already had an English show record, and Henry Bixby thought her son, Port Fortune's The Ace, the best-made Norwich he had ever encountered. Meanwhile All Kiff, though short-lived, became the first drop ear male Norwich to gain his AKC title. (It would be 45 years before another black and tan male attained that honor.)

For the next 20 years Jean Hinkle took an active interest in Norwich and was the original Club's first president in 1939. (Due to the War, the Club could not fulfill requirements for official recognition.) Jean bred and exhibited sparingly, but was an articulate judge, a knowledgeable Club member, and a generous benefactor. She presented the Port Fortune Bowl, named for her historic Cape Cod home, to the Club in 1954 after judging the Millbrook Match. This award was established for Best in Match winners to encourage breeding puppies of quality.

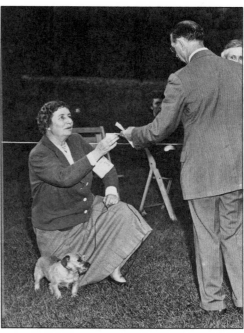

Figure 66: Wellesley match, 1949. Jean Hinkle receiving First Prize from Percy Roberts.

Other attributes notwithstanding, it is as a judge that Jean Hinkle will be long remembered, as will Mrs. William Constable, the venerable Scottish Terrier breeder, and Fanny Porter, the Cairn specialist. Fellow members, all, of the Ladies' Dog Club of Wellesley, Massachusetts, these astute judges put type at the top of their judging priorities, were patient with insecure exhibits, and were encouraging to novice exhibitors. All preferred drop ear Norwich, urged separation of drop ears from prick ears, and encouraged drop ear exhibitors to show their entries with the true Norwich temperament.

River Bend 1943 - 1973

Having grown up with animals in a close-knit extended New England family, Sylvia Warren was taught to assume responsibilities and learned early the importance of sharing. Selfless, witty, and outspoken, Sylvia served others in countless ways. In her youth she lost her hearing while nursing soldiers during the influenza epidemic of 1918. Between the wars she continued to work as a technician and built her charming home and peacefully situated stable in a bend of the Charles River near Dover, Massachusetts. An accomplished equestrienne, Sylvia used her gift with animals to help Irish friends who shipped her hunters and cobs that she polished in manners and turnout for grateful MFH clients from Massachusetts and Virginia.

In 1939, just as life at River Bend was about to change, Sylvia was given Bruff, a drop ear Norwich, by her friend Josephine Spencer. With the outbreak of World War II Sylvia founded the Warren Committee to relocate war-torn children. She gave up the horses, and by 1943 her dressing room had been temporarily remodeled into a whelping area for Bruff's "bride," a service in which it would continue for decades thereafter.

In the first Norwich litter raised at River Bend was a self-possessed male whose style and bold mien stood him apart. Tuff was the obvious pick of the litter, but Sylvia Warren tried not to show him favoritism because she was certain the former owner of both his sire and dam would exercise her right to best puppy and select him for herself. However, when the Partree breeder surprisingly went home with Tuff's sister, Sylvia was elated, and Tuff was soon launched on his special role in breed history. Though always grateful that Josie Spencer had not taken her favorite Tuff, Sylvia was never certain whether it had been through oversight or an act of generosity that this superb puppy was allowed to become the "sultan" of River Bend.

Figure 67:
First River Bend
champion, Tuff
CD, 1943, by
Bruff x Jenny
Pinch.

In competition Tuff gained his bench championship with ease and his CD with diligence. He was a popular sire and a busy house dog, for Sylvia had opened a superior boarding kennel during the War while sharing her home with three lively lads, refugees from the London Blitz. Tuff proved a sire of brains as well as beauty. He influenced both ear types by accident when one of his daughter's ears went up, and presto—a new line was begun! Years later another drop ear Norwich stud at

River Bend was Hunston High Flier. "Nobby," the black-eyed Alder son that Katherine Thayer had imported from Kay Southwick, became a favorite of Sylvia's after her sister's death. Nobby sired River Bend Tory UD, and the dominant Ch. Bethway's Tony. Though a woodchuck "got" him in the nose, Nobby never lost his desire to hunt and never missed Sylvia's long ritual dog walks.

Figure 68:
**River Bend
near Dover,
Massachusetts.**

Sylvia Warren took an active part in the canine world of show and Obedience through close personal and family contacts. Her brother had owned top Sealyham show dogs, including a homebred Westminster Best in Show winner. However, Sylvia's deafness made it expedient to allow her sister, Katherine Thayer, to take the position of secretary of the Norwich Terrier Club in 1948. Katherine could communicate her ideas and convictions, although she lacked Sylvia's more extensive breeding experience. On most Club matters the sisters agreed, although there was a brief disagreement when Sylvia branched out and bred prick ears. Katherine held to Miss M. S. S. Macfie's tenet that the only true Norwich were drop-eared.

Figure 69:
**River Bend Tory
UD, 1966.**

When an almost miraculous operation restored partial hearing, Sylvia Warren finally accepted a place on the Norwich Terrier Club board. After years of supporting Club events, she was persuaded to assume the presidency, and her energy and enthusiasm became an inspiration. Her organizational skills and special knack with animals, both two-legged and four-legged, suited her ideally for her office.

Sylvia practiced whatever she preached. She always handled her own dogs, and on one occasion mushed two miles through knee-high snow to Madison Square Garden after a record blizzard had crippled the surface transportation of New York City. Carrying her crated "Lacey" all the way to ringside, Sylvia was smiling when the judge gave her Reserve.

Though Sylvia Warren was awarded the Order of the British Empire by King George VI for her Warren Committee war efforts, it was the special citation from

Boston's renowned Angel Memorial Hospital that pleased her the most. The recommendation of her boarding kennel as a model to be studied was also a unique recognition of Sylvia's loving care of animals. Her warmth embraced every living creature on her land, and in the end she had the comfort of knowing that her "hobby" had attained an admirable worthiness in the eyes of all.

Her administrative aptitude was equally impressive, making it ironic that, after all her dedicated NTC work, her influence on the breed Club faded quickly. However, the founding of the American Norfolk Terrier Association (ANTA) in 1983 can be directly traced to the influence Sylvia Warren exerted on those who did heed her shining example.

Figure 70: Sylvia Warren, NTC president 1970.

While River Bend bred and owned champions of both ear types from 1943 until Sylvia's death in 1973, it was her dedication to the breed itself that inspired so many others to continue in her tradition.

Maplehurst 1945 - 1959

Although Pippin (1946) was her first champion Norwich, Katherine Thayer had known "Jones Terriers" since the late twenties. However, it was her sister Sylvia Warren's gift of this bitch puppy that opened a new chapter for drop ear Norwich.

Katherine Thayer was a person of strong convictions

and organizing abilities coupled with a love of nature and a deep respect for life. She quickly grasped the challenge that a numerically small breed offered and in 1948 was elected secretary of the Norwich Terrier Club. During her term in office the Club thrived, had prestigious judges for specialties and match shows, provided a monthly *AKC Gazette* column, published informative and detailed reports, and offered annual breeders' trophies.

Ring competition came naturally to Katherine, whose brother owned the famous Barberry Known Kennel. She associated the name of Maplehurst, her farm, with her Norwich when she became secretary of the Norwich Terrier Club. Breeders' bridges were built to Great Britain, and a son of Ch. Waveney Valley Alder's joined the Maplehurst pack to offer American Club members free access to this desirable bloodline.

On one trip abroad Miss M. S. S. Macfie, the noted Colonsay breeder, asked Katherine Thayer to handle one of two dogs she had entered in a class, then proceeded to deliver a running commentary on the judge and his choices in clarion tones. "We don't talk in the American ring," Miss Macfie was advised. "Then you must have expert judging," was her reply. Later it was through Katherine Thayer's efforts that a purse was made up to bring Marion Sheila Scott Macfie to judge the Norwich Terrier Club Specialty Show. It was a disappointment to drop ear exhibitors that so many prick ear exhibits at that show won top honors.

After the embarrassing ring debut of her first champion, who "turned turtle, paws akimbo and refused to budge," the mistress of Maplehurst became a talented handler. However, one most unique achievement still raises eyebrows among pedigree buffs. Johnny Cake of Maplehurst was registered as having two sires with the AKC after a series of letters and a personal appearance

Figure 71:
Katherine
Thayer with
River Bend
Hurry and Haste,
1954.

Figure 72:
Maplehurst
puppies, 1948.

at 220 Madison Avenue by his owner. In this unheard-of circumstance Katherine Thayer proved she would never perjure herself, and the American Kennel Club, which had originally objected to this most unorthodox registration, finally relented.

The loss of Katherine Thayer dealt a blow to all Norwich owners. She had given selflessly of her time and energies, promoting the dual aspects of the breed. Her own Maplehurst pack had been death on woodchuck and skunk, and she had avidly encouraged others interested in ratting and fox bolting. Her practical wardrobe, which varied little, consisted of lisle hose, stout walking shoes, and serviceable suits; but Katherine Thayer had soft and sensitive hands on a lead, and a varying pace to match that of her charges. In the ring her timing and presence were compelling. Her successes with others' dogs were notable; but with her own puppies she would sometimes resort to squeaky mice and get down on all fours, patiently encouraging the "squirmy worms" to pounce their prey.

Bethway 1951 -

The year was 1950 and Barbara Schilf Fournier, a resident of Bethany, Connecticut, was given a young Norwich drop ear bitch as a Christmas present by her friend and neighbor Elizabeth Spykman. This puppy, Kedron Cobbler's Biscuit, was the first Norwich "Bobby" Fournier had ever seen, but given her affinity for animals and her natural aptitude with them, it was not long before she found herself devoted to the breed.

At the suggestion of Katherine Thayer, Kedron Cobbler's Biscuit was bred to her grandsire, Ch. Tuff CD, and this auspicious union produced Barbara Fournier's first champion, Brigham Young, who became one of the cornerstone studs for Bethway Kennnels. In citing the successes of Bethway Barbara Fournier, with characteristic modesty, gives abundant credit to the astute advice not only of colleagues such as Katherine Thayer and

Figure 73:
NTC Specialty,
1966.
Ch. Bethway's
The Duke
and Ch.
Bethway's The
Dutchess, by Ch.
Bethway's Tony
x Ch. Bethway's
Scarlet, with
judge Marjorie
Bunting (Ragus)
and breeder/
owner Barbara
Fournier.

Elizabeth Spykman, who got her started, but to other dedicated Norwich breeders, such as the English judge Mrs. Ida B. Hardy. It was the latter who was so impressed with Ch. Bethway's Brigham Young at Westminster one year that she suggested that Barbara acquire from Miss M. S. S. Macfie Colonsay Kelly's Eye, the winning drop ear bitch who became Bethway's foundation dam.

While Bethway's prolific Ch. Brigham Young is best known for his son, Ch. Newry's McAleenan, Kelly's Eye produced innumerable illustrious descendants, including the champions Bethway's Pound and Bethway's Pence by the English import Ch. Ragus Jimmy Joe; Ch. Bethway's Tony by Hunston High Flier; Kelly's double-grandsons, Bethway's Mr. Chips and Mr. Kennedy—BOB at Westminster, 1962 and 1964, respectively—and the deep red Ch. Bethway's Pensum.

During the 1950s, at just the time when Norwich drop ears seemed at their lowest ebb of winning, Barbara Fournier and fellow breeders such as Mary Baird, Katherine Thayer, and Sylvia Warren can justly be credited with having brought drop ears back into the show ring and into recognition amidst the keenest of prick ear competition. A Bethway Norwich who stood out as one of the best representatives of the breed was Ch. Bethway's Ringo, among whose claims to breed recognition

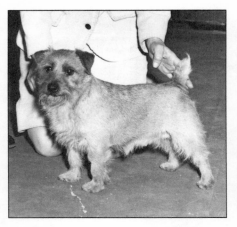

Figure 74:
(Left) **Ch. Bethway's Mr. Cricket by Ch. Bethway's John x Ch. Bethway's Cricket, Best of Breed, Westminster 1968.**

Figure 75:
(Right) **Ch. Bethway's Ringo, Best of Breed, 1973 Specialty.**

was his win at the Greenwich Specialty in 1973, going BOB over 58 competitors under the respected judge Mrs. John Marvin. Ringo's first Group placement had been in 1969, and after this start he had several others, including a Group I under Lydia Coleman Hutchinson. In addition to the Group wins of Ringo, Ch. Bethway's Aramis is acknowledged by Barbara Fournier as having been "probably the greatest sire at Bethway Kennels," not just for winning and placements but for "his get over the years."

Since moving from Bethany, Connecticut, to Santa Fe, New Mexico, in 1973, Bobbie Fournier has gradually diminished her breeding and boarding program by channeling her canine knowledge into the AKC world of shows and judging. Currently she is licensed to judge all terriers and awards Best in Show rosettes. She is also the founding president of the American Norfolk Terrier Association (ANTA) and founder of Santa Fe's only all-breed kennel club, Sangre de Cristo.

In her Santa Fe setting Barbara Fournier is still surrounded by her house Norfolk, although several are senior citizens and only three are now active producers. Nevertheless, her dedication to the breed remains unstinting, and today the kennels Anderscroft, C and J, Lyndor, Folklore, Neverdone, and Wintonbury are keenly indebted to Bethway for their beginnings. It is good news that Barbara celebrated our breed's anniversary year by raising a litter of four, and that her junior stud dog, Glori's Terrance, who is Bethway-bred on his distaff side, is now a champion.

Castle Point 1951 - 1989

Mary Baird's motivation to start a kennel was partly necessity and partly hobby sparked by opportunity. In order to preserve her Bernardsville family estate, the cottages and outbuildings had to be self-supporting, and winding down from horses to dogs made it easier for Mary to pursue

her interest in animal husbandry. So in 1951 the fieldstone carriage house and box stalls were converted into a capacious kennel complex, painted with the family racing colors, and a new era at Castle Point began.

Earlier forays into other breeds had proved unrewarding, but the memory of Snuff, the little hunt terrier Mary had once owned, persisted. It was on the way to the Ascot races in 1930 that the youthful Mary had stopped at Mrs. Phyllis Fagan's Windsor home in answer to an ad for hunt terriers in *The London Times*. Mary had paid "three quid" for the six-week-old Snuff, a black and tan, whom she regretfully had to leave with her friend Mollie Barnett when she returned to New Jersey from England. In time, Mollie bought Snuff a mate, Sneeze—another Fagan-bred black and tan—and several litters were produced by this bandy-legged pair, who were later recorded as Norwich Terriers, D.E. Snuff's intelligence and character were never duplicated in his immediate offspring, however. Snuff was "devoted but never sentimental, brave but not pugnacious." A first-class rabbiter, ratter, and retriever, he demonstrated common sense by retiring under tables during air raids. Fortunately Mary Baird was able to start her kennel with Snuff's descendants through Partree stock that became available due to Josephine Spencer's untimely death:

> As to my Castle Point Kennels, when Josephine Spencer died, I bought her fine son of imported Cobbler of Boxted, Partree Cobbler. He became a champion and I bred him to my best bitches, which was what she had told me

Figure 76: Ch. Bethway's Just My Bill by Ch. Elve Pure Magic and Bethway's Dolly Parton by Ch. Turkshill Brown Buccaneer. The dam of both is Bethway's Scarlet O'Fisty, 1984.

Figure 77: (L to r) Ch. Partree Sparkle, Ch. Castle Point Sylvia, and Ch. Castle Point Simon.

Figure 78:
Mary Stevens
Baird and
"Gambler,"1961,
with English
judge Esmée
O'Hanlon.

she had hoped for, just before she died. . . . I also bought her Ch. Partree Sparkle, whose picture appeared in your last year book, sitting on the top of a ribbon case, and she became my foundation bitch. She was by Ch. Cobbler of Boxted x Partree Chance and was whelped in 1948. I bred her to Sylvia Warren's Ch. Tuff, not only because he was an exceptional dog in every way, but also from sentiment. His grandfather was my original Norwich, Snuff, a black and tan I had owned in England in 1930. When I returned to this country I left him there with a friend, Air Commandant Dame Henrietta Barnett. He went through the War with her, sensibly took cover under a table during air raids, and died of old age.

From its establishment, Mary Baird had convictions about her kennel. A strong team of stud dogs, sturdy brood bitches, and a boarding facility for dogs she sold were maintained until the death of Bob Young, her indispensable kennelman, in 1985. Through the years few shows were attended, but the stud force at Castle Point was usually titled. Friends and fellow Norfolk breeders often helped exhibit the Castle Point studs; and Katherine Thayer, Anne Winston, and Priscilla Mallory all took turns with various future champions. Castle Point and its owner attended most Specialty shows and Westminster, but Mary Baird was hostess for numerous match shows, "education days," go-to-ground exercises, and Club meetings.

Always a stickler for correct small size, natural hunting ability, and drop ears, Mary favored judges with breed experience and still considers the points won by Ch. Bethway's Pound under Harry T. Peters, Jr., at the 1958 Specialty a most important win. She considered the late Percy Roberts the greatest breed authority ever to judge.

Ch. Castle Point Iguana (1969-1981) was the most influential of the homebreds, with seven champion get and one UD from eight different litters, plus winning descendants in both the show and Obedience rings. The latest Castle Point sire, and now veteran, Ch. Hatchwoods Creme De Menthe of Cracknor, was the best of the many imports Mary Baird acquired through the years. Over 300 puppies have been raised on her lovely estate, and their homes stretch across this continent and into Canada.

Mary Baird, past president of the Norwich Terrier Club, was a trained and experienced volunteer. She brought knowledge and a special perspective to meetings, as dogs were only one portion of a busy life bound up with the great educational foundation, the Stevens Institute, prison reform, state politics, family affairs, and a broad acquaintanceship. What luck for Norfolks that "three quid" was parlayed into superb pets for half a century.

Figure 79: Kennel at Castle Point, 1963.

Figure 80: Ch. Hatchwoods Creme De Menthe of Cracknor, by Swed. Ch. Cracknor Capricorn x Hatchwoods Peppermint, winning the 1981 Specialty.

Newry 1954 - 1974

Rita Haggerty was reared with show dogs, Irish Terriers, and Irish Wolfhounds owned by her father, Arthur McAleenan, in Madison, New Jersey. After marriage and city living, Rita returned to dogs when she

Figure: 81:
**Ch. Newry's Red
Fox as a puppy.**

moved to a farm in the heart of Long Island's duck-hunting country. Her first encounter with a drop ear Norwich was at a Labrador training session, when Dave Elliot's Ch. Woodchuck Of Wingan jumped out of the bird boy's truck and fetched a duck before Rita's "on line" Labrador was sent for his water retrieve. Woodchuck stole Rita Haggerty's heart, reminding her of her childhood Irish Terriers. The die thus cast, it was not long before Sweeny, an unforgettable little bitch of ambiguous ear carriage, bred by Henry Bixby's daughter, joined the Haggerty household.

The Haggertys remained active in retriever trials and raised drop ear Norwich as their house dogs. Foremost among these was Finnegan, a harsh-coated daughter of the aforementioned Woodchuck and Sweeny, and subsequently the founding dam of Newry's drop ear Norwich. Aided by Rita Haggerty's friendship with Barbara Fournier of the Bethway prefix, Newry, a small but significant kennel, also provided the founding dams for Badgewood (Ch. Newry's Mrs. McThing) and for Chidley (Shennanigans Of Chidley). At Turkshill, Quin Slocum's first drop ear, Crumpet, was also a Newry, and one who gave pleasure for 16 years.

Mt. Paul 1954 - 1975

Anne Winston's first drop ear Norwich was purchased as a pet. Castle Point Trivet, the result of an accidental breeding between champion littermates Castle Point Simon and Sylvia, proved a pioneer both as a dam and as an exceptional character. Within a few years Trivet's owner became very involved with breeding drop ear Norwich, and from 1961 through 1973 Anne Winston was secretary of the Norwich Terrier Club before becoming president, a position she held until 1977, when Ellen Lee Kennelly assumed the title.

Always a stickler for temperament, Anne made her ring debut with Mt. Paul Anderson from her first homebred litter. Defeating an international prick ear champion under respected terrier authority George Hartman,

Figure 82:
Anne Winston's first
champion, Mt. Paul Ander-
son (l) with his dam, Castle
Point Trivet, and younger
sister and brother, 1956.

"Andy" won on showmanship and rear propulsion, traits Anne always held in esteem. Andy's sire, George Pinch, a three-way descendant of Gordon Massey's and Henry Bixby's original 1936 imports, was a keen hunter and once spent 10 days in a collapsed culvert before being discovered. George Pinch's avid horseman-owner, Louis Murdock, had been reared with Jones Terrier imports from Market Harborough. Murdock was connected with the Essex Foxhounds, a pack that continued to use fox bolters, including the descendants of Ch. Mt. Paul Anderson, for years.

Figure 83:
Anne Winston
and Mt. Paul
Tulip at NTC
Specialty, 1974.

When Anne Winston expanded her breeding program in collaboration with her friends, Priscilla Mallory of the Wendover prefix and Mary Baird of Castle Point, Nanfan blood was added through a trans-Atlantic exchange. On a judging visit to the United States, Joy Taylor persuaded Anne to part with a charming young daughter of Gotoground Foxhunter in return for puppies from her English-whelped litters. Anne also acquired Ch. Nanfan Naiad, who became the first English and American champion drop ear and dam of the first Norwich D.E. to win an American Working Terrier Association certificate for going to ground.

Figure 84:
(L to r) **Ch. Mt. Paul Tulip, Mt. Paul Vesper, and Mt. Paul Rowdy.** *Photo © Constance S. Larrabee.*

As maintaining a second home became more demanding, Anne focused her special gift with puppies on developing one outstanding contender every year or two. Her breeding program was waning when Ch. Mt. Paul Rowdy won the 1974 Specialty Show, and her final litter carried the Mt. Paul banner in others' names. Ch. Mt. Paul Viking CG placed second in Group, then successfully competed in working terrier trials for his owner, Doris McGee. Mt. Paul Vanity produced pet puppies in Connecticut, including the dam of Ch. Annursnac Major Yeats, bred by Pliny Jewel III of Concord, Massachusetts. Mt. Paul Vesper, in succeeding litters by Ch. Elve Pure Magic, provided two notable foundation dams for others: Gaynor Green's Ch. Raggedge Best Bet for the Pennsylvania Greenfields Kennels, and Ch. Raggedge Are You Ready, Beth Sweigert's ratter and Group-winning Yarrow cornerstone.

When her term as Norwich Terrier Club president ended, Anne Winston also ended her association with drop ear Norwich and placed or pensioned her few remaining dogs.

Alden Blodget, NTC President 1955 - 1961

When Alden Blodget agreed to become president of the Norwich Terrier Club, he promised that neither death nor divorce would interfere with his term of office, and he kept his word to the letter. Alden enjoyed life immensely, and thus managed to be the embodiment of both "city slicker" and country squire. NTC match shows were held on his Nissaquogue farm in St. James, New York, and biannual Club meetings at the New York City studio apartment. His talented wife, the writer and actress Cornelia Otis Skinner, often would appear after meetings, adding sparkle and bright repartee to the atmosphere.

Experienced in dog clubs through Westminster, the Leash, and his field-trial Labradors, Alden Blodget could charm the most rigid of puritans. He used this power to conduct meetings with positive results, broadening the Norwich Terrier Club's base to prevent the bylaws from excluding from membership dedicated professionals. (Alden never subscribed to the so-called invasion-of-handlers threat.) He genuinely liked most dog lovers, whether amateur or "pro"; and he strongly believed NTC membership should be extended to anyone who had owned a Norwich for a year, whether blue collar or WASP. On a more personal level, Alden particularly adored his own favorite prick ear Norwich, the one-eyed Ch. John Paul Jones of Groton, his pet of 17 years.

When Alden Blodget stepped down as president of the Norwich Terrier Club, the active Club board had both drop ear and prick ear constituents evenly represented. However, the center of drop ear activity had by that time moved from Massachusetts to New Jersey, where an enclave of drop ear owners resided, among them the new Club president, Mary S. Baird.

Wendover 1955 - 1975

For 20 years Priscilla Mallory studied and bred drop ear Norwich with care and dedication. She was interested not in breed multiplication, but in improving conformation and correcting faults without sacrificing the breed's natural talents. Starting with Mt. Paul Bridgett, a younger sister of Mt. Paul Anderson's, she selected a yearling dog puppy from Esmée O'Hanlon when in England. Gotoground Foxhunter was bred once before being delivered to the Mallorys in London, and this union produced the great English showman Ch. Gotoground Widgeon Bunny. In the U.S., Foxhunter produced the trio of Wendover champions—Favor, Foxhunter, and Cobbler —as well as 48 other offspring.

Another farsighted Wendover import was Ickworth Moonlight, one of the first daughters of the great Ch. Ickworth Ready and dam of Nancy Parker's champion relay racer, the well-named Wendover Talent UD. Though other champions were produced at Wendover Farm in the rolling Somerset Hills, the Lyndor Kennel used Ch. Half Pound with success; and the last of the line, Ch. Wendover Torrent, influenced the present-day Surreys through their King's Prevention crosses.

Figure 85:
(Left) **Ch. Wendover Cobbler by Gotoground Foxhunter x Wendover Apple, 1964.**

Figure 86:
(Right) **Gotoground Foxhunter by Ragus Solomon Grundy x Gotoground Tiddlywinks.**

While Priscilla Mallory was promoting the drop ear cause and serving the Norwich Terrier Club, her sister in Virginia was building a world-class stable of racing brood mares. Ironically, neither lived to fully enjoy the fruits of their labors, which became more apparent with time. These sisters were both talented breeders, and there are several current exhibitors who savor their Wendover descendants, for only the soundest of stock earned Priscilla's carrydown Wendover prefix.

Morgan Wing, Jr., MB

Morgan Wing was a true dog lover. His prize-winning Norwich were woodchuck hunters of the first order; his gun dogs were workers at the pheasant shoots he ran; and his fame was enhanced by his enthusiasm for beagling and the triumphs of his Sandanona pack. With his encompassing good will, he became the American Kennel Club delegate from the Norwich Terrier Club in 1959, a position in which he worked actively until his death in 1974.

The Norwich and Norfolk Terrier Club is especially indebted to Morgan Wing for many important contributions. He streamlined the Club's ballot system. More importantly, he was responsible for persuading the American Kennel Club to work with the U.S. Department of Agriculture at all ports of air entry to familiarize personnel concerning laws on free entry for registered animal breed stock. This was no small feat and an obvious benefit to all breeders and fanciers who imported dogs.

In 1962 Morgan arranged for the American Kennel Club registration and showing of Norwich Terriers by separate ear type. This gave further impetus to England's formal separation of prick ears and drop ears into Norwich and Norfolk, respectively. In turn, he arranged for the recognition of imported English Norfolk in the AKC Stud Register. This significantly influenced drop ear lineage in the United States—particularly through Nanfan and Badgewood—for the next 15 years until breed separation here in 1979. All these achievements notwithstanding, it was Morgan Wing's warmth, radiant good cheer, and genuineness that marked his years with the Norwich Terrier Club.

Figure 87:
Morgan Wing with his daughters Lucia (l) and Jill (r).

Badgewood (U.S.A. Norfolk) 1969 -

During their 10-year business stay in England, the Philip S. P. Fells added first Norwich then Norfolk to their long-established Whippet kennel, Badgewood. The prefix had first been used by Betty Fell for her Sealyhams as a teenager in America before World War II.

Elizabeth West Fell's first encounter with drop ear Norwich was at the Westbury Kennel Club show in 1936, where she sighted Henry Bixby with Merry and Mark of Beaufin in tow. While judging terriers on her annual visit to the United States at the same Westbury show some 25 years later, Elizabeth was smitten by a red drop ear bitch, Ch. Newry's Mrs. McThing, who happened to be one of Merry of Beaufin's direct descendants. "Missy" returned with her new owner to England, whelped a bitch puppy in quarantine, and then joined the Fell's house dogs for the rest of her life. She twice won the High Rising Hardy Perennial Basket for Best NTC Veteran, while her granddaughter, Bonnie, was the first of her many champion Badgewood descendants.

The Fells returned to the United States from England in 1969, leaving behind dual CC winner Badgewood Bonnie, one of Ch. Nanfan Heckle's daughters, with Miss Alice Hazeldine. Bonnie went on to become an English champion and arrived on these shores in the spring of 1970 in whelp to Ch. Ickworth Ready. Bonnie then proceeded to produce the future Badgewood champion Blakeney and the remarkable brood bitch, Kings Lynn,

Figure 88: Elizabeth Fell with six Badgewood champions in 1976. In lap (l to r) King's Lynn and her dam, Eng. Am. Ch. Bonnie. On grass (l to r) Windmill Girl, The Huntress, Miss Alice, and Woodpecker Trail.

before gaining her own American championship. Alice Hazeldine also bred the Fells' leading stud dog and top breed sire, Am. Can. Ch. Ickworth Nimrod. "Nimmie" was selected by Philip Fell at a championship show, where he had the disadvantage of competing against his illustrious kennelmate Ickworth Ready. Nimrod sired four champions for Badgewood and eight champions for other American breeders.

Soon after the Fells' return to America Elizabeth was elected bench chairman for the Norwich Terrier Club, and Philip served on its board and as its AKC delegate. As Bethway Kennels moved to Santa Fe and the Wendover, Mt. Paul, and Aladdin kennels no longer competed,

Badgewood came to dominate the East Coast drop ear competition. In addition, the Fells' Ch. Monty Collins and Ch. The Huntress topped the prick ear Norwich competition at Montgomery County, Westminster, and Club specialty shows. Ch. Ickworth Bluemarking Saffron was wisely imported to broaden the Badgewood base, followed by a second bitch, Ch. Ickworth Penny Piece, also acquired from Alice Hazeldine. The sale of the latter was contingent upon the Fells' taking two other adult dogs, as Miss Hazeldine, at 80, had decided to retire from breeding Norfolks. The newcomers Eng. Ch. Ick-

worth Pathfinder and Ickworth Pennywise were never exhibited here, but were used at stud and remain happy, healthy senior citizens today.

The 1979 Badgewood Match proved a Club and family celebration. Recognition of Norfolk had been achieved, and the Norwich Terrier Club name changed to include both breeds. A Revere bowl was presented to Delegate Fell for his efforts, and Elizabeth Fell was elected to the NNTC board after eight bench-show years.

Figure 89: Ch. Badgewood Monty Collins, by Can. Am. Ch. Ickworth Nimrod x Ch. Badgewood King's Lynn, a winner of Groups, a Specialty, and BOB at Westminster and Montgomery County.

After Specialty Best in Show wins and numerous Group placements, Elizabeth Fell, except in the year following her husband's death, has attended shows only as a judge. However, perhaps this is a temporary arrangement, and hopefully the Badgewood prefix will return once more to the winner's circle.

Aladdin 1970 -

By 1970 Alice Ladd was ready for a change. Her Aladdin boxers had competed with success in the show ring and in Obedience, but a drop ear Norwich in local training class proved irresistible. So shrinking her sights, she abandoned breeding big dogs and acquired two Norwich D.E. bitch puppies from Mt. Paul and Castle Point.

A chance to attend Crufts in 1971 proved surprisingly fruitful. By no means a novice in canine affairs, the irrepressible Alice was thrilled by a separate entry of 28 Norfolk and made some interesting breed observations. Size was uniform, varying barely a quarter of an inch in height. The fabulous coat condition of English Norfolks made them look slightly overweight, but hands-on these dogs were hard as steel under very full coats. She found heads and fronts very good, tails much shorter than those of American Norfolk, and many long nails. Ch. Ickworth Ready was the impressive Best of Breed winner. Due to a post-show visit with Joy Taylor, Alice returned home with Ch. Nanfan Nogbad the Bad. Nogbad sired one of the breed's important English sires, Ch. Nanfan Nobleman, and Ch. Mt. Paul Rowdy was his most important American son.

Despite her breed enthusiasm, circumstances prevented this artistic needlewoman from pursuing her canine hobby, but her down-to-earth approach and humor always made Club meetings highly memorable.

NORFOLKS IN ART

(Right)
Ch. Wendover Half Pound by Jean Ross, 1971.

(Below)
A pastel of Ch. Biffin of Beaufin by Dorothy
Hallett, 1936.

(Below)
Painting of early terriers
once owned by Miss M.
S. S. Macfie and later
Mary S. Baird. Painted
by Hepper, an East
Anglian artist, 1857.

(Above) **Three colors of Norfolks—wheaten, black and tan, and red.** *Photo Frauke Hinsch, Windach, Germany.*

(Right) **Ch. Nanfan Crunch owned by Barbara Miller.** *Photo Donna J. Coss.*

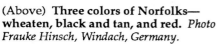

(Left)
"Come out and play some football, Ma!"
Photo Michelle Alton.

(Right)
Shannon Gaffney with Poole's Ide Pachysandra. *Photo Greg Siner.*

(Below)
Allright Magic Bee and Allright Julie Bee. *Photo Frauke Hinsch, Windach, Germany.*

(Above)
Ch. Dalcroft's Kyrie beside a lake.
Photo Christine Robinson, Ontario, Canada.

(Left)
Wally, the great impersonator, as a retriever.
Photo Roma Baran.

A NORFOLK FOR ALL SEASONS

(Above left) **Little Dickens of C and J.** *Photo Christine Robinson, Ontario, Canada.*

(Above) **Ch. Allright Magic Midge.** *Photo Frauke Hinsch, Windach, Germany.*

(Left) **Neverdone's Quick Pickwick.** *Photo Mrs. S. W. Holt.*

(Below) **Did you say bath?** *Photo Frauke Hinsch, Windach, Germany.*

3

NORFOLKS TODAY: UNITED STATES

This chapter records information from many of the active Norfolk fanciers in the United States. The date after each kennel prefix indicates when that kennel adopted the breed.

UNITED STATES

CALIFORNIA

Wonderwood (1978)
Jessica Jurich Relinque, Palo Alto, California

My life with Norfolks began in 1978 with my mother's Norfolk bitch, Leddington Folly. We were living in England at the time, and I decided Mother needed a dog of her own. Her birthday was coming up, and so I scouted around, investigating the suitability of various breeds. I had never seen a Norfolk in the flesh, but I knew the sort of dog we needed. It had to be a dog who would be equally comfortable in the cold drizzle of Buckinghamshire winters or curled up in front of the fire; this meant a sturdy easy-care jacket, and she had to be devoted and loving, but sensible and small enough for my mother to sling her under an arm and take her anywhere. Finally, above all I wanted a healthy, hardy breed.

Well, "Folly," as we called her, fit the bill perfectly—so perfectly in fact that I too became enchanted and set my sights on breeding and showing Norfolks. When my parents returned to the United States, I stayed behind and moved into an old World War II torpe-

Figure 90: Jessica James Relinque with (l to r) Ch. Wonderwood Barnburner, Ch. Wonderwood Wensday Addams, and Ch. Wonderwood Low Commotion Lu.

Figure 91:
Ch. Wonder-
wood Calliope
was BIS at the
1988 National
Specialty.

do boat on the Thames near Windsor Castle. I persuaded my mother to let me keep Folly in England temporarily (while she house hunted in California) and breed a litter from her. The result was my first champion, Wensday Addams, and her brother, Pugsley Addams, who now lives with my grandmother in New Jersey. I then registered my prefix, "Wonderwood"—a play on the name of the village in Buckinghamshire, Grendon Underwood, where it all started.

The following summer I began showing Wensday as a 6-to-9-month-old with some success. (The Windsor Dog Show was a pleasant walk from the boat.) My parents had by this time found a house, but instead of sending Folly out alone I decided that all the dogs and I

Figure 92:
Ch. Wonderwood Watch Her Strut.

Figure 93:
Ch. Wonderwood Megabyte.

would move to the West Coast to join them. Before leaving England I repeated the breeding on Folly, and she produced three puppies in my parents' new home in Atherton.

When I arrived here in 1981 showing Norfolks in California was nonexistent. I scoured the state looking for competition, but there was none. I found this difficult to believe, but the judges and terrier people with whom I spoke confirmed that there just weren't any Norfolks in the ring out here. The cloud had a silver lining, however, giving me an excuse to visit the East Coast once or twice a year to show or to breed a bitch.

Before long my Wensday's boundless charm had earned her a large following of admirers and would-be Norfolk owners. Wensday's one litter a year could hardly fill the growing demand, so the "imports" started arriving. We now have a significant geographical assortment of kennels represented in the San Francisco Bay Area: Bethway; C and J; Chidley; Max-Well; and Norvik. And we already have a new local prefix: David Cook and Bill Woodward are on their third Silverstone litter.

We held our first major in December 1984 and now have major competition on a regular basis. And the California Norfolks have been making a name for themselves on the national scene, with three on the 1985 list of Top Ten Norfolks in breed points. Sharon Curry's Ch. Chidley Bold Dust (Ch. Daffran Dusty x Ch. Chidley Jinx) was sixth on the list, with two California Group placements to his name. Cook and Woodward's Ch. Wonderwood Watch Her Strut (Ch. Hatchwoods Creme de Menthe of Cracknor x Ch. Wonderwood Wensday Addams) tied for seventh spot with her half-brother, Kathleen and George Eimil's Ch. Wonderwood Barnburner (by Ch. Surrey Sink or Swim). "Strut" was the only bitch to make the Top Ten, and she did her owners proud by taking Best of Opposite Sex at Westminster both in 1986 and 1988. My own Wensday took BOS at the 1985 Specialty and then capped the year by sharing a four-way tie for top-producing bitch.

The Norfolk owners here in the West are a keen and friendly group, and what started out as an informal luncheon to celebrate our first major in December 1984 has grown into an organized circle of fanciers meeting regularly. We joined forces with local Norwich owners and together formed the Middle Kingdom Alliance (MKA).

Of course what initially attracts most owners to Norfolk and Norwich is not their capabilities as show dogs but their irresistible charm. And so our Club's "fun day," held each May, includes events of interest to pet owners as well as exhibitors. Besides the obligatory match there are racing and go-to-ground events, Obedience demonstrations, and "talent contests." We all now eagerly look forward to this special day as an annual event.

CONNECTICUT

Anderscroft (1971)
Jane and Everett Anderson, Mystic, Connecticut

We registered our prefix, Anderscroft, with the American Kennel Club in 1971, the same year we bought our first Norfolk Terrier. Until that time we had been raising and exhibiting Labrador Retrievers.

We had thought about a second breed, but it was really our children that wanted a smaller, house-type dog. I had been raised with a very arrogant, pugilistic Irish Terrier as a child, but I fondly remembered him as a neat dog, and so we looked over the Terrier Group first. Finally it was narrowed to the Australian, the Border, and the Norfolk. Once we'd looked beyond the physical characteristics of the breed into the personality, there didn't seem to be any contest in our minds.

Finding a Norfolk bitch was harder, but I pestered Bobby Fournier (Bethway Kennels) enough that she finally sold us Bethway's Abbie, who soon became a champion and was lovingly known as "Dear Abbie"—someone you could tell all your troubles to.

Breeding Abbie and getting a bitch puppy from her was another tale, as she produced only one bitch puppy in her lifetime and that was in her first litter. I thought that this was going to be easy, and so sold that puppy—never to get another from Abbie!

Over the years we have bought other Norfolks, imported some, bred some, and have loved them all. At present we live with five along with our remaining Labradors; and we are now eagerly looking forward to extending our breeding program.

Folklore (1972)
Sheila Foran, Glastonbury, Connecticut

Folklore is a lap-size kennel. Its origins lie in a little girl's trip to her first dog show, where she saw her first drop-eared Norwich Terrier. It was love at first sight. Those drop-eared dogs were owned by Barbara Fournier, whose famous Bethway Kennel was then located in Bethany, Connecticut (this, long before "Bobby" made her westward trek to live in New Mexico).

Figure 94: Titanium Grenadier by Ch. Ferdinand the Warrior of Titanium x Titanium Golddust.

I, of course, was that little girl; and in 1972 I realized my dream of "someday owning one of those dogs" when I visited Bethway and was captivated by a 14-week-old male puppy. That first dog, Ch. Bethway's Joshua, was the foundation of my small group of Norfolks and remains the standard by which I judge all others. In many ways an "old-fashioned" type, Joshua possessed all the courage, spunk, and humor for which the breed is noted. A gentle dog, yet unafraid to protect his own territory, he was the epitome of what Norfolk should be.

Today at Folklore we dabble in the breed ring, in Obedience, in informal racing, and in go-to-ground events. We'll try anything, and we have fun doing it. Our current "top dog," Titanium Grenadier, joined us in 1987 courtesy of Eileen and Tom Needham, whose Eng. Ch. And Harry of Titanium, one of "Gren's" grandparents, is a leading sire in England.

Although we produce only occasional litters at Folklore, we continue breeding for the best in temperament and conformation. We will never be a large kennel, but we strive to be a good one.

Knollwood (1980)
Brunhilda Cohan, Avon, Connecticut

After rearing two litters from their Bethways family pet in the 1960s, the Cohans moved to Australia with May Apple. Settling in Connecticut upon their return to the U.S., Brunhilda's interest in Norfolk was rekindled. In 1982 Prince Igor of Knollwood, by Ch. Lyndors Pippin x Fiddle Dee Dee of Knollwood, gained his title. This Prince and his Nanfan bride are the foundation of Knollwood's operatic line.

Lyndor (1970)
Jerome and Doris Gerl, Bethlehem, Connecticut

Lyndor started approximately 29 years ago with Collies. At that time we lived in New Haven, Connecticut, and yearned to move out into the country. In 1970 we realized our dream and moved to our present residence in Bethlehem, a town where the cows outnumbered the people.

Our bitch, Bethway's Bell, was our first Norfolk Terrier. We purchased her from our dear friend Barbara Fournier. Bell was bred to Ch. Bethway's Aramis and produced one bitch, Ch. Lyndor's Flower Power ("Daisy"). Daisy was bred back to her grandfather, Bethway's Ringo, and produced Ch. Lyndor's Paper Moon ("Tatum"); Ch. Lyndor's Ring-O-Round ("Johnny"); and Lyndor's Georgy Girl ("Gigi"), who had to be spayed one point short of her championship.

With that awesome start it was our intention to develop the Lyndor style by outcrossing to other good lines and then inbreed to arrive at a dog with substantial bone, good coat, expression, and still be within the Standard. To date we have bred more than nine champions. It took three generations to produce Tatum, who proved to be an excellent foundation bitch, producing both Ch. Lyndor's Pippin (by Ch. Castle Point

Figure 95: Ch. Lyndor Mez-A-Mez, 1979, by Ch. Lyndor's Mister x Ch. Lyndor's Cricket, a Ch. Wendover Half Pound daughter.

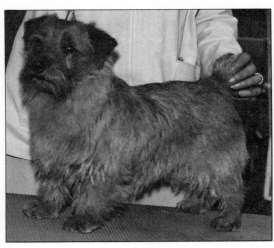

Iguana) and Ch. Lyndor's Mister (by Ch. Mt. Paul Rowdy). Pippin won Best of Breed at the first breed Specialty in June 1979 at one and a half years. And Mister holds a special place in our hearts. Although shown sparingly, he has won Best of Breed many times and is currently our most successful stud dog because of the look he puts on his puppies. Mister, bred to Ch. Lyndor's Cricket (another daughter of Daisy's by Ch. Wendover Half Pound), produced Ch. Lyndor's Mez-A-Mez, who was Winners Bitch at the second breed Specialty in 1980 at the tender age of seven months. Her litter sister, Neverdone's Jazz, owned by Mickey and Don Regula, went Reserve Winners Bitch at that same show. Ch. Lyndor's Mez-A-Mez and her two daughters by Pippin, Ch. Lyndor's Bewitched and Lyndor's Sabrina Fair, are now taking on the burden of the Lyndor name.

In conjunction with our planned breeding program, we are very selective in choosing buyers to whom we sell puppies. We try to make sure that all prospective owners are kind, considerate, and caring.

Tylwyth (1976)
Mary D. Fine, Storrs, Connecticut

Tylwyth is a very small kennel—actually not a kennel at all. (Tylwyth is Welsh for "household.") I acquired my first Norfolk in 1976 with the intention of showing in both breed and Obedience. That puppy became Ch. New Garden Eadith, Am. Can. UD, the first of my three Ch./ UD Norfolks. "Kelly" lists among her notable accomplishments three BOS's at the National Specialty, the third being from the Veterans' Class. One of her daughters, Ch. Anderscroft Tylwyth Trollop has also had considerable success in the conformation ring, handled by her owner, Jane Anderson.

My second Norfolk, Ch. Castle Point Mint, Am. Can. UD, CG, produced my first homebred Ch./UD, Ch. Tylwyth Just Chelsea, Am. Can.

Figure 96: Ch. New Garden Eadith, Am. Can. UD, First Ch., UD Norfolk and, to date, the only Norfolk to hold a Canadian UD as well as the AKC title.

UD, CG. "Chelsea" proved to be exceptionally trainable and became, at 18 months, one of the youngest, if not the youngest, terrier of any breed to earn a Utility title. She now has pointed and Obedience-titled offspring that are our hope for the future.

All of the Tylwyth Norfolks at home are shown simultaneously in breed, in Obedience, and in terrier trials. Above all, Tylwyth aims to produce a versatile Norfolk with plenty of spirit and hunting instinct.

Wintonbury (1968)
Dr. and Mrs. Donald G. Schroeder,
Bloomfield, Connecticut

We chose Norfolk Terriers for their enthusiasm for life. They also are good hunters and companions to our German Wirehaired Pointers. We have been breeding Norfolks for approximately 20 years and have had no difficulty in either breeding or whelping puppies. The late Wintonbury Streaker by Ch. Castle Point Iguana x Wintonbury Meg II, in addition to being a beloved house dog, was an outstanding stud who exerted a great influence on our line.

KENTUCKY

Whitehall (1980)
Mr. and Mrs. Frank Dean, Lexington, Kentucky

Martha and Frank Dean are known for their outstanding Irish Wolfhounds — sound dogs that are always owner-handled and conditioned. The Deans' first

Figure 97: (Left) **Ch. Todwil's Pac Man of Whitehall at six months.**

Figure 98: (Right) **Ch. Todwil's Pac Man of Whitehall by Ch. Elve Pure Magic x Ch. Todwil's Gentle On My Mind at two years.**

Norfolk litter, sired by Ch. Elve Pure Magic in 1982, was whelped by Ch. Todwil's Gentle On My Mind. Two of the puppies became champions and one, E.T., bred to Ch. Surrey Sink or Swim, produced the Leon Lussiers' first champion, Paprika of Whitehall, and the Deans' own Ch. Caper of Whitehall. The latter, bred to Ch. Chidley Magic Marker, is the dam of Ch. Sunoaks Foz of Whitehall in Texas and of another winner in California. Though Norfolk are the Deans' lesser breed, the occasional litter is reared in their house and many typey Whitehall puppies have winning ways.

Todwil (1972)
Glenn E. Wills, Shelbyville, Kentucky

The history of my Norfolks began with Ch. Todwil's Gentle On My Mind ("Jill"). Jill's story is rather unique in the annals of the breed. Jill is a Norfolk born to prick ear Norwich parents, Ch. Todwil's Burnt Cork (dam) and Eng. Am. Ch. Culswood Chipwood (sire). She had two litter brothers, Ch. Todwil's Jacks Or Better and Ch. Todwil's Red Woodchip. "Corky," Jill's dam, was bred to seven different sires and raised 25 puppies (22 of which finished their championships); but Jill was the only one with drop ears. I do know that other breeders got some drop ear puppies from Chipwood, Jill's sire, but on the positive side I must hasten to state that some of the soundest-moving rears I ever got also came from

Figure 99: Ch. Todwil's Jamie by Ch. Surrey Sink or Swim x Ch. Todwil's Gentle On My Mind.

Jill's litter. So much for her parentage. Jill was an exceptionally fine bitch, and at first her drop ears presented no problem because at that time both ear types were shown together as Norwich. She finished her championship in short order. However, I did wonder about her future as breed separation approached.

Jill was first bred while a "Norwich" to my own English import, Eng. Am. Ch. Norelston Mr. Chan. Two puppies were whelpe —a prick ear girl and a

drop ear boy—and both were sold as pets. The male was sold locally and remained a drop ear with good ear placement and carriage. The bitch went out of state, and at six months her ears were still erect and I'm sure they stayed that way.

When the breed was divided in 1979 I knew I had a problem. I wrote the American Kennel Club, gave a complete account of Jill's history and parentage, and asked their advice. In due time the answer came, a new registration certificate, officially changing Jill from Norwich to Norfolk. This opened up several possibilities. I was in England the summer prior to breed separation, and, anticipating what was to come, I had discussed Jill with some prominent breeders there. One of the most reputable stated that since drop ears were dominant over prick, Jill would most likely produce drop-eared puppies if bred to a Norfolk. Having been a college professor for the past 25 years, I was intrigued by the prospect of test-breeding to see if my bitch would breed true as a Norfolk. If she did, fine; if she didn't, the puppies would be sold as pets and that would be the end of it. In my enthusiasm I was totally unprepared for the attitudes and "tunnel vision" I encountered from a few members of the Norwich and Norfolk Terrier Club. I had recently been appointed to the board of governors of the Club, and one member of the board, without a meeting or discussion, suggested that unless I "disposed" of this animal I should not be allowed to serve. Every effort was exerted to get the AKC to reverse its action, and when this failed, the Club president wrote an article in the AKC *Gazette* warning breeders of this "terrible plague" that had been unleashed on the Norfolk breed and admonishing them to "examine pedigrees carefully." My biggest disappointment was that not one of the Club's leadership showed a flicker of positive interest in this unique situation. Genuine support came from a number of longtime breeders and judges, and I shall be forever grateful to Joan Read and Anne Rogers Clark for their support and assistance in specific aspects of my experiment.

Jill's first breeding as a Norfolk was to a local dog, Ch. Bethway's Jack. One puppy was sold as a pet and the other two finished their championships. The second breeding to Ch. Elve Pure Magic yielded two champions. One, Ch. Todwil's Pac Man of Whitehall, was Reserve Winners Dog at Montgomery County from the Puppy Class and went on to earn multiple Group placements. Jill's third breeding was a repeat to Pure Magic and again produced two champions. The bitch, as a puppy, went Best in Sweepstakes at the floating Specialty at Chain O' Lakes, and the dog went Best of Winners at both Devon and Montgomery County. Jill's last breeding before retirement was to the Clarks' Ch. Surrey Sink or Swim. Of the two champions from this breeding, Ch. Todwil's Jamie, a black and tan bitch, is truly outstanding. She finished at eight months with three consecutive four-point majors and had earned three Group placements before her first birthday. Her litter brother, Ch. Todwil's Dapper Dan, completed his championship the weekend after his first birthday.

The first of Jill's grandchildren are now on the show scene and doing well. One is finished and giving a good account of himself as a Special. Another is nearing her championship and will soon be ready to test the next generation!

MARYLAND

Surrey (1977)
Mr. and Mrs. James Edward Clark,
Centreville, Maryland

When our elderly miniature Dachshund house pet died, Constance Larrabee tried to persuade us to take a Norwich Terrier as a replacement. Of much greater interest to us was the Norfolk, Nanfan Corricle, that Constance had just imported from Joy Taylor in England. Corricle was, in our opinion, one of the best that we had seen. We hinted that when she was bred we would welcome a bitch puppy—not the best one, mind you, because she would be just a pet. We already had the Poodles, the Whippets, the English Cockers, the Smooth Fox Terriers, and the Beagles, and certainly did not need the responsibility of showing yet another breed.

After finishing her championship, Corricle went to Ch. Wendover Torrent and in May 1977 produced two red bitches. One went to South America, and King's Prevention Ahoy came to us, to be known as "Midget" and to be our constant companion. Midget was all we had hoped for — game, smart, funny, adaptable, and intensely loyal. At five months, we took her to the Club match as a gesture of support. She won the match under Jack Simm — a triumph for the less-popular drop ears! Midget finished by going Best of Winners at the National Specialty under James Reynolds and was defeated only once in her title quest.

Meanwhile Constance Larrabee put Corricle to her new import Eng. Ch. Ickworth Peter Pence, from which came King's Prevention Belinda, who in turn was bred to the very important Ch. Elve Pure Magic. That breeding produced a rich black and tan, King's Prevention Jolly Roger. Jolly Roger, one of the handsomest Norfolks we had seen, alas, was a monorchid. In our opinion his condition was traumatic rather than hereditary, and furthermore his quality was too great to pass up. So Jolly Roger came to Sealark Farm to join Midget and be an in-house stud should the need arise. We felt strongly that he should never be offered at public stud. About this time we heard of a well-bred Norfolk bitch in search of a home, and so Lyndor's Kizzy, by Ch. Lyndor's Mister, swelled our ranks to three.

Midget was bred first to the English import Ch. El Cid of Tinkinswood, producing Surrey Above Board. She went next to Jolly Roger and delighted us with Ch. Surrey Sailor's Delight, who won the Sweepstakes under Mrs. Anne Winston in 1981 and went on to win the National Specialty from the classes under Mrs. Pauline

Figure 100: Ch. Surrey Sailor's Delight, 1982 National Specialty winner.

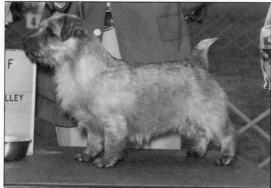

Ford the following year. Of greater import to us was a male in the litter, Ch. Surrey Sink or Swim, thought by many to be too much dog, but who proved to be an influential stud. He is, in fact, the top American-bred sire in the breed's history. Bred again to Jolly Roger, Midget produced Surrey Scrimshaw, a bitch of exquisite type, though criticized by some as too small.

Kizzy, bred to Jolly Roger,

produced Skiff and Dory. Skiff went to Jean Bryar's Norvik Kennels as a foundation dam, while Dory has remained an important part of the Surrey program. She has produced several champions, including Can. Am. Ch. Surrey Spinnaker and Surrey Frigate, who won the Sweepstakes under Mrs. Constance Larrabee the same day that Mrs. Joy Taylor chose her older sister, Surrey Binnacle, as Best of Winners at the Jubilee Specialty. Repeating the Kizzy/Jolly Roger breeding, we got two boys, Port and Sta'board. Port has done very well for his owners, Mr. and Mrs. Kazuhiko Hosaka, winning a National Specialty and the Breed at the AKC Centennial Show. Port became the first Norfolk since breed separation to win an all-breed Best in Show. Ch. Surrey Sta'board has also had a very successful career, winning the Breed at the Garden three times and topping the Terrier Group on several occasions.

Figure 101: Ch. Surrey Port owned by Mr. and Mrs. Kazuhiko Hosaka.

We look with much interest to Ch. Greenfields The Hustler, owned and bred by Ruth Cooper and Gaynor Green. The product of the Pure Magic daughter bred to Sink or Swim, he is of uncommon use at Surrey. It was he who sired the young Surrey Frigate out of Dory, who, after her Jubilee win, went on to finish in a single weekend. Remembering that Jolly Roger is by Pure Magic, one can see that The Hustler, out of a Pure Magic daughter, with a heavy infusion of King's Prevention Ahoy, knicks well with Surrey bitches. The Hustler was the second American-bred Best in Show Norfolk to be so honored, Surrey Port having been the first.

Surrey Norfolks, as a line, are still in their infancy. The establishment of an unmistakably recognizable type is a long and arduous task. We feel we have advanced to where certain attributes we feel important are beginning to surface on a regular basis. Someone was heard to say recently that they did not like "Surrey heads." This amused us a little, as we do not feel we have set a type in head. Nor do we feel we have yet stabilized size.

There are also certain structural features we would like to see improved.

And so "the beat goes on," providing the Clarks with pleasure, as they are devoted to the breed, its roots and its reasons, its size, and its temperament. Norfolks are, after all, companions and friends first, and if they can compete in the show ring that is an added plus. We hope only to continue what has gone before—to improve, but not change, the basic concepts of this charming breed.

Seneca Valley (1977)
Ann Erricker, Dickerson, Maryland

Anne Erricker's first drop ear Norwich was a Ch. Castle Point Iguana son with a harsh coat and a penchant for ratting. Anne's ability to maintain the sporting instincts and trouble-free coats of subsequent Norfolk litters has proved her reputation as a breeder. An occasional foray into the show ring keeps type stable. Seneca Valley Pooh, at his only show in 1983, was Best of Winners at the Montgomery County Specialty. Ch. Abbedale's Two Potato was bred at Seneca Valley, as was Red Mettle Sweet Bea, ANTA's 1988 Spring Racing and Go-To-Ground Champion at Kermit's Perch, Warrenton, Virginia.

Figure 102:
Ch. Abbedales
Six Gun by Ch.
Daffran Dusty x
Ch. Abbedales
Abigail Ray.

MICHIGAN

Abbedales (1969)
Joan Eckert and John Wood, Kalamazoo, Michigan

My love for Norfolks began 20 years ago while working for a kennel owned by Diana Gilmore. She owned four Norfolks (from Bethway Kennels in Connecticut) and occasionally boarded other Norfolks, so I gradually became well acquainted with the breed.

In 1969 I bought a bitch from Mrs. Gilmore that became Abbedales Tea and Crumpets. Two years later, with the help of Steven Hurt, I found Joan Read of Oyster Bay, New York, and her great stud, Ch. Elve Pure Magic. My bitch and Joan's

"T.G." proved to be two of the most important influences on my breeding program. Three puppies soon reared their lovely heads: Am. Can. Ch. Abbedales American Gigolo (Group winner and placer); Abbedales King James (the first certified Norfolk Hearing Dog); and Ch. Abbedales Abigail Ray, hunter supreme and dam of the 1985 National Specialty Best of Breed winner, Ch. Abbedales Six Gun. She also produced four other champions. "Abby" reared 31 puppies in 6 litters.

Our greatest satisfaction derives from breeding dogs that are as versatile in the field and on the race course as they are in the show ring.

NEW HAMPSHIRE

Kinsprit (1964)
Ellen Lee Kennelly, Peterborough, New Hampshire
In May 1970 Ellen Lee Kennelly met Nanfan Nutshell, who at the time was being hand-reared by Joy Taylor at Standall Cottage in England. Visiting with Sylvia Warren, who had already provided Ellen Lee with one drop-eared Norwich, the chance to import another puppy proved irresistible. Soon after, "Nutsy" arrived and sparked Ellen Lee's interest in both the breed and the Norwich Club. (She was later to serve as president.) Although Nutsy was not a ring candidate, she produced a champion in her first litter by a Heckle grandson, Ch. Castle Point Iguana. Kinsprit Nutcracker won his title handled by a junior at Westminster, with the Taylors watching fron ringside.

From Nutsy's second litter, Nancy Parker acquired the agile Kinsprit Token UD, who achieved notoriety in Obedience. Then, in 1979, she obtained a puppy bitch who became Ch. Nanfan Cornflower. Put to Ch. Hatchwoods Creme De Menthe, she produced Ch. Trownest Kinsprit Corncob CD.

Norvik (1980)
Jean Bryar, Meredith, New Hampshire
The Norvik prefix is well known among serious sled-dog racers, as its owner has competed successfully with her team of Huskies from New England to Alaska.

Wanting a smaller home companion, Jean Bryar selected Lyndor's Kizzy, a Norfolk bitch of good lineage and sound type. As the personalities of owner and pet proved incompatible, Kizzy became an important producer for the James E. Clarks' Surrey line. However, Kizzy's daughter, Surrey Skiff, by King's Prevention Jolly Roger, embodied both the character and conformation Jean Bryar wanted. In time, Skiff, a sister of the champions Surrey Port and Surrey Sta'board, also gained her championship and then proved her abilities as a brood. Among her winning offspring are Norvik the Witch, the first black and tan Norfolk bitch champion, and Julius F. Rumpf's foundation dam, Ch. Norvik Rightly So.

Now on her third generation of house-dog champions, Jean Bryar's select operation continues in limited competition, achieving high honors in the ring and at American Norfolk Terrier Association racing events.

NEW JERSEY

Jufelt (1982)
Judith Felton, Demarest, New Jersey

Judith Felton moved to the United States from England in 1983 with her family and two show-quality house dogs. In time the younger dog, Elve Black Shadow, joined the Domby Norfolks in Ohio, where he quickly became a champion. Judith Felton's other dog, Heathjul Christmas Robin, was shown by his owner in local competition. Robin gained his title in June 1986 and sired his first litter x Ch. Poole's Ide Mayflower Madam, later the dam of a trio of 1987 Jufelt hopefuls by Eng. Am. Ch. Jaeva Matti Brown.

Figure 103:
Ch. Heathjul
Christmas
Robin.

Poole's Ide (1976)
Greg Siner, Upper Montclair, New Jersey

Norfolk Terriers came into my life 12 years ago. I started with a cute bitch from the C and J Kennels of Carolyn and Jim Pyle. Since this Norfolk was just a pet and college was taking up most of my time, I didn't get involved with showing and breeding. After a few false starts, I acquired a bitch suitable for foundation stock from Joan Read in Oyster Bay, New York. Chidley Taboo, ("Nell"), by Ch. Daffran Dusty x Ch. Chidley Jinx, gained show points and in 1984 was Best Adult in the American Norfolk Terrier Association (ANTA) match under breeder Gaynor Green. Although an unfortunate accident ended Nell's show career, she was bred to Ch. Hatchwood's Creme de Menthe. The litter, the first to carry the Poole's Ide prefix, produced my first home-bred champion, Ch. Poole's Ide Beach Blanket Bingo.

Figure 104: Ch. Poole's Ide Mayflower Madam.

The second time I bred Nell was to a young dog I purchased from Enid Hallmark, Kilwinning Copperhead, by Ch. Daffran Dusty x Tridwr Red Riband. This breeding resulted in two more champions. The first to finish was Ch. Poole's Ide Mayflower Madam. "Mae" made her debut by being awarded Winners Bitch at the 1985 NNTC Specialty at seven months of age, finishing her championship a few months later. The second dog from this breeding to finish was Ch. Poole's Ide Big Chill.

In 1988 I am looking forward to exhibiting two new show prospects: Poole's Ide Pork Pie (Ch. Allright Magic Lamp x Chidley Taboo) and Poole's Ide Pachysandra (Eng. Am. Ch. Jaeva Matti Brown x Ch. Poole's Ide Mayflower Madam). Poole's Ide Kennel is also active in exhibiting and breeding Irish Water Spaniels.

NEW MEXICO

Bethway (1950—West 1974)
Barbara S. Fournier, Santa Fe, New Mexico

Barbara Fournier, a Norfolk breeder since 1950, has changed her focus in recent years from breeding and showing to judging. In the 1960s the kennel was at its largest with between 50 and 60 Norfolks of all ages in residence—possibly the largest kennel anywhere at that

YESTERDAY

Figure 105:
(Right) 1952, Beth-
way's first
champion,
Brigham Young.

TODAY

Figure 106:
(Left) 1987, Champion Glori's
Terrance by Nanfan Spartan of
Hoheit x Ch. Bethway's Cup Cake.

time. However, despite the shift of
activity, Barbara still maintains a
contiuous line. An historical account of Bethway Kennels can be
found in Chapter Two—American
Beginnings.

NEW YORK

Bear Hill (1983)
*Dr. Leon Lussier and Mrs. Patricia Lussier,
Selkirk, New York*

In 1983, at a New England summer show at which
their Welsh Terrier was being exhibited, the Leon Lussiers were captivated by a pair of Norfolk Terriers. Start-

ing with a pet from the Greenfields Kennels, the Lussiers went on the following year to seek a show-quality Norfolk. It was through the American Norfolk Terrier Club Information Circular (ANTIC) that they contacted Mr. and Mrs. Frank Dean in Kentucky and acquired their future first champion, Paprika of Whitehall. "Pappy" was soon joined by a stylish bitch puppy, Greenfields Cinnamon, also an easy future champion.

Success has followed success for these dedicated exhibitors, who have added Canadian titles to some of their homebreds, have won the annual ANTA (American Norfolk Terrier Association) match four times, with Ch. Paprika achieving a second and third place in all canine systems for point records in 1985, 1986, and 1987. The Lussiers readily credit Gaynor Green and Martha Dean, breeders of their foundation stock. They are justly proud of their homebred champions, Bear Hill's Mr. Pip and Miss Crisparkle, among others. An important recent addition to Bear Hill is Eng. Am. Ch. Ragus Pass the Buck, acquired in the spring of 1987.

Figure 107: (Left) **Second-generation home-bred Ch. Bear Hill's Toby Crackit by Ragus Pass the Buck x Ch. Bear Hill's Miss Chrisparkle.**

Figure 108: (Right) **Ch. Paprika of Whitehall by Ch. Surrey Sink or Swim x Todwil's ET of Whitehall with Dr. Leon Lussier.**

C and J Kennels (1965)
James and Carolyn Pyle, Freeville, New York

We have always been "dog people." My family had Irish Setters and Jim's family raised American Cocker Spaniels, so it has always been natural for us to have dogs in our lives.

In 1960 we started showing and breeding Rottweilers. Then, wanting a small breed that would get along well with the Rotties, we purchased our first Norfolk Terrier from Barbara S. Fournier in 1965. Nora was our foundation bitch and the first Norfolk (then called drop ear Norwich) to be on the cover of the AKC *Gazette* in January 1986.

We have bought several other Norfolks from Bobby Fournier and have never regretted doing so. We attribute the dark eyes and lovely ear sets of our dogs to the Bethway line. It was always a pleasure and a learning experience to drive to Bethany, Connecticut, to visit Bobby and her beautiful dogs.

It is a pleasure to report that C and J Kennels has introduced many new and happy owners to the breed; and through our methods of socialization, we have maintained the happy character and temperament of the breed.

Chidley (1974)
Joan R. Read and Barbara R. Ege
Oyster Bay, New York

Dogs have always been a part of my life. I grew up with a succession of my mother's Irish Terriers, my own Labradors, and other breeds belonging to my sisters. Multiplying our pets came naturally, as many members of our family raised dogs. One aunt was a true dog breeder and Best In Show judge. She had general advice on line breeding to impart, and attending shows with her was always a stimulating experience, although for

Figure 109: (Left) **Ch. Chidley Dandelion,** top breed winner for two years. Owner: Barbara Ege.

Figure 110: (Right) **Ch. Chidley Jinx, dam of three champions.**

me, field work with Labradors proved more challenging.

The gift of a Norwich bitch in 1951 rekindled my terrier ties. Her size and spirit suited me since I could no longer handle big dogs in the field. After many years as a Norwich breeder-exhibitor, judge, and AKC *Gazette* columnist, Norfolks entered my life. Though my first Norfolk purchase proved a false start, I discovered a young bitch puppy, Shenanigans of Chidley, from the last Newry litter. Then followed a 10-week-old male import from Michael Crawley's first Elve litter, thanks to a shrewd tip from Marjorie Bunting in England. These fortunate purchases gave me sturdy foundation stock which shaped the course of Norfolks here for the next decade. My Crawley import, Elve Pure Magic, or "TG," proved a boon to other breeders. He was a character in his own right, a compact, masculine dog who exerted dominant influences for many current kennels, including Abbedales; Anderscroft; Glenelg; Greenfields; Raggedge; Surrey; Todwil; Wenwagon; Whitehall; and Yarrow.

In the autumn of 1982 the eight-month visit of the English import Eng. Am. Ch. Daffran Dusty reinforced TG's influence in five of these kennels. "Dusty" returned to England an American champion and gained his international status in 1985. These two U.K. bred dogs were leading sires before 1987 when our German import, Ch. Allright Magic Lamp CG, started his influential rise. Now our developing strength is shared by four generations of bitches to further benefit breeders, both at home and abroad.

Most fortunately for Chidley my daughter, Barbara R. Ege, donates her time and talents to our dogs, the breed, its club, ANTA (the American Norfolk Terrier Association), and to ANTIC, the Norfolk quarterly. Along with Beth Sweigart, the show dog star maker, we all enjoy raising happy winning pets for sport and spoiling.

Max-Well (1974)
Barbara Miller and Suzann Bobley
East Hills, Roslyn, New York

A breeding program is like a child. You conceive it, give birth to it, protect it, watch it grow, guide it, and set up goals — but above all are proud of it.

Figure 111:
Barbara Miller
and Ch. Max-
Well's Christmas
Crackers. *Photo
Margaret Miller.*

Figure 112:
Ch. Nanfan
Crunch at Mont-
gomery County
Kennel Club
Show, 1986.

My co-owner, Suzann Bo-
bley, and I began with Soft-
coated Wheaten Terriers in
1967; but in 1974 after being introduced to Ch. Badgewood
Monty Collins at the home of
his handler, Jack Simm, I
brought the first Norfolk Terriers to Max-Well. The male
was entirely of Badgewood
breeding, and the bitch was
sired by Monty Collins.

Our breeding program be-
gan. All bitches were to live at
my home. (They still do.) All males were to live at Sue's.
The first Max-Well Norfolk litter was a batch of five lively charmers. We continued to produce large litters until
one day our beginner's luck changed. We've also had litters of one whelp. Have we had problems? Doesn't eve-
ryone who breeds dogs over an extended period of
time?

Basically, however, we've been fortunate. We've
bred no indications of hip dysplasia, as we've routinely
x-rayed all of our stock. The mouths on our Norfolk are
intact, having the required scissors or level bite. At Max-
Well we breed for soundness and temperament. If we
happen to produce beauty as well, we show it off in the
ring. Max-Well has produced 13 champions to date. The
reigning queen of the brood bitches, Ch. Max-Well's Liberty Bell, has produced a total
of six titled get.

And then there is our star,
Ch. Nanfan Crunch. "Crunch"
was bred by the famous English
Norfolk breeder Joy Taylor, and
from the moment he arrived, I
knew that he would make Norfolk history here. He earned his
championship, guided by Peter
Green and Beth Sweigart, and
then I afforded him every opportunity by placing him under
the care and guidance of the

young professional Susan DePew. Crunch is a three-time Best of Breed winner at Westminster, and the only Norfolk Terrier to have placed in the Westminster Terrier Group in two successive years (1987 and 1988), before retirement at age four. He is the top Norfolk in breed history, having gained 14 all-breed Best in Shows, over 50 Terrier Group wins, countless Group placements, and the Number 4 or Number 5 Terrier under the two recognized point systems, respectively. One win that I cherish was at Montgomery County in 1986, when English breeder-judge Gilean White awarded Crunch the Specialty BOB ribbon. Crunch youngsters who have earned their championships are a credit to the terrier world.

We also own and breed top stud dogs. Eng. Am. Ch. Jaeva Matti Brown, bred by Martin Phillips, arrived on these shores directly after his third Best of Breed win at Crufts in 1987. He is the only Norfolk to have placed Reserve to the Terrier Group winner at this prestigious show, and he is also a leading English Norfolk stud. In America he has sired many offspring, and some of these have achieved major points from the Puppy Classes. Matti has been awarded many Terrier Group wins and a Best of Breed under Norwich breeder-judge Edward Jenner at the Montgomery County Kennel Club Show in 1987. I know Matti will sire many more puppies to enhance the quality of the breed. Watch out World: Matti's daughter, Eng. Ch. Clockwise of Jaeva, BOB at Crufts in 1988, whom I own, has already gained Terrier Group placements and her first Best in Show.

But does this truly matter? Not to us. Records are the "gravy" for a job well done, and the show ring is just that — a showcase. What concerns us above all else is the happiness and soundness of our Max-Well puppies. Just knowing they are loved and well cared for in their new homes is the greatest satisfaction of all. As Max-Well Norfolk walk into the future, their past speaks for itself.

Neverdone (1969)
Dr. and Mrs. Donald P. Regula, Schenectady, New York

Neverdone Kennels started in 1955 with Labrador Retrievers, and in 1969 we purchased our first Norfolk Terrier, Wendover Quest, from Mrs. Priscilla Mallory.

After breeding and showing sporting breeds for 14 years, an injury caused us to search for a smaller breed. With my childhood sport of fox hunting, the dual purpose of the Norfolk seemed to match our new desires.

We have expanded by leaps and bounds in the years following. We have whelped 14 Norfolk litters, with a total of 42 puppies. Whelping problems have been minimal, with only two caesarian sections to date.

Our Norfolk these days total five (our "walking carpet") and are companions to our English Setters. Living with our Setters, we can truthfully say that the Norfolk is certainly a "large dog in a small package."

Reidmar (1984)
Nat R. LaMar, Brooklyn, New York

Figure 113: Nat LaMar with Anderscroft Henna LaMar, 1985.

I've never yet known a southern family who didn't love animals—dogs in particular—and mine was no exception. My boyhood menagerie in Atlanta included a succession of Chow-Chows and wonderful Am-erican Cockers. Years later, in the 1960s, I met my first Norwich Terrier when I came to New York after college to look for a job in publishing. I encountered him one summer evening in a chic East Side bistro. "Oinkers" was a prick ear Norwich, and he belonged to Patricia Hemingway, a lady who was not only extraordinarily intelligent and glamorous, but a great restauranteur and dog fancier. Pat eventually advised me in the purchase of my first Norwich prick ear, a Whinlatter bitch whom I bred to the Upland Spring line of the late Mrs. Howe Low. Before I knew it I had produced a litter—of one (you heard me, one), who went on to become Ch. Spicer's Jones, top-ranking Norwich in points for 1969.

As I continued to edit books and breed my occasional litters of prick ears I kept noticing, out of the corner of my eye, Barbara Fournier's Bethway drop ear Norwich. This was not just because they were top-quality dogs and were winning all over the place, but because they had a kind of pixilated intelligence and rascality that I couldn't escape. (What I was sensing, without knowing it, were some of the distinct differences between Norfolk and Norwich.) Then came a period in prick ear Norwich development when everything seemed to look like a little teddy bear. That was when I stopped "littering" and took some time off to think.

Figure 114:
Waiting for Nat.

Five years ago, after 15 years of Norwich, I acquired my first Norfolk—an Anderscroft (Jane and Everett Anderson) bitch by a Bethway sire. "Henna LaMar" is no champion, nor will she ever become one; but she is typey, red, and as bright as a new coin. With Chidley Charm, a de facto champion I purchased later from Joan R. Read, I've now acquired two bitches that are producing at the very least a line of wonderful pets. Each has whelped three litters so far, and the news from all quarters is decidedly good: delighted, happy owners. My current, and more difficult, goal is a more carefully developed breeding program that will produce better dogs. Meanwhile, I could not have imagined the fun, harassment, time, and just plain sweat that my "new beginnings" in this distinctly different breed, my Norfolk, have yielded.

Rightly So (1982)
Julius F. Rumpf and Virginia Hedges
Sag Harbor, New York

This successful show kennel of Norfolks is owned by the serious young handler, Julius F. Rumpf, with the dedicated help of Virginia Hedges in Sag Harbor, New York.

Learning about the breed through the Surrey dogs of the James Edward Clarks, Fritz Rumpf acquired his foundation dam from Jean Bryar of the Norvik prefix.

Figure 115:
Rightly So
Carbon Copy.

This red bitch, Rightly So, finished her championship at the Montgomery County Specialty in 1983. That same year Virginia Hedges acquired a Norfolk companion from a local veterinarian, and a collaborative interest in the breed was established.

Ch. Norvik Rightly So, Fritz Rumpf's foundation dam, has been bred to a succession of champions and has produced winning show dogs in every litter. "My goal as a Norfolk breeder," Fritz says, "is to come up with a typey animal that will do well in the show ring, but also will be able to go to ground properly."

While still a class dog at the 1988 Norfolk Specialty Show, Ch. Rightly So Original Sin, by Ch. Surrey Sink or Swim x Ch. Rightly So Henbit, won the Sweepstakes. Then he bowed to his seven-and-one-half-month-old kennelmate Rightly So Carbon Copy, who was judged both Winners Dog and Best of Opposite Sex by Mrs. James E. Clark. "Copy" doubles on the Rightly So foundation bitch out of her Ch. Max-Well's Lone Ranger daughter.

Noted for its immaculate presentation, Rightly So has used a broad spectrum of outside studs to produce its animated, tidy show dogs. To date, Ch. Rightly So Right Now is an international champion, with titles in Puerto Rico and Mexico.

Sage (1957)
Prudence Read, Bedford Hills, New York

Since 1957 Prudence and Peter Read have owned five producing companion bitches and have reared "a mixed bag of charming puppies every year or two. Some were fluffies, many were black and tans, two are bench champions, and a sprinkling have attained Obedience titles."

Cricket, their first Norfolk, developed from a "stringy black and tan puppy to a beauty—a terror to woodchucks and a loyal friend to her family." Cricket defended her property around the clock, had plenty of honest scars, and set the standard in courage, humor, and wisdom for future Sage denizens.

The Reads started their line with Joy of Jasmine Jones, a red bitch purchased from Mrs. Fifield Workum. Sired by Ch. Bethway's Mr. Kennedy, Jasmine's dam also hailed from early imports and the Jones-named line of the pioneer Virginia breeder Frederick Warburg. Through the careful choice of compatible studs for color, conformation, and personality, Pru Read's personal "kitchen venture" thrives. Puppies remain in their sporting environment until the Reads are "convinced that potential owners have better places for the Sage puppies that will encourage their development."

Today Ch. Sage's Solomon Seal CDX is working toward his Utility degree, while his black and tan niece is already a truly game vermin exterminator with show potential.

Figure 116: Eng. Am. Ch. Ragus Brown Smudge.

Turkhill (1971)
Mrs. H. R. Slocum, Glen Cove, New York

The Slocums' first drop ear Norwich "Crumpet"—charming and somewhat Chaplinesque—came from Mrs. Rita Haggerty. Their next, a compact Nanfan, came from England but, sadly, died of an obstruction. Then, in 1976, as an anniversary present, Eng. Ch. Ragus Brown Smudge joined the Slocums and created a niche in Norfolk history. After becoming an International Champion, "Smudge" produced, in three litters, three bench champions and a CD winner. Her line continues today with many titled offspring for Pliny Jewell's Annursnac Kennel; the Joseph Mattisons' Cybele Kennel; and Joan Eckert's Abbedales Kennel.

Yarrow (1980)
Beth Sweigart, Oyster Bay, New York

I was given my first Norfolk, Raggedge Are You

Figure 117:
Ch. Raggedge
Are You Ready—
"Muffin"—and
Beth Sweigart.

Ready, in the fall of 1980. She was bred by John Mandeville and came to me when she was one and a half years old. "Muffin" was a spectacular show dog and loved every minute of being in the ring. She was Best of Breed from the classes at Westminster in 1981 and was the first Norfolk bitch to win a Group at the Bryn Mawr Kennel Club Show under Mr. William Kendrick.

Because Muffin loved dog shows and I loved showing her, her career as a brood bitch got off to a late start. Of the seven puppies she has produced, five have completed their championships: Ch. Yarrow's Ruff N' Ready; Ch. Yarrow's Everready; Ch. Yarrow's Remarkable; Ch. Yarrow's Whiz Bang; and Ch. Yarrow's Top of the Mark. Currently Muffin has three champion granddaughters.

Because I believe strongly that Norfolk puppies do not fare well in a kennel environment but should be raised as house dogs, I have never kept very many at one time; nor have I raised many litters. With the help of my mother and Joan Read at Chidley, all my litters have been raised as house dogs. I feel that socializing them at home better prepares them for life as a show dog or as someone's special pet.

Norfolks are naturally happy and easygoing companions. Whether or not you ever breed a litter or enter your Norfolk in a show, just having one to own and love is in itself a most rewarding experience. This is why I feel my Muffin has truly become my "best friend."

NORTH CAROLINA

Barwood (1980)
Barbara A. Runquist, Greensboro, North Carolina

Because I was looking for a small house pet that would fit in a townhouse environment, I went to see Swithun, a Norfolk bred by John H. Beeler of the New Garden prefix. Swithun immediately pulled one of the typical Norfolk cons. Looking for a home, he would do anything to please you; after he got it everything had to be on his terms.

In sheer self-defense I enrolled Swithun in Obedience class. I was then encourged to enter him in Obedience trials. Taking a natural "ham" into the ring is a humbling experience. They perform to please the audience, not you. One thing I have found is I cannot rush my dogs. They will learn at their own pace and in their own way. They really enjoy attending class and are disappointed if they can't go.

New Garden Swithun acquired his CD in July 1979 and his CDX in May 1981. Castle Point Bark gained his CD in March 1982, and Barwood Lord Darby finished his AKC championship in October 1984.

New Garden (1965)
Anne C. Beeler, Greensboro, North Carolina

After World War II in England, I saw a photograph of a Norfolk puppy (in a teacup) in *Country Life* magazine and fell in love. Mrs. Richardson sold me two—a half-brother and sister.

My late husband, John H. Beeler, owned our first brood bitch and thus was always "the breeder." We bred two champions—Ch. New Garden Godiva and Ch. New Garden Eadith, owned by Mary Fine. Eadith excels in the Obedience ring also and has the Utility Degree (UD) both in Canada and the United States. New Garden Swithun has a CDX, and New Garden Dunston, bred by Patricia Adams Lent, has a CD.

Pennywhistle (1982)
Mary B. Rand,
Brown's Summit, North Carolina

Pennywhistle was started by Mary Rand in 1982 when she imported Nanfan Summer Sweet, a bitch puppy. Since then she has acquired a bitch and a dog from Nanfan and has established her own breeding program.

Mary Rand's first Pennywhistle litter was whelped in 1985, and the first home-bred champion, Pennywhistle Razzle Dazzle, finished in 1986. Pennywhistle's breed-

Figure 118:
Ch. Pennywhistle
Razzle Dazzle.

ing aims are to preserve the Nanfan "look" and to produce sound dogs with good temperaments. The Rands and their Norfolks have just moved into new quarters, where the dogs have the run of 70 acres which they share with a large beaver colony.

Figure 119:
Rightly So What Now.

OHIO

Buckeye (1985)
Richard and Kay McKinstry, Athens, Ohio

After Rightly So What went Winners Dog at the NNTC Specialty Show in 1985, the Richard McKinstrys acquired for their young champion a bride, Rightly So What Now, daughter of Eng. Ch. Ragus Bantum Cock and, like her mate, bred by F. J. Rumpf. From this union the McKinstrys' established Golden Retriever kennel now boasts its own homebred Norfolk champion, a black and tan, Buckeye Huckleberry, from their first litter.

Domby (1984)
Anthony Gabrielli and Wayne Palmer,
Cleveland Heights, Ohio

Figure 120:
Ch. Domby's Mrs. Cornelia Pipchin.

Experienced with other breeds, it was Tony Gabrielli's and Wayne Palmer's hope that their first Norfolk bitch puppy, Pool's Ide Beach Blanket Bingo, would grow up to be showworthy. Within weeks of her arrival they also acquired an overweight, mature male import, Elve Black Shadow. After careful exercise and conditioning, Shadow became the first male U.S. black and tan Norfolk champion, and Bingo, by Ch. Hatchwoods Creme de Menthe of Cracknor x Chidley Taboo, gained points and starred at terrier racing. Today their original Norfolk pair are both champions, and have a daughter, Dom-

by's Mrs. Cornelia Pipchin, whose litter brother is being trained as a hearing-ear dog. The supportive interest of the Domby prefix has effectively helped the breed and exhibitors in the Ohio area and at many out-of-town ANTA events.

OREGON

Landmark (1986)
Franzi Corman, Yamhill, Oregon

After years of experience with a large working breed, Franzi Corman discovered Norfolks. Her six-month wait for one ended in May 1986 when she flew East to collect a recently weaned puppy, her future champion, Yarrow's Jasmine. This happened at the Jubilee Specialty Show and it was a day to remember as Jasmine's sire, Allright Magic Lamp, was Best of Winners and her granddam, Ch. Raggedge Are You Ready (Beth Sweigart's "Muffin"), won the Veteran's Class.

Figure 121: Ch. Yarrow's Jasmine.

A year later the successful breed stud Ch. Chidley Magic Marker traveled to Oregon to become a Landmark house dog. While still co-owned by Helen Brann in Connecticut, "Mark" now enjoys the space and affection denied many show dogs. Most recently, Jasmine's half-sister from Yarrow and an Allright bitch puppy from Germany have joined Franzi's winning homebred Ch. Landmark Magic Legacy from Jasmine and Mark's first litter.

PENNSYLVANIA

Greenfields (1980)
Gaynor E. Green, Bowmansville, Pennsylvania

My foundation bitch is Ch. Raggedge Best Bet ("Bebe") by Ch. Elve Pure Magic x Mt. Paul Vesper. I didn't choose Bebe, she chose me. I'd had a pet Norwich before, but she was shy and hadn't gotten along with Binny, our Sealyham house dog. We were fortunate to obtain Bebe from John Mandeville in September 1980.

Figure 122:
Ch. Raggedge
Best Bet.

She was 15 months old and walked into our house and became Binny's companion until he died in 1984.

I bred Bebe, whom I'd finished in 1981, to Ch. Hubbestad Wee Johan, and she whelped three puppies that were big, fat, and strong. However, when they were 15 days old they contracted a virus and in two hours all three were dead. That was a sad and traumatic experience; but I bred Bebe again—this time to Ch. Surrey Sink or Swim. She again had three pups, again whelped naturally, and the entire litter survived (including me). Bebe is a super mother, and has passed this down to all her daughters.

Bebe's second litter produced Ch. Greenfields Abigail and Ch. Greenfields Tea and Crumpets, both of whom I finished in 1983. The other bitch in the litter went to the Mandevilles. That year I again bred Bebe, this time to Ch. Daffran Dusty, and she whelped five puppies and successfully raised them all. Out of that litter three were shown, and I finished Ch. Greenfields The Gambler in 1985. In 1985 I also finished Ch. Greenfields The Hustler, who is out of another litter by Surrey Sink or Swim.

I think that for the comparatively few years that I've been involved in Norfolks I've been relatively successful. I have bred five champions and finished six, including Bebe. All my Norfolks are co-owned with Ruth Cooper. I only raise one or two litters a year and am very selective about seeing dogs to good homes. In fact, that is my main concern. I try not to fool myself and become "kennel blind."

VIRGINIA

Glenelg (1972)
Deborah C. Pritchard, Middleburg, Virginia

While fox hunting in Virginia in 1972, I met a Norwich and fell in love. I didn't notice whether the ears were drop or prick; I was simply charmed by the personality and hardy appearance. Returning home to New Jersey, I was lucky enough to find a breeder, Mrs. Basil Stetson, and a drop-eared bitch puppy, Sionnach Nora, virtually in my own backyard in Princeton. Seventeen years later I still have Nora's line including puppies out of Glenelg Parsley. These, of course, are Nora's great-great-grandchildren.

Nora's grandson, Ch. Glenelg Tuff Too, is the only dog I have shown. With the noted handler Peter Green's help, Tuff finished his championship, and with Damara Bolte he went Winners Dog at Westminster in 1981. In 1982 he went Best of Breed at Westminster.

While living in New Jersey I always bred into Mary Baird's Castle Point line. After moving to Virginia I acquired King's Prevention Damara, a daughter of Ch. Nanfan Corricle, from Constance Larrabee. The best breeding I've had was between Damara's daughter, Glenelg Magic Curry (Ch. Elve Pure Magic x King's Prevention Damara) and Ch. Chidley Magic Marker, a Pure Magic grandson. I believe this combination of the Nanfan and Ragus lines, bred in this country, is responsible for some of the most successful Norfolks seen in the ring over the past four to five years.

Wenwagon (1977)
Linda and Edwin Plummer, Warrenton, Virginia

My mother always had a dog when I was growing up, a Beagle, a Poodle, and a Maltese, so when I had my own place I of course wanted a dog of my own. A friend of my mother's had a Cairn Terrier that I much admired, and typical of me, I found myself in a pet shop looking at what I thought was a Cairn. The hard-sell manager of the shop knew a sucker when he saw one and had me holding the four-month-old puppy in no time. By the time he told me it was a Norwich Terrier, I didn't care what breed it was, but he did talk me into buying the valuable and informative book **How To Raise And Train A Norwich Terrier** by Barbara Fournier. This I read over and over again until I could find other literature on the breed. My pet shop find, "Honey," was a prick ear Norwich, and I had fun tracing her ancestry

Figure 123:
Chidley
Lark.

and learning all about the breed after finally meeting breeders in Washington D.C. and Berryville, Virginia.

Ten years later I met my first Norfolk Terrier at Constance Larrabee's King's Prevention Kennels in Chestertown, Maryland. Having just lost my beloved Honey, I fell in love with this independent, crazy character, so unlike my first Norwich, who had been painfully devoted to me. King's Prevention Belinda is a caricature of a Norfolk—really neither a Norwich nor a Norfolk. Her ears slowly but surely went straight up and are like great antennae, constantly watching TV, her favorite pastime. She had three litters of puppies—the last two by caesarian—and then was spayed. Most of her puppies inherited her prick ears, but one that didn't is King's Prevention Jolly Roger, sired by Ch. Elve Pure Magic, who has done very well siring puppies for the James E. Clarks' Surrey Kennels.

By this time I was very interested in the breed and had developed a close friendship with the knowledgeable breeder and canine historian Joan Read, who enthusiastically shared with me her wealth of information and eventually sold me my second Norfolk, Chidley Lark. Lark is an attractive daughter of Ch. Daffran Dusty out of one of my favorite Norfolks, Chidley Pooka. She is the foundation dam for all Wenwagon stock, which includes my first homebred champion, Wenwagon Fergie. Lark spends most of her time training for Norfolk races by chasing squirrels with my white Poodle and Eddie's black and tan Norfolk, Ch. Chidley Magic Moon, her constant companions.

WEST VIRGINIA

Hobbitshire (1984)
Clay and Betty Price, Beckley, West Virginia
Hobbitshire Kennels is small and new to the breed. Our foundation bitch, Abbedale's Taters and Tea (Ch.

Abbedale's Two Potato x Abbedale's American Hillary) is only three and a half years old. Her first ("A") litter by Nanfan Whistle (a full brother of Ch. Nanfan Crunch) produced two champions: Ch. Hobbitshire Anne of Abbedales for Joan Eckert, and our own Ch. Hobbitshire Allyson. The latter started her show career at seven months by winning a 5-point major, always competing from the Bred By Exhibitor Class.

Our second litter was struck by a Parvo tragedy and only two of the five survived. We have since had litters sired by our Ch. Abbedales Fox Shadow (Ch. Elve Black Shadow x Ch. Abbedales Six Pence), the "main man" here. With very novice grooming (I didn't know until after he had finished his championship that the longest hair on his ears should be removed) and an owner-handler who had never before been in a show ring, "Shadow" won Best Puppy at ANTA's 1986 Soirée Match in Leesburg, Virginia. He finished his championship at 13 months, with most of his points coming from the Puppy Class, handled exclusively by Clay Price.

With this start and the bloodlines we have—Abbedales, Elve, Nanfan, and Daffran—we hope we are on the way to what we want. Our bitches are free whelpers and ideal mothers. The most important thing, of course, is that we love our dogs. Those we have sold have all gone to loving homes, and all have the temperament that is so very important.

OTHER STAUNCH BREED SUPPORTERS

Capstone	CA	Roger Cutler
Charnwood	MN	Mr. and Mrs. Chas. Leavitt III
Cybele	MA	Mr. and Mrs. Jos. Mattison III
Hartleigh	NJ	Phyllis Hart
Lime Tree	NY	Mr. and Mrs. Robert V. Lindsay
Mayfair	CA	Kathleen Eimil
Pinchbeck	NJ	Susan M. Ely
Queens Gate	NY	Sarah Dombroski
Windsong	CT	Helen Brann

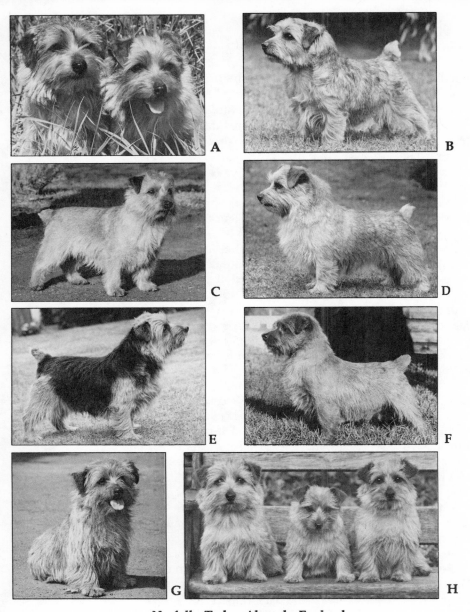

Norfolks Today: Abroad – England

Figure 124: (A, l to r) Titanium Fanciful by Ragus Whipcord x Ch. Titanium Just Fancy, 1980, and her dam, Titanium Gold Digger, 1982 .

Figure 125: (B) Ch. Heathjul Christmas Cracker by Ch. Salad Burnet of Vicbrita x Elve Pure Joy.

Figure 126: (C) Ch. Pipridges Templar, 1974, by Ch. Nanfan Nobleman x Pipridges Innis.

Figure 127: (D) Lees Sweet Briar, 1979, by Ragus Brown Sauce x Lees Rudbeckia.

Figure 128: (E) Elve Witch King by Ch. Ragus Browned Off x Elve Mimosa Bunce.

Figure 129: (F) Int. Ch. Ickworth Kythe of Ryslip, 1970, by Ch. Ickworth Ready x Ickworth Bluemarking Katriona.

Figure 130: (G) Ch. Crackshill Hardy by Ch. Ragus Whipcord x Nanfan Nightcap of Crackshill.

Figure 131: (H, l to r) Vicbrita's Bergamot, Tussie Mussie, and Star Anise. All are by Ch. Salad Burnet of Vicbrita x Sweet Cicely of Vicbrita. *All photos © Sally Anne Thompson.*

4

NORFOLKS TODAY: ABROAD

The following kennels and dogs illustrate the influences and interrelationship of Norfolk parent stock throughout the world.

We are grateful to: Eileen Needham, England; Eva Valinger, Sweden; Frauke Hinsch, Germany; and Margot Johnson, Canada, for their collected data.

ENGLAND

In 1964 after breed separation into Norwich and Norfolk Terriers in the United Kingdom, Norfolks were dominated by a handful of kennels including Nanfan, Ickworth, and Ragus. In the last few years this has changed, and now several newer dedicated exhibitors and breeders have joined the ranks of those prepared to persevere in the breed. It is mainly these newcomers we shall consider here.

Figure 132: Int. Ch. Nanfan Sweetcorn by Ch. Nanfan Heckle x Nanfan Sickle.

Cracknor

This prefix, famous in Sweden, came to England in 1977 when Elizabeth Matell returned there to work for *Dog World*. She brought with her two dogs. One was Cracknor Capricorn, owned jointly with the Swedish breeder Mrs. Haglund and the only foreign-born Norfolk to win a CC in England. Capricorn was returned to Sweden after having sired only one English litter, to Cherry Howard's Peppermint. The second Matell Norfolk was the Swedish and

Norwegian Champion Nanfan Sweetcorn, litter brother of the famous Ch. Nanfan Sweet Apple. "Corn" gained his title in 1980, becoming the thirteenth champion offspring of the then Top Sire, Ch. Nanfan Heckle. In 1982 Sweetcorn's son, Cracknor Candidate, went to Germany, where he has been a dominant breed force and in 1985 was World Champion. (See "Sweden" for further Cracknor information.)

Crackshill

Coming to Norfolks from Cocker Spaniels, Barbara Ritchie won her first CC in the breed in 1978, making up her first champion, Crackshill Hardy, in 1980. Hardy, of half-Nanfan, half-Ragus breeding, is the sire of Martin Phillips's Ch. Jaeva Matti Brown. Ritchie also bred Ch. Ragus Bow Bells.

Figure 133: Eng. Am. Ch. Daffran Dusty by Ickworth Bacardi x Daffran Dallus.

Daffran

Daphne Thacker won her first Challenge Certificate in Norfolks in 1975, making up her first champion, Daffran Dana, in 1977. At the last show of the year in 1979 her second champion, Daffran Dallus, a leading winner that year, followed. In October 1982 dual CC winner Daffran Dusty left England to join Joan Read's Chidley Kennels in Oyster Bay, New York, as guest stud, returning to England an American champion with one German and ten American champion get. "Dusty" won his qualifying CC in 1985.

Elve

Michael Crawley, whose wife, Lesley, partners her mother, Mrs. Marjorie Bunting, in the Ragus prefix, won his first CC with Ch. Ragus Browned Off in 1976. Browned Off had already gained his title while with the Ragus Kennel, but was Top Stud in 1982 and 1983 under Mr. Crawley's ownership. The first Elve litter contained Am. Ch. Elve Pure Magic, an outstanding sire in the U.S., and Elve Pure Joy, dam of Ch. Heathjul Christmas Cracker and Am. Ch. Heathjul Christmas Robin. Successes with two further Ragus exhibits followed: a bitch,

Ch. Ragus Brown Cider (made up in 1979, a seventh champion offspring of her dam, Ch. Ragus Brown Sugar), and a dog, Ch. Ragus Brigadoon (made up in 1980 and exported to Sweden soon afterwards). In 1981 Michael Crawley won a first CC with homebred Elve Poppy Bolger, who was the year's Top Winner. In 1985 another homebred bitch, Ch. Elve Esmeralda Took, gained her title; and yet another bitch, Ch. Elve Ruby Puddifoot, qualified for her title at the last show of the year in 1987.

Figure 134: (Left) **Ch. Elve Poppy Bolger by Ch. Ragus Brass Tacks x Ragus Busy Lizzie.** (Right) **Ch. Ragus Browned Off.**

Hatchwoods

Under this prefix, belonging to Cherry Howard, Hatchwoods Humbug (litter sister to Am. Ch. Hatchwoods Creme de Menthe of Cracknor) a double CC winner, received her first CC in 1980. Humbug's son, Hatchwoods Bugsy Malone, took the CC and Best in Show at the NTC Championship Show in 1986. Cherry Howard's painted trophies have frequently enhanced American Norfolk Terrier Association (ANTA) events in the United States.

Jaeva

Martin Phillips took his first CC in the breed with Jaeva Bizzi Lizzi (Ch. Jaeva Matti Brown's granddam) in 1981, and bred Ch. Ragus Bijou (qualified in 1982). Since then this kennel, founded on Ragus stock, has qualified Ch. Jaeva Bisto Brown (1984), the first champion with the Jaeva prefix; and the 1985 Top Winner, Ch. Jaeva Matti Brown (three times Best of Breed at Crufts). Also qualified was the 1986 Top Winner, Ch. Jaeva Brown Sauce, and top-winning bitch, Ch. Nathan's Sparring Partner of Jaeva (bred by Jon Rudkin). Phillips was the Top Breeder/Kennel in 1986, with Ch. Matti Brown a leading stud dog. In 1987 he made up two more bitches, Ch. Clockwise of Jaeva (bred by Tina Bentley) and homebred Ch. Jaeva Brown Treacle, whilst Ch. Brown Sauce proved himself to be one of 1987's leading studs.

Figure 135: **Hatchwoods Bugsy Malone, a CC winner, by Int. Ch. Nanfan Sweetcorn.** *Photo: © Sally Anne Thompson.*

Figure 136:
(Left) **Martin Phillips with Ch. Nathans Spar-
ring Partner of Jaeva by Ch. Vicbrita Bergamot
x Janning Merry Maid.**
Photo B. Miller.
Figure 137:
(Upper right) **Ch. Jaeva Brown Sauce by Eng.
Am. Ch. Jaeva Matti Brown x Rass-Ma-Tass of
Jaeva.** *Photo Dalton.*

Figure 138:
Lowmita Wren,
dual CC winner,
by Ch. Timber-
falling King's
Crown x Nanfan
Candycorn.

Lowmita

Dorothy Buck Dorkins took her first CC in the breed in 1977 with Ch. Nanfan Nectarine (made up in 1980). Unfortunately, Nectarine died at an early age. Mrs. Dorkins bred Ch. Lowmita Hazelnut in her first litter of Norfolks and was a leading breeder in 1982 and 1983.

Nathans

Jon Rudkin qualified his first champion, the black and tan Ch. Nathans Genisis Ragusa Prince, by winning CCs at three successive shows in 1985. Genisis was the fourteenth champion offspring of the then 13-year-old Ch. Ragus Whipcord.

Pipridges

David Saltmarsh, a former NTC committee chairman, qualified Ch. Pipridges Templar (his first show dog) in 1977 and followed with a second champion dog, Ch. Pipridges Hustler, in 1985.

Newthatch

Richell

Figure 139: (Left) Ch. Newthatch Blue Bell of Jaeva by Jaeva Brown Sauce x Newthatch Folly. Owner: Martin Phillips. Breeder: Pat Keen.

Figure 140: (Right) 1988 Crufts CC winner Ch. Richell Coffee Playboy by Ch. And Harry of Titanium x Daffran Dinky with owner Rita Mitchell.

Pottawotames

This kennel, whose prefix was taken from the name of a North American Indian tribe, won a first CC with owner Joyce Turner's Roses of Kenwunn of Pottawotames in 1983; but it was not until 1986 that the kennel qualified its first champion, homebred Ch. Pottawotames Rdainyanka, the sixteenth champion offspring of Ch. Ragus Whipcord.

Ryslip

Elizabeth Cartledge took her first CC in Norfolks in England in 1973. She then went on to qualify her Ch. Nanfan Wedding Present (who was in fact a wedding present from the *Dog World* staff, where Elizabeth worked, when she married Joe Cartledge). Then, in 1975 Int. Ch. Ickworth Kythe of Ryslip began his show career in England before being sent to Sweden. On his return to the U.K., he qualified for his English title in 1976. From Ch. Nanfan Wedding Present came homebred Ch. Ryslip Lovebug, Best in Show at the NTC Championship Show in 1978. In 1979 another homebred bitch, Ch. Ryslip Lucy Lastic, gained her title. Ch. Ryslip Mixed Blessings, although owned and exhibited by Jane Miller of the Brio Scottish Terriers, was bred at Ryslip. She was Best in Show at the Club Championship in 1979 and 1980, making wins for Ryslip at that show for three successive years by mother and daughter. The first homebred male to gain his title from the kennel, Ch. Ryslip Here Comes Trouble, qualified in 1984.

Squirreldene

Mr. and Mrs. Roger Thomas, whose prefix is well known for Norwich Terriers, qualified their first Norfolk bitch, Ch. Ragus Buckshee of Squirreldene, in 1986. Buckshee was top-winning bitch of 1985.

Timberfalling

Edwina Hart, after winning a first CC in the breed in 1968, qualified five champions: Timberfalling Santa Maria (in 1969); Ch. Timberfalling Red Spruce (in 1970); Ch. Timberfalling Saligna Gum (in 1972); Ch. Timberfalling Red Cedar (in 1976); and Ch. Timberfalling King's Crown (in 1979). King's Crown is behind the winning line of the Lowmita Kennel.

Figure 141: Brenda Daniel's Titanium Lyrical, winning a CC with breeder Mrs. Needham and Lesley Crawley.

Titanium

This kennel, owned by Tom and Eileen Needham, in 1981 qualified Ch. And Harry of Titanium, top-winning

dog that year, and went second place on the Club Kennel Table. In 1982 Ch. And Harry's daughter, Ch. Titanium's Just Fancy, gained her title. The kennel was third on the Club Kennel Table in both 1983 and 1984, with two further champions qualifying in 1984: Ch. Titanium Fanciful and Ch. Ferdinand the Warrior of Titanium. For three years Ch. And Harry was one of the breed's leading stud dogs and had 21 first-prize-winning offspring in the show ring. His record continued through 1987 and 1988.

Vicbrita

This kennel, owned by Miss Gilean White, twice president of the Norfolk Terrier Club, won its first CC in 1965 with that year's top winner, Vicbrita Nanfan Nutmeg, whose daughter, Ch. Vicbrita Costmary, was top winner in 1967. Costmary's son, Ch. Salad Burnet of Vicbrita, qualified for his title in 1975, after being top winner himself in 1974. Salad Burnet's son from the last litter he sired, Ch. Vicbrita Bergamot, gained his title in 1986.

Wemcroft

Sylvia Way took her first CC in the breed in 1973 and had the distinction of taking both CCs at Crufts in 1977 (a first CC for both dogs: Wemcroft Astronaut, who qualified for his title in 1978; and Nanfan Cradle). This was the first time any kennel had won both CCs at this world-famous show.

MORE ENGLISH KENNELS, 1988

Baktwin	Mr. and Mrs. K. T. Watkins
Brenin	M. S. King
Delladale	Judith Vaughn
Dykefoot	Barbara & Ken Petrie
Elmsgarth	Elizabeth G. Parsons
Endane	Miss Phillips and Mrs. Johns
Franfoy	Frank, Jo and Katy Foy
Hanleycastle	L. W. R. Clements
Kson	Mr. and Mrs. S. A. Hiller
Janning	J. C. Harding
Leddington	D. Blandford
Lees	Pat L. Curties
Nanfan (see History)	M. Joy Taylor
Newthatch	Pat Keen
Oasthopper	Eddie and Chris Howes
Osmor	O. Morris
Penorth	David and Annette Penny
Pinecourt	Mrs. M. Cooper
Ragus (see History)	Marjorie Bunting and Lesley Crawley
Richell	Rita Mitchell
Rubaiyat	R. G. and Anne Wood
Starcyl	Mrs. McCrystal
Spindletop	Olive and William Denyer
Tyka	Dorothy and Jean Gledhill
Valstar	Mr. and Mrs. Derek Carter

Figure 142: Sylvia Way holding Ch. Wemcroft Astronaut.

AUSTRALIA

During the 1970s several key dogs with Nanfan, Leddington, and Cracknor prefixes went to New South Wales and South Australia to form a strong nucleus for future show winners. In 1981 Warren and Carol Goldsworthy had great success with Aust. Ch. Craigend Romany Rebel, a grandson of two dominant studs, Ch. Nanfan Nobleman and Ch. Ragus Whipcord. Two other familiar dogs, Leddington Captain Cook and Int. Ch. Nanfan Sweetcorn also share honors through their winning descendants; and more recent imports include Nanfan Cheesecake. Familiar prefixes are the Goldsworthys' Craigend; Bet Millhouse's Penfillan; and Joyce Thorne's Summerplace.

GERMANY

Allright

In 1976 in Windach, Germany, a tall and slender young stable assistant, Frauke Hinsch, started her Norfolk career by breeding the import Ickworth Penny Ha' Penny, a bitch she acquired from a racehorse trainer in Munich. Through correspondence and travel, contact was made with other Norfolk owners in Germany, Holland, and Switzerland, and "Penny's" offspring by a Cracknor and a Ragus stud were exhibited by their new owners.

Soon Frauke's enthusiasm brought her in touch with Norfolk breeders in England and America, whom she visited through the Young Farmers' program before starting her veterinary studies. By 1982 she had the foundation bitch from Penny she'd been hoping for, by Ick-

Figure 143: (Left) **Int. Ch. Allright Firecracker by Ickworth Sandstorm x Ickworth Penny Ha'Penny.** *Photo © Sally Anne Thompson.*

Figure 144: (Right) **Dr. Frauke Hinsch and friends.**

worth President — a breeding Alice Hazeldine had originally planned. Following the English Jubilee Specialty in 1982, Elizabeth Matell parted with her promising young winner, Cracknor Candidate, after neighbors complained about "Tubby's" appetite for live chicken dinners. The following year on a judging visit to the United States Frauke went home with a bitch puppy, Chidley Magic Carpet. Today a licensed veterinarian with a flourishing grooming business, Frauke Hinsch is the leading continental Norfolk breeder and a regional officer for the collective terrier clubs.

Among the champions at Allright are: Int. Ch. Cracknor Candidate, World Champion in 1985; homebred Int. Ch. Allright Firecracker, World Champion in 1986; and Ch. Allright Magic Midge, 1987 winner of the breed continental record entry. In America Ch. Allright Magic Lamp, Midge's litter brother, was an all-breed Best in Show winner and sired five champions in 1987.

Despite a busy schedule, Frauke Hinsch has published a comprehensive history of Norfolk and Norwich for the Terrier Kennel Club, travels internationally to shows (with and without dogs), and has plans for a continental breed club.

Figure 145: Third-generation homebred Ch. Allright Lancelot.

Figure 146: Int. Ch. Ragus Bellario by Ch. Ragus Whipcord x Ch. Ragus Brown Sugar. *Photo © Anne Roslin-Williams.*

Le Piqueur

S. Peter's Basset Hound kennel, Le Piqueur, added Norfolk Terriers in 1976 with the acquisition of Eng. Ch. Ragus Bellario and Ragus Spiced Cider. Among Le Piqueur's successful homebreds are the champions Agamemnon, Curry Cream Girl, and Curry's daughter, Ebony Ella, World Champions in 1980, 1981, and 1984, respectively.

Red Pepper

In 1985 Ulrich Berg of Hamburg, after careful searching, finally located two bitches for his start in Norfolks. In June 1988 Pipridges Sicco, the English import by Eng.

Figure 147:
Red Pepper
Krambambuli by
Gammelgard
Saxe x Allright
Kincsem.

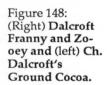

Figure 148:
(Right) **Dalcroft
Franny and Zo-
oey** and (left) **Ch.
Dalcroft's
Ground Cocoa.**

Ch. Heathjul Christmas Cracker (bred by David Saltmarsh), and the German-bred winner Allright Kincsem were joined at Red Pepper by the American winner Chidley Beechcroft Cricket, a double descendant of Eng. Am. Ch. Daffran Dusty.

NEW FANCIERS

Through the enthusiasm and show exposure of their pioneer breeders, Norfolks have recently gained favor with other German owners. In 1987 Gainsay Airproof, a Finnish import was exhibited by Britta Pepper, whose parents own the West Highland White kennel, Peppermint; and two promising Norfolk puppies from Allright and Red Pepper have joined the Von Tinsdal Kennels of Scottie and Westie fame.

CANADA

In the early 1970s the P. S. P. Fells vacationed in Canada with a pair of their favorite drop ear Norwich Terrier winners and returned with a championship for Am. Ch. Ickworth Nimrod. He is believed to have been the first titled drop ear Norwich in Canada. It was not until 1977, just two years before breed separation in America, that Canadian Norwich D. E. achieved official recognition as Norfolk Terriers.

Dalcroft

In 1978 Margot and Norman Johnson added a pair of Norfolk bitch puppies to their Dalcroft Dalmation kennels in Ancaster, Ontario. This pair, bred by Pamela Scaife of the Northsea prefix, had been noticed at an Obedience class, and one puppy, Northsea Dunval Half-a-Bob, was already well on her way to her championship. Grounder, by Ch. Badgewood Blakney x Marmalade of Ragus, proved an invaluable

foundation bitch for the Johnsons' Norfolks. Bred to Badgewood Tweedle Dee, she produced their first home-bred champion, Dalcroft's Ground Cocoa, among other winning progeny.

In 1984 Dalcroft imported a bitch, Jalaska Periwinkle, from Scotland; and in the following year Am. Can. Ch. Chidley Mumbo Jumbo, an American outcross and sire of black and tans, joined the Johnsons. With their enthusiasm for Norfolks, Margot and Norman Johnson are providing breeding stock for new Canadian fanciers from Niagara to Newfoundland.

Northsea

In 1977 two Norfolk pioneers were imported into Canada from England by Pamela Scaife for her Northsea Kennels in Ontario. This early foundation stock figured prominently in the beginnings and growth of Norfolk popularity in Canada.

SWITZERLAND

Roughrider

The B. Thulins, who live near Fribourg, started breeding their Norfolk in 1976 from Nanfan and Cracknor stock. Among their present dogs are Ch. Cracknor Conqueror, an Int. Ch. Nanfan Sweetcorn son, and recent Scandinavian imports from the Of Course and Gainsay kennels.

DENMARK

Gammelgard

Lone Holm's kennel in Jutland started with a Norfolk puppy, now Danish Ch. Nanfan Siskin, and a littermate of Eng. Am. Ch. Nanfan Sandpiper. With other dogs from Germany and Scandinavia, this breeder is off to a good start.

Tjeps

The J. and J. Corneliussens are well-known Cairn breeders who started to exhibit their Norfolk, All-

Figure 149: Ch. Allright Sir Francis Drake.

right Sir Francis Drake, in 1987. He ended the year as the top Danish winner and was Best in Show at an all-terrier event in Germany. The Corneliussens have since added a Swiss bitch from the Roughrider Kennel of the Thulins, a German lass from Ulrich Berg's Red Pepper prefix, and an Eng. Am. Ch. Jaeva Matti Brown son, bred by Beth Sweigart of Yarrow, Oyster Bay, New York.

SCANDINAVIA
Elizabeth Matell and Eva Valinger
(Adapted from Club publications)

In 1964 the landmark action of the British Kennel Club created the Norfolk Terrier. That same year Colonsay Red Mouse and Colonsay Punk arrived in Sweden.

Through her friendship with Miss M. S. S. Macfie, Mrs. Hammarlund of the Dallas Dalmation Kennels imported and exhibited the first Norfolk in Scandinavia, and her original pair of Colonsays produced the first Swedish-bred Norfolk champion, Dallas Nickel Note, in 1966.

Soon the Dallas dogs found ring competition from the well-known Golden Retriever prefix Sandemars, owned by Mrs. Braunerhjelms, from Mrs. Ohms's Hubberstad, and from Elizabeth Matell's Cracknor. These three Swedish breeders worked together, first using imported stock mostly from Ickworth, Nanfan, Ragus, and Ravenswing. Sadly, Mrs. Hammarlund was forced to give up her Norfolks due to an allergy, although her Dalmations continued in their prominent breed position.

In 1974 the Swedish Norfolk Terrier Club was formed with 100 members, some of whom also owned other terrier breeds. That year 63 dogs were entered in the Club show in June under English Specialist judge Alice Hazeldine. The Club now holds two open shows a year but still does not offer Challenge Certificates. Total registrations rose from 19 in 1968 to an average of 50 per year at present.

A strange twist binds several of Sweden's most influential imports to England in an interesting way. Although Ickworth Kythe was bred in England, he first became a Nordic champion, then returned to win his English title at the age of six. In England he sired, among other CC winners, Ickworth Pennywise, who joined the Badgewood Kennel in America. Int. Ch. Cracknor Capricorn also competed as a Nordic champion and became the first foreign-bred Norfolk to win an English Challenge Certificate in 1978. He sired the popular Am. Ch. Hatchwoods Creme de Menthe of Cracknor before returning to Sweden. The third and most important Norfolk of these multinational contenders came from the famous English champion Nanfan Heckle's last litter. This was Elizabeth Matell's Int. Ch. Nanfan Sweetcorn. "Corn" had a show and stud career in Scandinavia before he and his owner emigrated to Kent in 1978, where he quickly gained his English championship. The move to England was a severe loss to both the breed and breeders in Sweden, for Elizabeth had been their leading and most enthusiastic exhibitor.

Luckily, Cracknor stock was, and is, helping others at home and on the continent. Sweetcorn's son, Int. Ch. Cracknor Canterbury (x Ch. Bluemarking Santolina), a slow-maturing, but long-lasting male, won the Swedish show at nine and a half years under a Specialist judge and has proved to be a top producer.

Figure 150:
Int. Nord. Ch.
Cracknor
Canterbury.

Figure 151:
Ch. Ragus
Buttermilk.
Photo © Anne
Roslin-Williams.

Another dominant sire that came to Sweden was Eng. Ch. Ickworth Ready's son, Eng. Ch. Ragus Buttermilk. The Int. Nordic Ch. littermates, Ickworth Jingle and Jewel, were also by Eng. Ch. Ready. In addition, Eng. Ch. Ragus Shady Lady, an important brood bitch, arrived in Sweden in whelp to her grandsire, Eng. Ch. Ragus Whipcord, in 1979. She was followed by Int. Ch. Ragus Betsy Trotwood and Eng. Ch. Ragus Brigadoon.

Until the 1980s the Scandinavian Norfolk history was that of Sweden, but now the Swedish must

share their laurels with Norwegian and Finnish breeders of high-quality Norfolks. In Finland, the "of Woodhill" suffix and the Lecibsin Kennels of Jukka Kuusiste began in the 1970s. But it was Paivi Avotie's Gainsay prefix that became known throughout Scandinavia. Starting with Int. Ch. Jailbait of Woodhill (by Buttermilk's son Ch. Rough 'n Ready) and a couple of Lecibsin bitches, Paivi Avotie had great success. And she found an outstanding sire in her Norwegian black and tan, Int. Ch. Stall Mascot Airmail (by a son of Eng. Ch. Ragus Whipcord x Eng. Ch. Ragus Shady Lady). Petter Födstad's Stall Mascot Kennels of Norway made its way through a black and tan bitch, Ch. Cantab Black Velvet (also by Ch. Rough 'n Ready), and Ch. Nanfan Category, littermate of the English champions Nanfan Catmint and Nanfan Cat's Cradle. Velvet was Airmail's dam, and her even more famous offspring was Ch. Stall Mascot Baloo (by Category), who was Norway's 1985 Dog of the Year for all breeds. Baloo tragically died young, leaving few puppies. One of these was Am. Ch. Tickatee Catchascatchcan (with Category as grandsire on both sides).

Baloo's father—Nanfan Category—brings us back to Sweden, where Category's son, Int. Ch. Guestlings Catch a Star (x Int. Ch. Redriff Rambling Rose, a granddaughter of Sweetcorn), was Top Norfolk in both 1986 and 1987. Catch a Star seems headed toward becoming Swe-

Figure 152: (Left) **Ch. Nanfan Category and** (right) **his son** **Ch. Stall Mascot Baloo.**

den's next top producer, with champions in almost every litter to date. His breeder, Susan Bjorkfall, started her line based on two half-sisters from Inger Lundstrom's Redriff Kennels. Both bitches were out of Int. Ch. Ragus Betsy Trotwood, and they quickly led her Guestling prefix to the forefront of Swedish Norfolks.

Noteworthy among the Swedish prefixes are:

Figure 153:
Int. Nordic Ch.
Guestlings Catch
A Star.

Cantab	Marita and Kenneth Eliasson
Easy	Anna-Lena Holmquist
Guestling	Susann Bjorkfall
Lurifax	Barbro Karlsson
Of Course	Irene Sober
Road Stars	Agneta Bostrom
Sandemar	Ylva Braunerhjelm
Redriff	Inger Lundstrom
Truffles	Gunilla Ericsson
Vantans	Inge Pettersson

In general, Scandinavian Norfolks are of correct size, type, and conformation with good heads and expressions, although some carry soft, abundant coats. Less than a handful of breeders keep dogs in kennel runs, and they always guard closely the typically friendly Norfolk temperament. Most Scandinavian Norfolks live as pets, whether show dogs or not. Together, various Scandinavian kennel clubs register some 75 Norfolks a year. Let us hope that with Norway's ban on exhibiting dogs docked after June 1988 and Sweden's January 1, 1989, docking ban the steady progress of the breed will not be slowed. As the Swedish Kennel Club itself is not anti-docking, it does not intend to use police action at this time.

Figure 154:
Successful breeding is always a combination, or balance, of theory and practicality.

5

BREEDING:
HEREDITY, SELECTION, AND COMMON SENSE

Dog breeding is far from an exact science. As a matter of fact the old adage, "Breed the best to the best and hope for the best," is repeated only slightly tongue-in-cheek by those who have had experience in this often frustrating, occasionally rewarding, endeavor.

This chapter is not intended as a definitive presentation on how to breed champion-quality dogs. Rather, it presents the opinions of a variety of successful breeders, both in this country and abroad, and offers their views on selecting a stud dog, developing a strong bitch line, and various other aspects of "the mating game." Breeding references to championship titles will refer to the country of origin.

IDEAL VS. REAL:
A MATTER OF BALANCE
Tom Horner
Dog World, August 15, 1980 (Adapted)

> Never fool yourself into thinking your dogs are better than they are just because they belong to you.

Breeding top-quality dogs is a long, slow process. First, as a breeder the one thing you must never do is to fool yourself into thinking your dogs are better than they are just because they belong to you. That dispells any hope of progress. First and foremost, be honest about your own dogs.

Second, successful breeding is always a combination, or balance, of theory and practicality. While the theoretical side of breeding is going on, there must be *selection*. It is no good mating two animals apparently compatible on paper unless they are also well-matched on points. You may have two champions with the same faults—all champions have their share—which would make for a ridiculous mating; the faults would just marry up and reappear for generations, like the good points,

Figure 155:
**Surrey Binnacle
by Ch. Surrey
Sink or Swim x
Surrey Dory, 1986.**

and the breeder would find himself making no progress, or more likely, going backwards.

Balancing good points and faults is by no means exact. When heads become a little longer, backs have a nasty habit of becoming longer too. A little more bone can bring coarseness in its train, and so on. The test of a true breeder is being able to weigh these varying points so that the result is both a typey and balanced dog.

Finally, it is absolutely necessary as a breeder to know your breed standard, and to have a clear idea of just what you are trying to achieve. Always select towards your ideal. It is very unwise to take risks with any functional failures, such as fertility, temperament, mothering capacity, soundness, and movement. It is also very unwise to continue with a line of bad whelpers.

Such points as color patterns, eye color, and pigmentation—unless completely wrong—are of far less importance than the essentials, and can be corrected by the choice of a suitable sire or dam. The "essentials" can be summed up as type, substance, and soundness; balance; conformation; movement; and temperament. These qualities are the ones that are of paramount importance in the planning of any truly effective breeding program.

IMPORTANCE OF GENETICS
IN BREEDING

*Joy Taylor, Nanfan Norfolks,
Malvern, Worcestershire, England © July, 1986*

It is with some hesitation that I write this chapter, knowing that it will be read by more knowledgeable breeders than myself, but with the hope that it may perhaps help new breeders to found a sound basis for a future breeding program and to understand that the greatest stud dog is only able to influence a *total* litter of puppies if the bitch's pedigree is compatible with his own.

Dog breeding is a craft concerned with the maintenance and improvement from generation to generation

Figure 156:
Joy Taylor with a team of Nanfans and Lisa, Mrs. Geir Petersen's daughter.
Photo © Sally Anne Thompson.

of the desired qualities of soundness, breed type and temperament, and the maintenance and improvement of these qualities in succeeding generations with the elimination through breeding of those qualities which are held to be undesirable. To achieve this end it is necessary to lay down a breeding plan many generations in advance, and with this in mind the *breed standard* of any breed should be regarded by responsible breeders as virtually unchangeable.

Until quite recently "type breeding" was practiced by many breeders; i.e., breeding like to like regardless of pedigree, or more frequently breeding a bitch with, for instance a poor shoulder, to a dog who excelled in shoulder. The result could only be successful if not only preceding generations of the dog were deliberately set to this specific characteristic, but if it also complimented the attributes carried by forebears of the bitch. Like, on its own, will not produce like; inheritance goes back further than one generation and characteristics are inherited from *all* the ancestors. The shoulder in question might

Figure 157: **Eng. Ch. Nanfan Nimbus**

Breeder and Owner: Mrs. M.J. Taylor. Whelped: April 6, 1960.

This pedigree of Eng. Ch. Nanfan Nimbus illustrates how the recessive line (on the dam's side to Waveney Valley Alder) is taken up and back to become dominant and recessive, with influence on both lines.

			Ch. Waveney Valley Alder
		Ragus Solomon Grundy	
			Ragus Sweet Sue
	Gotoground Foxhunter		
			Ch. Waveney Valley Alder
		Gotoground Tiddly Winks	
			Ragus Merry Maid
Ch. Gotoground Widgeon Bunny			
			Elel Spruce
		Ch. Waveney Valley Alder	
			Pennie of Waveney Valley
	Ragus Merry Maid		
			Colonsay Didlum Buck
		Congham Merry Moth	
			Congham Lizzie
ENG. CH. NANFAN NIMBUS			
			Colonsay Hudson
		Colonsay Bimp	
			Colonsay Flaming Orion
	Elel Spruce		
			Bulger of Boxted
		Sparkie	
			Colonsay Bunderbust
Nanfan Nettle			
			Elel Spruce
		Ch. Waveney Valley Alder	
			Pennie of Waveney Valley
	Nanfan Bramble		
			Colonsay Flip
		Nanfan Candy	
			Colonsay Full Con

well be improved in one puppy in the first generation, but the improvement could well slip back in the following generations, especially if the improvement is carried on a recessive line. Planning and knowledge must therefore be laid down before a breeding program is established if type is to be reliably settled right through a strain. The desired factors and attributes must be doubled up in the previous generations to produce soundness, type, and temperament on which to establish the future generations.

The doubling up of desired factors can be done in two ways, by "inbreeding" or by "linebreeding." Linebreeding was once described as something you did yourself, but was "inbreeding" if someone else did it. The two are in fact very different. *Inbreeding* is the close breeding together of related dogs, e.g., daughter to father. *Linebreeding* is deliberately setting characteristics and type through four or five preceding generations and breeding back to the original type, e.g., breeding daughter to great-grandfather in a pedigree pattern going upwards and backwards from the bitch line to the dog, at the same time breeding a second separate partially outcrossed line which shares a common ancestry with a dog and bitch already related, for use to the foundation dog or bitch.

Both inbreeding and linebreeding intensify all quali-

Figure 158:
Ch. Nanfan
Heckle, 1963,
by Nanfan
Nimble x
Nanfan Hayseed.
The most
prepotent
Nanfan—sire
of 13 champions.
*Photo © Sally
Anne Thompson.*

```
                                                    Ch. Waveney Valley Alder
                                  Ragus Solomon Grundy
                                                    Ragus Sweet Sue
                 Gotoground Gunner
                                                    Ch. Waveney Valley Alder
                                  Gotoground Tiddly Winks
                                                    Ragus Merry Maid
   Gotoground Moley
                                                    Colonsay Bimp
                                  Elel Spruce
                                                    Sparkie
                 Ch. Waveney Valley
                 Aldersister
                                                    Colonsay Cady
                                  Pennie of Waveney Valley
                                                    Tanner of Waveney Valley
```

NANFAN NIMBLE
(Sire of 8 champions, including Nanfan Heckle)

```
                                                    Ragus Solomon Grundy
                                  Gotoground Foxhunter
                                                    Gotoground Tiddly Winks
                 Ch. Gotoground Widgeon Bunny
                                                    Ch. Waveney Valley Alder
                                  Ragus Merry Maid
                                                    Congham Merry Moth
   Ch. Nanfan Nimbus
                                                    Colonsay Bimp
                                  Elel Spruce
                                                    Sparkie
                 Nanfan Nettle
                                                    Ch. Waveney Valley Alder
                                  NanfanBramble
                                                    Nanfan Candy
```

```
                                                    Ragus Solomon Grundy
                                  Gotoground Foxhunter
                                                    Gotoground Tiddly Winks
                 Ch. GotogroundWidgeon Bunny
                                                    Ch. Waveney Valley Alder
                                  Ragus Merry Maid
                                                    Congham Merry Moth
   Nanfan Nimrod
                                                    Colonsay Bimp
                                  Elel Spruce
                                                    Sparkie
                 Nanfan Nettle
                                                    Ch. Waveney Valley Alder
                                  Nanfan Bramble
                                                    Nanfan Candy
```

NANFAN HAYSEED
(Dam of Heckle and 3 other champions.)

```
                                                    Colonsay Bimp
                                  Elel Spruce
                                                    Sparkie
                 Ch. Waveney Valley Alder
                                                    Colonsay Cady
                                  Pennie of Waveney Valley
                                                    Tanner of Waveney Valley
   Hunston Hedge Warbler
                                                    Colonsay Fagwagger
                                  Hunston Herald
                                                    Colonsay Dizzy
                 Hunston Heralda
                                                    Colonsay Griffin
                                  Hunston Ha'Penny
                                                    Polly Flinders
```

ties, good and bad, and should never be practiced with stock that you suspect could be unsound or of poor type and temperament. Inbreeding can be successfully carried out in very skilled hands by a breeder *with his own stock*, as the risks involved can be offset by a thorough knowledge of all attributes and failings known to the breeder of his own stock. Linebreeding is safer and probably more successful in a small breed as it will not be as important to bring in a completely outcrossed (unrelated) line to the foundation stock, but possibly to use instead a partially outcrossed line that shares a common ancestry with a dog and bitch already related. This type of breeding is easier to control if all unsoundness is not known to you, or you suspect it may not be; and it is more certain to get the dominant and recessive genes in exactly the right place in the pedigree where they are most needed.

The progeny of inbreeding will have only a short-term effect on future generations, and not only because of the need to outcross rapidly, a process in which you lose much of the advantage gained. The progeny of linebreeding are more lasting in their influence. This is the discovery of heredity in its simplest form. The first cross, or breeding, shows only one of the characteristics of the parents—which is the dominant member—but the second generation has the dominant characteristic and also the recessive, the two being necessary to establish future type. If a dominant characteristic alone is present, only one out of three puppies at most will breed true, and while we all welcome a "fluke flyer" occasionally, he will be of little use to his breed or to his owner's breeding program if he cannot throw his type into future generations. This law of inheritance and characteristic was discovered in 1865 by Gregor Johann Mendel in experimentation with plants. The reasons for it were not known until later when August Weismann discovered that the animal and human body consisted of billions of individual cells, and that the center of each cell contained a minute rod, which he called a *chromosome*, which carried characteristics of the parents. The first cell of each fertilization contained one complete set of chromosomes from each parent, male and female. He discovered that growth was established by the splitting of these cells into 2, 2 into 4, and so on. Each time a cell was split the original male and female chromosomes were handed down exactly as in the first case. The chromosome was the unit of heredity.

> The progeny of inbreeding will have only a short-term effect on future generations. The progeny of linebreeding are more lasting in their influence.

In the early 1900s a young biologist named Thomas Morgan took Mendel's work a stage further, experimenting with fruit flies, whose rapid reproduction made it possible to collect data over 25 generations in the space of only one year. Through this work Morgan discovered that every animal and plant has a characteristic number of chromosomes and that this number is invariably the same. He also discovered that inheritance comes in groups as though some of them are linked together. These heredity elements are called *genes*. In the original cell of every new organism the male and female genes lie opposite each other. In this manner a male gene controlling pigmentation lies opposite the female gene controlling pigmentation, and so on. It is now known that a part of the male chromosome can be interchanged with the same part of the corresponding female chromosome so that the paternal chromosome then contains elements of the maternal, and the linkage group is broken. As only the dominant elements will be inherited by the first generation this will not alter the characteristics of that generation, but the change will be seen in the second generation when the offspring will inherit features of *both* grandparents. This is known as *crossing over*. It is in this "crossing over" or change—as well as in sex predetermination—that the possibility of "bending" characteristics to become dominant or recessive is carried out.

As only the dominant elements will be inherited by the first generation this will not alter the characteristics of that generation.

The genes and grouping of genes within the chromosomes are entirely responsible for the growth and inherited characteristics of each individual, animal, and human. As yet scientists have found no way of simply changing the structure of the genes in any organism except bacteria, so that the breeder's craft in striving for desired characteristics must rely on doubling up and strengthening through successive generations the genes carrying the desired qualities and to lose or drown the undesired ones. It should be remembered that the grandparental line is always more important than the parental line due to crossing over, and the influential planning is worked out in the great-grandparents' line. It is at this stage that the second separate and partially outcrossed line can be usefully brought in to double up on the attributes already achieved, and to improve the weaknesses which were anticipated when the secondary line or lines, were planned.

Research has been carried out on "pedigree patterns" in animals in an effort to establish sex linkage with dominant and recessive elements. In cattle it is often successful to work the pedigree in a circle, the "uncle" and "aunt" line being the most likely to carry the desired dominant elements. In dog pedigrees the bitch line is generally carried upwards and backwards

Figure 159: (Left) **Ch. Nanfan Thistle.** *Photo © Sally Anne Thompson.*

Figure 160: (Right) **Foxhunter's Tally Ho bred to Ch. Nanfan Heckle produced Ch. Nanfan Thistle.** *Photo © Constancee S. Larrabee.*

```
                              Gotoground Gunner
              Gotoground Moley
                              Ch. Waveney Valley Aldersister
      Nanfan Nimble
                              Ch. Gotoground Widgeon Bunny
              Ch. Nanfan Nimbus
                              Nanfan Nettle
Ch. Nanfan Heckle
                              Ch. Gotoground Widgeon Bunny
              Nanfan Nimrod
                              Nanfan Nettle
      Nanfan Hayseed
                              Ch. Waveney Valley Alder
              Hunston Hedge Warbler
                              Hunston Heralda
```

CH. NANFAN THISTLE, 1969

```
                              Ch. Waveney Valley Alder
              Ragus Solomon Grundy
                              Ragus Sweet Sue
      Imp. Gotoground Foxhunter
                              Ch. Waveney Valley Alder
              Gotoground Tiddly Winks
                              Ragus Merry Maid
Foxhunter's Tally Ho
                              Ch. Ragus Jimmy Joe
              Ch. Bethway's Pound
                              Ch. Colonsay Kelly's Eye
      Gum Drop
                              Ch. Castle Point Simon
              Gee Gee
                              Ginger
```

through the dog line. If the grandparent and great-grandparent lines have been correctly established, it is likely that the dominant genes will be carried more heavily by the male line and reinforced by the female. When outcrossing, therefore, it is usually preferable to outcross a bitch to a line-bred dog who shares the same common ancestry which is known to be sound and dominant in the required characteristics. In a small breed it will probably be necessary to accept a weak or undesired line on the dam's side, which is more likely to be recessive, and in this case in the following generation to breed a dog from this litter back to the original bloodline; the dam's line on the sire's pedigree of the puppy in question should in this instance also be recessive.

Pedigree is important, but no kennel can be established entirely by the breeder working on a piece of paper. It is essential to have the eye to be able to recognize the type towards which the planning is aimed; to study your dogs with a dispassionate eye and to recognize their faults and shortcomings; and to study the progeny of other kennels, and to see the pattern of dominant and recessive genes emerging; and above all to only be content when every puppy in every litter is identical

Figure 161:
A daughter of Gotoground Foxhunter, imported from the U.S., with a small dose of outcross on a recessive line and bred to Ch. Nanfan Heckle produced Ch. Nanfan Thistle. Then Thistle bred to Ch. Nanfan Sickle produced Eng. Ch. Nanfan Summerstorm (see photo) and Am. Ch. Nanfan Stormcock.
Photo © Sally Anne Thompson.

```
                                    Gotoground Moley
                     Nanfan Nimble
                                    Ch. Nanfan Nimbus
        Ch. Nanfan Heckle
                                    Nanfan Nimrod
                     Nanfan Hayseed
                                    Hunston Hedge Warbler
Ch. Nanfan Thistle
                                    Ragus Solomon Grundy
                     Gotoground Foxhunter
                                    Gotoground Tiddly Winks
        Foxhunter's Tally Ho
                                    Ch. Bethway's Pound
                     Gum Drop
                                    Gee Gee
```

ENG. CH. NANFAN SUMMERSTORM AND AM. CH. NANFAN STORMCOCK

```
                                    Ch. Nanfan Heckle
                     Ch. Nanfan Nogbad the Bad
                                    Ch. Nanfan Needle
        Ch. Nanfan Nobleman.
                                    Ch. Nanfan Heckle
                     Ch. Nanfan Noctis
                                    Nanfan Nobility
Nanfan Sickle
                                    Nanfan Nimble
                     Ch. Nanfan Heckle
                                    Nanfan Hayseed
        Ch. Nanfan Snapshot
                                    Moortop Rinty
                     Gayrunor Golden Spangle
                                    Gayrunor
```

Figure 162: Eng. Ch. Nanfan Nobleman (photo) was bred to Ch. Nanfan Snapshot, who produced Nanfan Sickle. Sickle bred back to Ch. Nanfan Heckle produced Ch. Nanfan Sweet Apple; and Sweet Apple bred back to Ch. Nanfan Nobleman produced Ch. Nanfan Sugarlump. *Photo © Sally Anne Thompson.*

```
                                               Nanfan Nimble
                           Ch. Nanfan Heckle
                                               Nanfan Hayseed
          Ch. Nanfan Nogbad the Bad
                                               Gotoground Moley
                           Nanfan Needle CC
                                               Ch. Nanfan Nimbus
```

CH. NANFAN NOBLEMAN

```
                                               Nanfan Nimble
                           Ch. Nanfan Heckle
                                               Nanfan Hayseed
          Ch. Nanfan Noctis
                                               Nanfan Buckwheat
                           Nanfan Nobility
                                               Ch. Nanfan Nimbus
```

Figure 163:
**Chs. Nanfan
Catmint and Cat's
Cradle (1981).**
*Photo © Sally Anne
Thompson.*

```
                                      Nanfan Nimble
                        Eng. Ch. Nanfan Halleluia
                                      Nanfan Hayseed
            Eng. Ch. Nanfan Ninety
                                      Gotoground Moley
                        Nanfan Needle
                                      Eng. Ch. Nanfan Nimbus
     Eng. Ch. Nanfan Sweet Potato
                                      Nanfan Nimble
                        Eng. Ch. Nanfan Heckle
                                      Nanfan Hayseed
            Eng. Ch. Nanfan Sweet Apple
                                      Eng. Ch. Nanfan Nobleman
                        Nanfan Sicle
                                      Eng. Ch. Nanfan Snapshot
```

CHS. NANFAN CATMINT AND CAT'S CRADLE *

```
                                      Nanfan Nimble
                        Eng. Ch. Nanfan Halleluia
                                      Nanfan Hayseed
            Eng. Ch. Nanfan Ninety
                                      Gotoground Moley
                        Nanfan Needle
                                      Eng. Ch. Nanfan Nimbus
     Eng. Ch. Nanfan Copycat
                                      Eng. Ch. Nanfan Heckle
                        Eng. Ch. Nanfan Thistle
                                      Foxhunter's Tally Ho
            Eng. Ch. Cinnamon of Nanfan
                                      Eng. Ch. Gotoground Widgeon Bunny
                        Gotoground Cuckoo
                                      Eng. Ch. Hunston Hedge Betty
```

**This pedigree
also refers to
Int. Ch. Nanfan
Catagory and
Am. Ch. Nanfan
Crunch.*

to the standard to which you have planned. This then is successful linebreeding.

All breeders know that nature is a fickle jade, but if we can understand a little of what lies behind heredity the odds against us are perhaps evened out to fairer proportions. Future generations of breeders may well be given all the answers, and our "Eldorado" to produce the perfect animal within our breed will be given to them by science on a plate. I doubt if they will have the satisfaction in producing their perfect specimens that we achieve in raising our not-such-perfect ones. Nor will they know the adventure of striving to capture the one elusive combination that eludes us in every generation.

RECESSIVE TRAITS

Color: The Black and Tan

In Norwich and Norfolks, undoubtedly there was more than one original source for color. A study of pedigrees reveals black and tan producers: Tobit (1925), a founding drop ear sire; Smudge (1926), himself a prick ear black and tan; and Babbling Binks (1925), another early drop ear sire. All three share a common ancestor, Pepper, on one side of their pedigree but are unrelated on the other side. A fourth black and tan sire was the first prick ear champion male, Farndon Red Dog (1933) who like the above came from Jones and Trumpington stock but is not a recorded descendant of Pepper's.

During the 1930s black and tans were prevalent, and one of each ear type became an English champion. Miss M.S.S. Macfie, who soon dominated the drop ear Norwich contingent, did not care for the color, associating it with soft, profuse, wooly coats. A number of dogs of this color came to America before World War II, and in 1940 the black and tan import Ch. Colonsay All Kiff was the first drop ear dog to win an AKC title. The first American champion, Merry of Beaufin, a red, carried the black and tan recessive gene and produced black and tan get. After this period the color all but disappeared, at least from the show ring, in both countries and ear types.

Ch. Red Wraith (1951), the first English drop ear champion after World War II, also carried the black and tan recessive, which was manifested in his grandson,

BLACK AND TANS

Figure 164:
(Above) Tommy, 1925, bred and owned by Mrs. Phyllis Fagan. Descended from her "Brownie," 1912, ancestor of Ch. Tuff.

Figure 166:
(Below) Hunston Holy Smoke, 1955, by Rednor Gay Caballero x Jubilant of Shervage. Breeder: A. Grimwood. Owner: Kay Southwick. First postwar black and tan English show winner with champion descendants today.

Figure 165:
Snuff, 1931, Mary Stevens Baird's first drop ear hunt terrier—later registered. Bred by Mrs. Phyllis Fagan.

Figure 167:
Eng. Ch. Ryslip Mixed Blessings, 1977, by Ch. Ragus Brown Herb x Ch. Ryslip Love Bug. Breeder: E. Cartledge. Owner:Jane Miller. Winner of 2 Club Specialty shows and 10 CCs.

Figure 168:
Eng. Ch. Ragus Whipcord, by Ragus Humphrey Bear x Ragus Who Dat, leading breed sire with 16 champion get. First black and tan champion.

Hunston Holy Smoke, owned by Kay Southwick, who liked the color. "Smoker" (1955) and Red Duster of Redlawn, a black and tan carrier used by Marjorie Bunting of the Ragus Kennels, did much to keep the color popular in England. In America Ragus Jimmy Joe sired Ch. Bethway's Pound (1957), a popular black and tan producer for Mary Baird's Castle Point prefix in New Jersey. In England the first postwar champion Norfolks of this color were Ch. Ragus Whipcord (1973) and Ch. Ragus Blackberry (1979), while the first American-bred black and tan Norfolk champion was Ch. Norvick the Witch (1985).

Among breeders today red is still the favored color, yet there are quality black and tans in ring competition everywhere. The once-elusive color gene is now widely found in many lines. Although it was formerly believed that "those horrid coats" (hairy bears) were linked to black and tan coloration, no genetic connection between these charming "sports" and coat color has been proven.

Coats: "Fluffies" or "Hairy Bears"

On rare occasions a whelp appears in a litter whose soft, single coat grows straight, long, and profusely. Commonly called "hairy bears" or "fluffies," these puppies' soft coats can be parted to reveal the tender skin. Despite efforts to eliminate this particular coat type, it still turns up periodically in Norfolk and Norwich Terriers.

Originally, fluffies were thought to be linked to the black and tan color pattern, perhaps inherited from an early Yorkshire Terrier cross. Certainly, we still see occasional traces of coats that may be long, flat, and silky, or harsh with vestiges of silky hairs in their furnishings. Others may have traces of a topknot on the forehead.

Unlike Yorkies, however, fluffies have a coat texture similar to today's larger soft-coated terriers that share with Norfolk common ancestry from early Irish Terriers. Whatever their origin, fluffies have been recorded since Norwich (both drop ear and prick ear) were recognized in 1932. There is good reason

Figure 169: Jacks or Better, 1966, a true fluffie, by Bethway's Mr. Kennedy x Bethway's Bridget, and a double descendant of Ch. Tuff, who carried the gene.

Figure 170:
COLOR DOMINANCE
Note: Red is dominant—black and tan recessive.

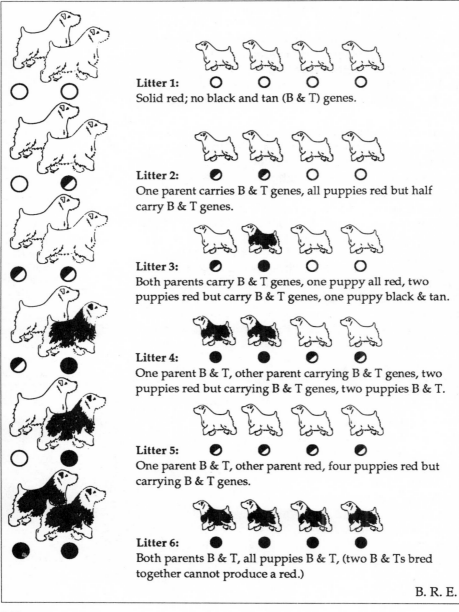

Litter 1: O O O O
Solid red; no black and tan (B & T) genes.

Litter 2: ◐ ◐ O O
One parent carries B & T genes, all puppies red but half carry B & T genes.

Litter 3: ◐ ● O O
Both parents carry B & T genes, one puppy all red, two puppies red but carry B & T genes, one puppy black & tan.

Litter 4: ● ● ◐ ◐
One parent B & T, other parent carrying B & T genes, two puppies red but carrying B & T genes, two puppies B & T.

Litter 5: ◐ ◐ ◐ ◐
One parent B & T, other parent red, four puppies red but carrying B & T genes.

Litter 6: ● ● ● ●
Both parents B & T, all puppies B & T, (two B & Ts bred together cannot produce a red.)

B. R. E.

Figure 171 & 172: Trisha, 1988, a long-haired Norfolk *before* and *after* hand stripping. She is not believed to be a true fluffie.

to believe they are descendants of either the influential black and tan sire Pepper (thus the once-presumed color link) or the unregistered Midge, dam of Tobit and granddam of Ch. Biffin and of Peggotty and Witherslack Jane. At any rate, soft and silky coats were both considered a serious—even disqualifying—fault under the 1947 American Standard.

The simple recessive gene that controls hairy bears is often carried undetected for generations by hard-coated parents. Fluffies, while adorable, are severely handicapped if they like to hunt among briars and burrs. Soft coats require regular grooming and monthly haircuts for comfort and health. Since fluffies are capable of producing normal coats and are so appealing, it seems unlikely the gene will ever become extinct.

In the distant past, some of the breed's most personable characters produced fluffies. Today, after a long hiatus, the number of hairy bears is again on the rise, thanks in part to two popular, typey international champion sires—one a Norfolk and the other a Norwich.

Figure 173: Two puppies, 1983, by Eng. and Am. Ch. Daffran Dusty. Puppy on the left shares Ch. Ickworth Ready as the common ancestor.

EAR CARRIAGE: A MIXED HERITAGE

All Norfolk ears are not alike in size, shape, and placement due to the breed's diverse roots and recent separation from its prick-eared brethren, the Norwich. Until 1964 in England and 1979 in the United States the interbreeding of both ear types was permitted, though sparingly practiced.

When the Norwich Terrier was rec-

ognized in England in 1932 both the erect- and pendulous-eared dogs had their following. Gradually the two separate ear types developed, with the drop-eared having a larger concentration of genes back to Biffin of Beaufin (1932) and Tobit (1928) rather than to the prick-eared cornerstones Smudge (1926) and Ch. Farndon Red Dog (1933).

Figure 174: Minx of Fuzzyhurst, Colonsay Musical Box, and Colonsay Junior, England, 1958.

CONTROL THROUGH CAREFUL BREEDING
Marjorie Bunting, Ragus Kennels, Kilsby, Northamptonshire, England

Some people seem surprised that Norfolks' ears can be troublesome. It is not really surprising when you remember the different types of ears in their background. Apart from crossing prick and drop ears in the early days, there was a Staffordshire Bull Terrier cross (rose ears) and Bedlington Terrier cross (long ears) in the '20s. The white bitch Ninety, owned by the Lowe family at the beginning of the century, was said to be a cross between a Smooth Fox Terrier (high-set ears only lightly dropped) and a Dandie Dinmont (again, long ears). A Wire Fox Terrier type bitch was also used at this time (like Smooth Fox Terrier ears).

Wensum Kennels: Magnus Helga, Zob, Wiky, and Snorri, U.S.A., 1956. Note lack of furnishings on these early dogs in both pictures.

With so much variety in ear type and carriage it often surprises me that we ever get correct ears at all. Like all faults, it is impossible to actually breed it out short of spending a lot of time and money experimenting. It will

only be controlled if all breeders are careful to breed a Norfolk with a poor ear carriage of any sort *only* to one with a perfect ear carriage, and so far as possible only keep those puppies for breeding which have correct ears and ear carriage. However, the possibility of one being born with incorrect ears at anytime in the future will always be there.

CHOOSING A STUD DOG
*Ruth E. Corkhill, **Redash Kennels**,*
Birmingham, England

Choosing a stud dog is a matter for great care and consideration, with plenty of time spent deliberating the virtues and vices of various dogs. Above all, avoid hasty selections a few days before the bitch is to be mated!

Here are a few basic guidelines:

1. Write out your bitch's pedigree — preferably in a split pedigree book so you can copy the pedigrees of possible stud dogs into the top half of the book and see at a glance the resulting pedigrees of the planned litter.
2. List all the faults and virtues of your bitch or her line.
3. Try to list the faults and virtues of possible stud dogs. Do this by observation (and handling, if possible) at dog shows, visiting kennels, talking to owners and breeders, and by studying photographs. You will find conflicting information, no doubt, and you will have to make up your mind whom to believe and form your own opinion, especially if you cannot examine the dogs yourself.
4. See as many progeny as possible from the stud dogs being considered, and find out the pedigrees of their dams to compare them to your own bitch. If you are an inexperienced breeder, it is probably best to use a proven stud who has shown what sort of progeny he can produce. In Norfolks, the choice of stud dogs is limited due to the breed's small numerical size, so you won't have an enormous list to wade through.

Figure 176: Am. Ch. Elve Pure Magic by Ragus Bitterman x Eng. Ch. Ragus Brown Cider, 1980.

5. In the ideal mating, the stud dog should be better than the bitch. From your list of studs eliminate those with the same faults as your bitch. You should try to compliment the

A

B

C

D

RAGUS DOMINANT SIRES

The Ragus stud team has a history of success, as selected breeders outside of England have benefited from Mrs. Bunting and her daughter Lesley Crawley's long-established policy to part with proven champions.

Figure 177: A. **Ch. Ragus Whipcord, 1971, first black and tan champion and sire of record 16 champion get.** *Photo © Anne Roslin-Williams..*

Figure 178: B. **Ch. Ragus Brown Herb, 1977, by Ch. Ragus Whipcord x Ch. Ragus Brown Sugar,** sired Ch. Ryslip Mixed Blessing before going to Holland. Herb's brother, **Ch. Ragus Bellario, 1974,** helped establish the breed in Germany while his sister, **Eng. Am. Ch. Ragus Brown Smudge, 1973,** produced further AKC champions. *Photo © Anne Roslin-Williams.*

Figure 179: C. **Ch. Ragus Blacksmith (1982), by Ch. Ragus Browned Off** (Whipcord and Brown Sugar's most influential son) x **Ch. Ragus Blackberry,** was the leading breed sire in 1984 and 1985.

Figure 180: D. **Eng. Am. Ch. Ragus Pass the Buck, 1984, by Ch. Ragus Blacksmith x Ch. Priestess of Ragus,** sire of **Ch. Bear Hill's Toby Crachit,** a black and tan in his first litter.

Figure 181: E. **Ch. Ragus Bantum Cock, 1983, by Ch. Ragus Blacksmith and Ragus Back Chat,** an English specialty show winner and sire of **Am. Ch. Wonderwood Caliope, 1988 NNTC Specialty Show.**

E

faults of your bitch with the virtues of the stud dog. In some instances it may be necessary to forgive a minor fault in both animals provided they compliment each other everywhere else.

6. Now examine the pedigrees closely. You probably should eliminate from your choice any dogs with the same parent or parents as your bitch (that is, full or half-brothers). That sort of inbreeding should be left to experts.

Linebreeding, or the mating of two related dogs, may be carried out, but only after discussion with those who know the common ancestors in the pedigrees. Since linebreeding means, literally, breeding always to one line of ancestry, it involves the "doubling up" of genetic characteristics. The dog or bitch whose name appears repeatedly throughout a three- or four-generation pedigree is the one on which you are linebreeding. This method will produce favorable results only if the dogs and bitches that consistently reappear in the pedigree are themselves excellent examples of the breed. The more times a dog appears in the pedigree, the stronger its influence for good or bad. Therefore find out as much as possible about the ancestors in the pedigrees of both your bitch and the stud dog before deciding on a mating. To do this read all you can, look at as many pictures as possible, and question older, more experienced breeders who may remember ancestors of these dogs as well.

Another approach is outcrossing. This is when two completely unrelated dogs are mated. A mating that may appear to be an outcross as far back as the third generation may actually recover linebreeding of animals in the fourth and fifth generations. I would say in Norfolks, no mating is a true outcross as the gene pool (that is, the number of different hereditary lines) is relatively small.

Having finally decided on one or two possible dogs, ask their owners what *they* think. If they are experienced, they should be able to advise you if the prospective mating is suitable or not. Also ask the advice of the breeder of your bitch, as he or she should know what to expect from her particular line. The final decision is yours, but be sure it is the result of careful observation, diligent and thorough research, and the soundest professional advice

> The more times a dog appears in the pedigree, the stronger its influence for good or bad.

THE ICKWORTH INFLUENCE (ENGLAND)

Alice Hazeldene's preference for weather-turning coats was exemplified by her first champion. She believed "good coats are rather dominant," and ears "somewhat difficult to cope with."

A

Figure 182: A. **Ch. Ickworth Ready, 1967, the top winner and universal breed influence.**
Figure 183: B. **Ch. Ickworth Pathfinder, 1973, by Int. Ch. Ragus Buttermilk, a Ready son, x Ch. Ickworth Proper Pretty, an Orderley Dog granddaughter.** *Photo © Sally Anne Thompson.*
Figure 184: C. **Int. Ch. Ickworth Kythe of Ryslip, 1971, a Ch. Ready son and sire x Ickworth Bluemarking Katriona.** *Photo © Sally Anne Thompson.*

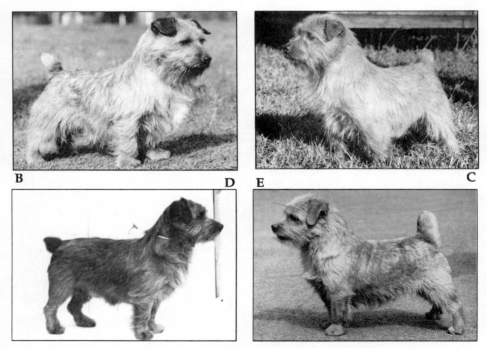

B

D **E**

C

Figure 185: D. **Ch. Colonsay Orderley Dog, 1960, a grandson of Ch. Waveney Valley Alder and Ch. Colonsay Junior. He won 19 CCs.**
Figure 186: E. **Eng. Am. Ch. Ickworth Pretty Piece, 1976, by Ch. Ickworth Kythe x Ch. Ickworth Penny Piece by Ch. Ready x Ch. Ickworth Proper Pretty.** *Photo © Sally Anne Thompson.*

you can obtain.

SELECTING A BROOD BITCH
Tom Horner, Dog World (Adapted)

Probably the most important step the would-be breeder of high-quality dogs has to make is the choice of the first brood bitch or bitches. A kennel is only as good as its producing females. A single bitch able to consistently produce high-quality offspring can be the cornerstone of a successful breeding operation.

Foundation bitches are just that: foundations of a breeding plan. All future generations will be descended from them, inheriting their good qualities and their faults, while the breeder "plays the field" of available stud dogs, changing from one line to another as the need arises. Both pedigree and appearance call for expertise to be exercised in making the choice. A well-bred bitch's pedigree will exhibit a number of typical animals in the first three generations. If there are no champions close behind the bitch, it is unlikely she is of the high quality a breeder needs.

In selecting a first brood bitch it is important to look first and foremost for a typical specimen. She does not have to be outstanding, but should be thoroughly characteristic of correct breed type and of good quality. A good all-around specimen should be chosen rather than one with a fantastic head or coat, for example, and nothing much else to recommend her. If you choose a generally faulty bitch with some extravagant merit as a foundation, you will find her faults constantly recurring and may lose the outstanding feature while trying to correct her ordinary flaws. With the all-around bitch, you have little to correct, only the trimmings to add.

Buying a young puppy from a very successful kennel

Figure 187: Ch. Wonderwood Wensday Addams by Leddington Captain Cook x Leddington Folly, and her son, Ch. Wonderwood Lo Commotion Lu, by Ch. Surrey Sink or Swim, owned by Jessica Relinque.

may be a good way to start, but puppies are unpredictable. As one famous breeder used to say, "They change so, dear!" The little model that at 8 or 10 weeks looks like a sure champion too often turns out to be nothing of the sort, while her plainer sister, whom you passed over, may turn out to be the star. Few breeders, however experienced, can tell how a seemingly promising puppy will eventually turn out. Thus a typical choice: Gamble on a promising puppy or take, say the grown, plainer litter sister of an excellent bitch the breeder is keeping.

Above all, in looking for a foundation bitch go for the best quality available. In the pedigree and in the individual, you cannot make a silk purse from a sow's ear. You just can't breed quality dogs from substandard bitches.

BROOD BITCH AND
THE TAIL BITCH LINE
Jane Anderson, Anderscroft Kennels, Mystic, Connecticut

The more books and articles you read on breeding and the qualities to look for in a brood bitch, the more confused you can become. Over the years of breeding both Norfolk Terriers and Labradors, however, I have come to some fairly definite conclusions about what I look for and want in a good brood bitch.

It would certainly be ideal to start your breeding program with a bitch that is near-perfect—perhaps even a champion—with a pedigree that is carefully line-bred in just the right manner, emphasizing all the good qualities and minimizing any faults and unsoundnesses. But realistically, how many of us have started that way? How many bitches of such quality are there? Believe me, they are few and far between; and in most cases, they are owned by breeders and are not for sale.

Fortunately, by looking hard and choosing carefully for soundness and type it is possible to find a bitch that —although far from perfect—fits the standard reasonably well, has a decent pedigree, and, if bred to the right stud dogs, is capable of producing much *better* than herself. If it has been your good fortune to find such a bitch, then you have probably chosen a foundation dam whose tail bitch line will be true to the structure and character

Above all, in looking for a foundation bitch go for the best quality available.

of the breed.

By *tail bitch line* I am referring to what will be the lowest line on the pedigree of each of your bitch's offspring. I firmly believe that it is this line that is the most important and influential part of a breeding program. A number of earlier books on breeding and the qualities and influence of the brood bitch seem to adhere to the theory that there is an equal genetic inheritance from the sire and dam, each giving their offspring 50/50 right down the line in terms of type, temperament, and all the qualities for which you are breeding. Although some people still hold to this belief, my own experience certainly has not confirmed it. Obviously it is imperative that much thought and emphasis be given to choosing the right stud dog for a bitch. In doing this you look for a prepotent dog who stamps his get with his own best characteristics and compliments the good qualities of your bitch. But consider for a moment that a well-used Norfolk stud dog in his lifetime can probably sire close to 30 litters. On the other hand, even a well-used Norfolk brood bitch will probably produce five litters in her lifetime. So we are speaking about an average of perhaps 15 puppies of a bitch against possibly 100 of the stud dog. From this it is evident that if the bitch line —consisting of your foundation dam and those bitches you keep that are directly descended from her— is producing quality, typey puppies from different stud dogs, then you have "solid gold."

Figure 188: (L to r) Ch. Bethway's Portia, her daughter, Ch. Bethway's Scarlet, and her granddaughter, Bethway's Little Scarlet.

If you can continue with bitches in this manner, your line will carry, and even improve, for many generations, making attainment of your goals easier and more rewarding.

BREEDING IMPORTED STOCK
W. Ronald Irving, Popular Dogs, October, 1974

The problems for the American breeder of terriers seem to me to be greater than those of the equivalent

British breeder—particularly in certain breeds. Distances between dogs and the lack of density of terrier population is bound to cause problems in arriving at the correct and yet convenient breeding formula. But perhaps the most difficult thing is the fact that so many dogs have been imported to the U.S. over the years, which means that the dogs appearing in the pedigrees of terriers being bred from are not well known to either the owner of the stud dog or the owner of the brood bitch. This must cause problems in judging how to eliminate certain faults and how to improve upon certain virtues. Behind each dog there are several generations of ancestors, all of whom are important, and breeders who have seen and known the faults and virtues of these ancestors must be in a better position to make breeding judgments. Besides this point, is it not the case that the importance of the Group win in the U.S. coupled with the advantage in the Group ring as opposed to bitches, has meant that far more top-quality dogs have been imported over the years than top-quality bitches? Perhaps a few more really good bitch imports could do a great deal to improve the depth of quality and could erode considerably the apparent advantage that Britain seems to hold in many terrier breeds. It is a plain fact that one good stud dog and a selection of good brood bitches is a far more valuable base for a kennel than one good brood bitch and a selection of good stud dogs. Naturally the British are aware of this too, and perhaps that is why they are generally more prepared to part with their good dogs rather than their good bitches. I think I agree with John T. Marvin that the way to improve the Terrier Group in depth is to pay more attention to importing the right dog or bitch rather than to import the top-winning dog or bitch. "Top-winning" is not always best from a breeding point of view.

Figure 189: Visiting stud dog, 1987-1989, Eng. Am. Ch. Jaeva Matti Brown by Ch. Crackshill Hardy x Jaeva Bobby Sox. Breeder/owner: Martin Phillips (England) and Barbara Miller (U.S.A.).

GENETIC TRAITS

1. Behavior patterns are hereditary. Breed for them.
2. Dark eyes are dominant over light.
3. Short coats are dominant over long.
4. Sparse coats are dominant over thick.
5. Lack of undercoat is dominant over the presence of undercoat.
6. Wire coats are dominant over straight.
7. Coarseness of coat is dominant over softness or silkiness.
8. Longer coats seem to go with darker color.
9. In breeding short-legged dogs, the results are legs of intermediate length, with short legs incompletely dominant over long.
10. Tight feet are dominant over hare feet, short feet over long.
11. Separate sets of recessive genes control each jaw and the number and size of a dog's teeth.
12. Missing teeth are recessive, but more than one factor controls tooth development.

DOMINANT TRAITS: RULES OF THUMB

1. The trait does not skip a generation.
2. Only individuals who carry the trait display it.
3. There is less danger of continuing undesirable dominant traits than with undesirable recessives, due to visibility of the former.
4. The inheritance formula for each individual is quite certain.

RECESSIVE TRAITS: RULES OF THUMB

1. The trait may skip one or more generations.
2. Only those individuals who carry a pair of the determiners display the trait.
3. An animal carrying only one determiner can be discovered only by being mated to another carrying the same determiner.
4. To be evident, the trait must come from both sides of the family.

HEREDITARY EXAGGERATIONS
Tom Horner, Dog World, 1985

Concentration on a single point, by even one breeder, will almost certainly lead to degeneration in other parts of the breed concerned, and if that breeder is a strong character who strongly promotes his wrongly made or exaggerated stock, the problem will quickly become widespread with dire results for the breed.

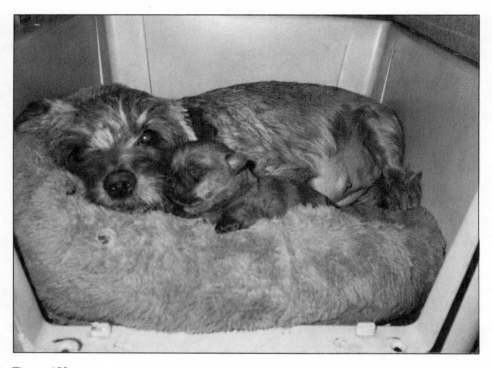

Figure 190:
Ch. Wonderwood
Wensday Addams
and her son, Ch.
Wonderwood Tur-
bo Plus by Ch.
Hatchwood's
Creme de Menthe.
Note the use of an
airline crate as a
whelping facility.

6

FROM MATING TO WEANING

RESPONSIBILITIES OF BREEDING
Carolyn Pyle, C and J Kennels, Freeville, New York

We can think of the genetic fundamentals that influence selection of a sound foundation bitch or a prepotent stud dog as the *theoretical aspects* of breeding. But there is a practical side of breeding as well, without which all the pedigree patterns and knowledge of canine genealogy will be ineffective. It is this practical knowledge that takes the business of dog breeding out of the stud book to the mating pen and on into the whelping box. This is the area where common sense and learning to profit by one's (and others') mistakes are most important.

When to Breed
Whether you are buying a bitch puppy or are lucky enough to acquire a "pedigree-perfect," proven adult dam for breeding, it is important for you to know that your bitch is in excellent health, and that her dam and granddam are problem-free whelpers. This is helpful in developing a good producer for your line.

A maiden bitch should not be bred until her second season, or until she reaches at least 16 months of age. Time is a better yardstick than the number of seasons, because what you are seeking is physical and mental maturity appropriate to the demands of motherhood. It is also important that you breed your bitch at a time convenient for your life-style. Look ahead to the date when she will whelp to see how it fits your schedule. Remember, the puppies will be with you for about three months and will require at least three meals a day. Before the season in which you breed your bitch make sure she has been wormed and is up-to-date on all immunization boosters. If it is her first breeding she should also have a rectal examination to confirm a normal pelvis.

> It is practical knowledge that takes the business of dog breeding out of the stud book to the mating pen and on into the whelping box.

Stud Service

Have in mind well in advance at least one or two choices of stud dog. Contact the dog's owner ahead of time to confirm availability. A usual breeding arrangement for Norfolk is a service charge at the time of mating, with the stud fee payable after the litter is whelped and the registration form signed. There may be additional charges if board and transportation are involved. In some cases the owner of the male may elect to take a puppy instead of the customary stud fee. Whatever the terms, they should be clearly understood and agreed upon by both parties before the mating.

Since it is customary for the bitch to go to the stud, the closer the location of the male geographically the better. You may have to transport your bitch by car or ship her by plane to her destination. This is done regularly by breeders. Just remember that every dog shipped from one state to another needs a health certificate, which you can easily obtain from your veterinarian. If your bitch must travel, ship her in good time for her to settle down in her new surroundings.

The stud owner should make arrangements to care for the visiting bitch either at home or at some nearby safe facility. This is a serious responsibility, as visiting Norfolks are often "only" dogs and house companions. A bitch should be housed in her own individual crate lined with a white towel or paper; water should be always available, and she should be exercised in an enclosed, preferably covered, run. In turn, stud dog owners appreciate having visiting bitches arrive free of fleas and internal parasites, with their coats tidy around and below the tail.

"The Season Is Upon Us"

Although the canine estrus cycle, or heat, occurs about once every six months, Norfolk bitches are notably unpredictable with their seasons, often varying from four to nine months between heats. A normal heat usually starts with a bloody discharge and a slowly swelling vulva. After a week to 12 days the color usually lightens and clears. This begins the period during which your bitch is ready to be bred. Despite this rule of thumb, Norfolk can vary in their fertility periods from 24 hours

You may have to transport your bitch by car or ship her by plane to her destination. This is done regularly by breeders.

to several days. Some bitches show color for *three weeks* before being ready to breed! Others have so-called silent seasons, with no apparent discharge, but are in standing heat and ready to breed as soon as the vulva swells. Veterinary texts give the variation in canine estrus from as few as 3 to as many as 21 days.

When in heat Norfolk bitches are unusually flirtatious. A sure sign that a bitch is ready to be mounted and bred is when she stands and backs up to the male repeatedly, holding her tail to one side. Some veterinarians and breeders use vaginal smears to pick the correct breeding date. However, a single smear is useless as an indicator, while a series is sometimes also inaccurate and costly as well. To repeat our rule of thumb: A bitch with normal bloody discharge is usually ready to breed when the color lightens and clears.

For best results, breed your bitch to an experienced male. First, put the bitch in with the stud and let them play and get to know each other. This get-acquainted period may last an hour or, on the other hand, a union or "tie" between the two might well occur within minutes. Whatever the time interval, the bitch will be bred when she is ready and when the male is genuinely "interested" in her, not when *you* are ready or when "the book" says so. A proven stud dog will know just when to breed the bitch, and when that moment arrives she will stand and be receptive.

Professionals and kennel owners often prefer a table-trained stud. This method takes two people: one to hold the bitch in position, the other either to encourage the stud, or guide him, if necessary. An inexperienced stud, if a house dog, usually performs better when his owner is not visible. Terriers, as their name implies, like to be on the ground.

Artificial insemination is also an AKC-approved method of breeding. Live semen can be used, provided the proper procedures are followed; however, not all veterinarians are experienced in this field, so it is wise to plan ahead. The use of frozen semen is also permitted, although to date, 1989, its success rate is less than satisfactory.

A bitch that refuses to mate should not be force-bred. Avoidance or lack of interest on either her or the

The bitch will be bred when she is ready and when the male is genuinely "interested" in her, not when *you* are ready or when "the book" says so.

stud's part may be nature's way of saying there is something wrong with the bitch—thyroid problems, small vagina and birth canal, improper ovulation, or other factors.

The "official" gestation period for a bitch is 63 days from conception to day of whelping; but there can be considerable variation, both earlier and later, from this norm. After breeding you may not be able to tell whether your bitch is in whelp for five to six weeks (about three weeks before delivery). At about five and a half weeks you should be able to detect pregnancy by the pinkish tinge and slight enlargement of the nipples and breasts, and possibly by a thickening of the abdomen. If by the sixth week your bitch's appetite and water intake have increased markedly, you can be reasonably sure she is in whelp.

Allow the pregnant bitch to exercise and lead a normal life.

Allow the pregnant bitch to exercise and lead a normal life. Feed her well, but don't overfeed so she gets obese and flabby. Allowing her to exercise will create good muscle tone and strength, which she'll need for whelping.

There is a wide range of due dates for whelping, and most bitches are deliberately bred more than once during a heat cycle. Just because a bitch mates at 2:00 p.m. on a Tuesday doesn't mean she conceived at 2:00 p.m. on Tuesday. So don't panic if she doesn't whelp at 2:00 p.m. on the sixty-third day after breeding. As long as she is healthy, she will whelp when the pups are ready to be born.

WHELPING
Sylvia Warren, Norwich Terrier News,
Spring 1969 (Adapted), Dover, Massachusetts

There are two schools of thought on the whelping of puppies. The first gives the bitch a box in the cellar, . . . [lets] nature take its course, and is not too concerned about the bitch's future or the survival of all puppies. The second takes into account all emergencies, demanding from the owner much loss of sleep (puppies are usually born in the middle of the night) and extra effort to prevent avoidable mishaps. Experienced breeders will have their own approach to whelping, but for those who have never been near a dog in whelp before, the best advice is: Be prepared. All things are possible. The bitch may be a "natural mother" able to cope with a litter of five without effort, or she may need help from you or your veterinarian.

Most bitches have definite ideas about where to have their puppies — either in a hole in the woods, under the porch, on your living room sofa, or in your bed. For her sake, and for your own, these fancies must be frustrated! One week before the bitch is due to whelp choose a warm, quiet room in which to place the whelping box. It is wise to let the bitch spend four or five nights in the whelping box, and her days too if she tends to stray. The normal gestation period is 63 days, but bitches tend to whelp in advance of the expected date. A bitch, if late, should be checked by your veterinarian to make certain that the puppies are alive. Alert your veterinarian in advance of whelping. A normal bitch needs no help, but *only* a veterinarian can give the assistance needed if complications arise.

It is assumed that your bitch, checked before and after breeding, is worm free. The only time to worm her is *before* breeding. Regular exercise during pregnancy is a must. One bitch I know walked one mile each day, including the afternoon on which she produced a litter of four healthy puppies.

Puppies should be kept really warm for the first two weeks of their life, gradually reducing the temperature to a steady 60°- 65° in winter. In getting prepared, the following whelping-room list is helpful:

1. Whelping box
2. Bowl of water
3. Clean newspapers
4. Clean towels
5. Clock
6. Plastic garbage bag(s)
7. Sterilized scissors
8. Heating pad
9. Hot water bottle or small heating lamp
10. Shoe box or small carton (to keep puppies safe if bitch is restless)

How do you know when the time has come for your bitch to whelp? The signs are many. Her temperature

Alert your veterinarian in advance of whelping. A normal bitch needs no help, but only a veterinarian can give the assistance needed if complications arise.

will usually drop to subnormal about 12 hours before whelping time. (Normal is 101°–102°.) She will be restless, go off her food, and start scratching up a nest in the newspapers with which you have covered the bottom of the box about two inches deep. (Note: Some bitches "nest" or scratch around in their whelping box days or weeks before they whelp if they have access to their box.) Next, the bitch will usually start panting, slowly but steadily, and squinting her eyes as she pants. Make sure she has plenty of water. Now is the time to darken the room, place the electric heating pad under the box, and leave her quietly alone, checking at brief intervals to see if all is well.

Canine labor is a two-stage event, the first lasting 6 to 12 hours and characterized by a drop in body temperature and uterine contractions that won't be visible to the bystander, although the bitch's restlessness and panting will be obvious. Stage two, when the fetuses begin to move through the birth canal, is characterized by the straining and voluntary contraction of abdominal muscles. This is when awareness on your part is essential. If four hours pass without the appearance of a puppy, or if more than two hours elapse between puppies, trouble may be brewing. When a bitch in stage two constantly *strains* for more than one hour without producing a pup, she needs medical attention. If the birth canal proves to be normal but contractions have ceased (uterine inertia), the veterinarian may administer intravenous calcium and oxytocin, a hormone that stimulates uterine contraction. If the patient does not respond to this therapy, a caesarian section may be necessary.

If four hours pass without the appearance of a puppy, or if more than two hours elapse between puppies, trouble may be brewing.

If the first puppy arrives with ease within one hour of straining, leave the bitch alone. She prefers it and is capable of coping in a most self-sufficient way with the whole litter. Do not fuss; keep her quiet, and keep your watchful eye on her in case of need. If she does not take care of a puppy as soon as it is born, tearing away the membrane surrounding it with her teeth for the pup to breathe, biting the cord and licking the pup warm and dry to stimulate its heart and lungs, and feeding it immediately as soon as its first cry signals that all is well, then you must take over.

In this emergency act fast. As soon as the puppy in

CERTIFIEI

Name of Dog **CH ABBEDALE'S MAGIC CHELSEA**

Breed **NORFOLK TERRIER**

Date Whelped **MARCH 5, 1989**

CRACKNOR CANDII
7 VDH 45

ALLRIGHT HUCKLEBERRY FINN
3 VDH 47

ALLRIGHT CHILCC
8 VDH 17

Sire-1 **CH ALLRIGHT MAGIC LAMP**
RB035603 12-86 RD (WGR)

CH DAFFRAN DUST
9 RA785250 8-83

CHIDLEY MAGIC CARPET
4 RA849806 RD

CHIDLEY POOKA
10 RA685401 8-83

CH ELVE PURE MA
11 RA451400 1-79

CH ABBEDALE'S AMERICAN GIGOLO
5 RA565882 5-82 RD

ABBEDALE'S TEA
12 RA376086 9-79

Dam-2 **ABBEDALE'S AMERICAN CREME**
RA873240 12-89 RD

CH HATCHWOODS C
13 RA639251 11-81

CH TURKHILLS CREME OF ABBEDALE
6 RA682260 7-83 RD

TURKHILLS PATTY
14 RA532955 1-82

The Seal of The American

this pedigree has been co

PEDIGREE

Sex **FEMALE**   Reg. No. **RB314713**

Color **RED**

Breeder **CONNIE BEACH**

NANFAN SWEETCORN
15KCSB 1885BM
NANFAN COUNTRY COUSIN
16KCSB 2718BP
ICKWORTH SANDSTORM
17VDH 15
ICKWORTH PENNY HA'PENNY
18VDH 1
ICKWORTH BACARDI
192525 BN C510011D4
DAFFRAN DALLUS
20722BN C250672C8
CH ELVE PURE MAGIC
21RA451400 1-79 RD (UKG)
SHENANIGANS OF CHIDLEY
22RA247737 11-79 RD WHTN
RAGUS BITTERMAN
233920BJ 49363/75
RAGUS BROWN CIDER
241858BK 138936/75
BETHWAY'S POPOVER
25 R867630 2-73 RD
BETHWAY'S MUFFIN II
26 R867629 2-73 RD WHTN
CRACKNOR CAPRICORN
272998BM C92220C2
HATCHWOODS PEPPERMINT
283422BJ 33514/75
CH ELVE PURE MAGIC
29RA451400 1-79 RD (UKG)
CH RAGUS BROWN SMUDGE
30RA232356 10-76 RD (UKG)

GIRL

UKG)

UKG)

CRUMPETS

DE MENTHE-CRACKNOR
(UKG)

Date Issued **10/20/93**

its sac slides out, gently pull the membrane away from the pup's head and strip it off. Then, leaving one inch attached to the puppy, gently cut the umbilical cord with sterilized scissors. If scissors are not available, twist the cord to sever it; but using your forefinger and thumb, first *clamp off* one inch of the cord nearest the pup's abdomen, and then pull the excess cord from that point so as not to create an umbilical hernia.

The towels and wash rags are useful here—it would be slippery work without their aid. Quickly wipe the pup's nose and mouth free of mucus (when taking its first breath this must not be drawn into the lungs.) If lifeless, rub the puppy briskly with a rough towel and try mouth-to-mouth breathing. Don't give up. A seemingly lifeless puppy can often be brought around with warmth and friction. Once active, start it sucking by gently squeezing a drop of milk from one teat and holding the puppy to the nipple. Let the bitch lick it and take an interest in it between pups. A newborn cannot survive more than its first three hours without milk. Once the bitch starts nursing the first pup, instinct will usually take over and she will know what to do with the rest of the litter. This first milk, or colostrum, is extremely important, because it contains all the antibodies needed by the pup to fight disease.

> If lifeless, rub the puppy briskly with a rough towel and try mouth-to-mouth breathing. Don't give up. A seemingly lifeless puppy can often be brought around with warmth and friction.

The afterbirth, or placenta, is expelled for each pup born, either with or after the puppy. It is usually attached to the other end of the umbilical cord. The bitch eats it for nourishment and it stimulates milk production. She will sometimes do this first before doing anything else, gobbling up the placenta and working her way down the umbilical cord. She will then start tearing open the sac and cleaning the puppy. A good brood bitch may seem very rough with her newborn, rolling it around and licking it voraciously. It may even look as if she will gobble up the pup, but keep calm, as this is very good for the puppy and for her. She will stop as soon as the puppy starts crying and will settle down to nurse until labor starts again.

Norfolk litters vary in number from one to six puppies, the average being three or four. When the litter is complete the bitch will relax, settle down, and nurse. Later pick her up, being careful no pups are clinging to her, and take her out for a short walk. On her return offer her water or water sweetened with honey. Put fresh paper in the box, discarding all damp and soiled paper, and make sure the box and puppies are dry. Feed the mother four moderate meals daily and keep the box clean and *dry*, changing the papers as often as necessary.

At birth most Norfolk puppies weigh between five and seven ounces. Few two-ounce puppies survive, and dams of very large puppies (nine ounces) may need assistance in whelping. Healthy puppies should double their birth weight by eight days and open their eyes within two weeks. If there are no complications the bitch and her litter should be checked by the veterinarian the day after whelping or when the pups' tails are docked and dew claws removed on the fourth day. If the puppies need supplementary feeding, ask your veterinarian to recommend a good formula. (I use Esbilac.) Your veterinarian or even local pet shop should be able to sell you a nursing kit. Supplemental feedings are not usually necessary with an average-size litter and should only be given on medical instruction.

Norfolk litters vary in number from one to six puppies, the average being three.

At night use a night light and by day keep the whelping box shaded from strong light until the puppies' eyes open on about the twelfth day. The bitch may want to use newspapers on the floor near her box, as she will be loath to leave the pups even for a short walk that first week or two. She will have to be carried out or taken on a lead for a walk several times a day. When the pups stagger to their feet—an enchanting sight—tack a small piece of carpet securely down in half the box. This helps get their hind legs under them, giving them more grip than the slippery paper. As soon as they are ready to climb out of their box, at about four weeks, move them to a three-sided box, screening off a small area so they can move around more freely. At six weeks they will be on the brink of weaning and independence.

PRE-ECLAMPSIA ("MOUTHING PUPPIES")

A bitch will normally always clean her puppies after they nurse in order to stimulate elimination. And a puppy cannot eliminate without stimulation until it is about three weeks old. However, at any time after whelping a calcium shortage sometimes causes a bitch to constantly and obsessively "mouth" and clean her pups. This constant mouthing and carrying them about while panting, shivering, and looking "wild-eyed" is a definite sign of trouble. A bitch not able to settle down long enough to nurse her puppies is probably suffering from pre-eclampsia.

An injection of calcium gluconate may be necessary to avoid eclampsia and save both dam and the puppies. (A second injection may also be necessary.) Veterinarians have discovered that TUMS, the popular commercial antacid that comes in tablet form, is also an excellent source of readily absorbable calcium. One TUMS tablet given daily during the last two or three weeks of pregnancy and the first two weeks after whelping can be highly effective in avoiding calcium deficiency.

A bitch not able to settle down long enough to nurse her puppies is probably suffering from pre-eclampsia.

TWITCHING PUPPIES
Marjorie Bunting
Norfolk Terrier Newsletter, Autumn 1985

If you stand and watch a litter of pups during the first days after birth, you will see them "twitch" in different parts of their bodies. This is a sort of jumping movement and can sometimes be so strong it lifts the puppy off the bottom of the box. Only healthy puppies twitch in this way, and while they do so there is little to worry about. So watch them every day to make sure they are vigorously twitching. If they *don't*, or if they *stop* after having twitched to start with, then something is wrong, even though the pups may look fat and healthy. Sometimes getting an antibiotic into them immediately will save them. But unfortunately it is not always easy to convince your veterinarian that antibiotics are necessary, as the pups may look all right and many veterinarians surprisingly do not know the importance of twitching.

TAIL DOCKING

The tradition of docking has long separated the British terrier and shepherd breeds from their long-tailed Scottish counterparts. Originally, England levied a tail tax on hounds and lap dogs belonging to landowners, but the working ("cur") dogs of drovers and ratcatchers' terriers were docked to prove their tax-free status. The tail tax was abolished in 1867, but the practice of docking has continued. Today the practical reasons for docking are debatable, but so are the arguments that it maims and causes trauma.

In 1987 England made tail docking optional to the Norfolk Standard. The Norwegian government in July 1988 banned from competition all dogs docked after that date. Sweden has set January 1989 as its deadline for prohibiting docking; but policing cooperation with the kennel club there has yet to be established. These innovations notwithstanding, the majority of English and American Norfolk breeders continue to prefer docking for its trimmer, sportier effect.

Norfolk pups should have their tails docked from four to six days after birth. Many breeders do their own docking, but inexperienced Norfolk owners sometimes leave docking to the veterinarian, deferring to his or her judgment as to length. This can cause problems because often a veterinarian may not be familiar with the breed, and the medical "rule book" fails to allow sufficient length as required by the Norfolk Standard. The result? An otherwise well-balanced Norfolk with a "stub" instead of a respectable tail. The correct rule is practical and simple: The tail of a Norfolk should always be left long enough to be firmly grasped by your hand.

The tail of a Norfolk should always be left long enough to be firmly grasped by your hand.

There are several docking methods that, when done correctly, are bloodless and virtually painless. Special scissors, needle-nosed pliers, a razor, or a scalpel are all effective docking instruments. When being cut, a puppy's tail should be held at what would be the "one o'clock" position on a clock's dial. A good rule of thumb is to leave slightly less than half the tail or enough to just cover the genitals. Some Norfolk puppies are born with a dark (or light) "band" strategically located about halfway along their tails. If your pups have this marking, use it as a guide when deciding on the length you want. Remember, though, that *not every puppy's tail should be cut the same length.* This is because some have short, fat tails; some have long, thin ones; and tail sets differ. When docking, never take what appears to be the "pick of the litter" as your first candidate. If you make a mistake on the first one, you'll probably do a calmer, better operation on the next.

If your whelps are docked professionally, your veterinarian should be happy to let you decide where each tail should be shortened. It's much better to have a client who has participated in the decision-making process than one who laments later, "Oh, you *ruined* my puppies!" And finally, bear in mind that it's far better to leave too much tail than too little. After all, you can always humanely shorten a tail that's too long, but you can never lengthen a too-short one!

DEW CLAWS

Although the "roots" of the front dew claws are deep, they can be removed from inside the front legs (and hind, if present) with a curved nail scissor at the same time puppies' tails are docked.

If not removed or kept trimmed, these claws, which grow in a curve, can lock and prevent a digging terrier from extricating itself from below ground. Above ground, dew claws can catch in brush and tear the attached pads, causing profuse bleeding. Rear dew claws are rare, vestigial, and ugly in a short-legged dog. Caution: Always have a styptic powder or pencil handy in case removal causes bleeding.

If not removed or kept trimmed, these claws, which grow in a curve, can lock and prevent a digging terrier from extricating itself from below ground.

WEANING

After three weeks of age, you will want to start weaning your puppies. Choose a time when the mother has been away from the puppies and mix a little softened puppy chow (there are many excellent brands on the market) with some warm water, or water mixed with evaporated milk or buttermilk. The mixture should be soupy, and its temperature warm to the touch. If the pups are well fed they will not be interested in this first food, but if they're hungry enough they should go to it right away. A low, flat dish, such as a teacup saucer, is a good starting bowl. Put a drop on your finger and put it to the puppy's tongue. Then direct the puppy to the bowl. After about four days you can start adding very lean ground beef to the mixture. Add enough hot water to the ground beef to liquify and warm it before mixing it with the puppy chow. Feed the puppies this mixture twice daily for the first week as they also continue nursing, and then three to four times daily.

Don't panic if the puppies also help themselves to their mother's food. Between six and eight weeks the brood bitch may start regurgitating her dinner to the puppies. This is perfectly normal and is her way of introducing them to solid food. At a certain point in the puppies' development (usually between seven and eight weeks) their dam's milk can cause loose stools. This means they are now weaned and should be separated from her at feeding times and at night. The dam, however, should be allowed to play with and instruct her offspring for as long as they remain with her. Norfolks are devoted mothers, and this playtime should not be discouraged.

> Norfolks are devoted mothers, and playtime should not be discouraged.

THE MODERN WHELPING BOX
Linda Plummer, Wenwagon Kennels,
Warrenton, Virginia

I always intended to build a whelping box with removable sides, metal edges to prevent chewing, and so on, but when the time came the box wasn't built and the puppies wouldn't wait. I've always used small molded fiberglass airline crates as beds for my Norfolks, and bitches feel comfortable whelping in these containers due to the privacy of a bottom, top, and three sides and an open metal grate in front. For whelping, I now use a bigger-than-Norfolk-sized fiberglass crate and let an experienced bitch whelp in the crate fully assembled, knowing she is capable of handling things by herself. For a first-time whelper, I simply remove the top of the crate. When this is done the metal grate or front door comes off and can be put aside until you want to reassemble the crate. This allows the bitch to be surrounded on three sides, with a small lip, or edge, at the open front (which keeps newborns from crawling out); and I can see inside with easy access. These crates are much easier to clean than wood, an added advantage.

Best of all is the way the airline crate adapts to all stages of puppy growth. In the beginning I use either the bottom half or the fully assembled crate, depending on the bitch. For the first two to three weeks I keep the bottom lined with washable bathroom cotton carpet or old towels. (I discard the newspapers as soon as all the puppies are born because even newborns need traction to nurse.) The bitch keeps her puppies absolutely clean for about the first three weeks, so the carpet or towels need washing only every two or three days. Depending on the time of year and room temperature, I place a small heating pad underneath the carpet and/or towels and set it on LOW, making sure the pups have space to get away from the pad if they become too warm. The heating pad can be removed after the first two weeks or when you see the pups no longer using it. Chilled puppies will usually let you know they're cold by crying, whimpering, and squirming, even if they're getting enough to eat.

After the first two or three weeks, I take the top I removed from the crate and attach it (with its hand screws) to the bottom section, *lengthwise.* In other words, instead of screwing it back on the top, I put the crate's two sections together, front-to-front, connecting the *front* of the bottom to the *front* of the top. This creates a long, two-sectional box with a low ledge in the middle. One half is lined with the washable carpet and the other half with newspaper. As early as three weeks the puppies will start eliminating on the newspaper side and eating and sleeping on the carpet side. As soon as they can eliminate on their own they're strong enough to climb over the little ledge between the two sections of the crate. This gives them the feeling they are getting away from their "den." I discovered this by accident when I wanted to make the box bigger because the puppies were getting more active. I use a fairly large crate (Retriever or Shepherd size), and with some bitches I place a small, very low stool next to the box so the bitch can jump in and out or just sit on the stool and "look in" on her puppies without actually getting in. The puppies can't get out because the sides of the box are about two feet high.

When I start weaning the pups, I feed them on the newspaper portion because weanlings are very messy,

Chilled puppies will usually let you know they're cold by crying, whimpering, and squirming, even if they're getting enough to eat.

and as soon as they have "taken care of business," they crawl back over to their carpet and play and sleep until it's time to eat again. This large crate arranged in two sections is big enough for a Norfolk litter until they are about six weeks old. I've used this method for years and recommend it to anyone I know having a litter of puppies, and people always call me the day they see their puppies crawling from the carpet to the newspaper at three weeks of age. The puppies keep themselves clean because they always sleep and play on the carpet section and eliminate on the newspaper section. Even after they're weaned and racing around outdoors, I still put them to bed in their whelping box (on the carpet side) and find clean puppies in the morning. I've also discovered from the owners of my puppies that they adapt naturally to this "crate method" of housebreaking later on because they are used to not soiling their beds. Try it — you'll like it!

> No matter what your aims as a breeder, every Norfolk puppy deserves the opportunity to become a companion. Norfolks do not flourish without human attention.

THE RIGHT HOME

No matter what your aims as a breeder, every Norfolk puppy deserves the opportunity to become a companion. Norfolks do not flourish without human attention. This is an easy goal to achieve. If all your puppies are not spoken for, contact other Norfolk breeders, your breed club publication, or your local dog club. Nationwide the demand for Norfolk Terriers outweighs the supply, as the average litter is only three.

Although many Norfolk pups are bred from titled stock, are home-raised and thoroughly socialized, few are of championship caliber. Despite its pedigree no Norfolk puppy can be considered a show prospect until it has its permanent teeth, can set its ears correctly, or has proven itself in the ring. Customarily, show prospects are confirmed by experienced exhibitors and professionals.

As the constant demand for Norfolks continues, breeders can afford to selectively match each puppy with its future owner. Though overcharging is a lamentable temptation, responsible breeders rely on their intuition and affection for their terriers before parting with a puppy at any price.

Norfolks thrive in the country, city, and suburbs as long as they have the companionship of people. When relocation proves necessary, these terriers are also very adaptable to change.

PUPPY "CARE PACKAGE"

It is comforting to send each puppy off with a "care package," including:

1. The "papers" (AKC litter registration application, pedigree, and veterinary records indicating dates of shots and wormings)
2. Feeding information (what the puppy has been eating, how much to feed, and how often)
3. A three-day supply of food(s)
4. List of useful Norfolk publications and where to obtain them
5. One or two safe toys and rawhide chews
6. Show lead

New owners are always grateful for this "puppy packet," and it gives the breeder the satisfaction of knowing the puppy will feel at home and be well cared for immediately and at minimum expense.

Despite its pedigree no Norfolk puppy can be considered a show prospect until it has its permanent teeth, can set its ears correctly, or has proven itself in the ring.

Figure 191: One or two safe toys might be included in a puppy "care package."

Figure 192:
Puppies are cute, but their needs make a long list.
Kalle and "Mandy," Sweden.

7

YOUR NEW NORFOLK

MALE OR FEMALE?
*Sheila Foran, **Folklore**, Glastonbury, Connecticut*

As conscientious breeder and prospective pet owner meet, the inevitable question arises, "Which makes a better pet, a dog or a bitch?" Common belief dictates that females make the best pets because—or so the story goes—they are smarter, cleaner, and more loving than males. Case closed. But before we endorse sexist stereotypes and relegate the boys to the show ring or breeding shed, let's take a closer look at the issue of sex as it pertains to Norfolks.

The attributes of intelligence, cleanliness, and personality are not linked to sex alone. Rather, they are specific to individual dogs, and there may be substantial variation in habits and behavior, even among same-sex littermates. For a pet owner to reject a puppy solely on the basis of its sex is a mistake. This is particularly true in a breed where litters may be scarce and choices limited.

Figure 193: Ch. Ferdinand The Warrior and his daughter Titanium Gold Digger. *Photo © Sally Anne Thompson.*

It seems that males may be quicker to learn than females, but they're more easily bored by formal training. This general tendency of males to mature more slowly than females, both physically and mentally, should not be confused with lack of intelligence. As adults all Norfolks seem equally bright.

Cleanliness is obviously a concern to anyone who has a dog living in the house. As males mature, they begin "marking" their territory by lifting their legs. Most male dogs can successfully learn that what is acceptable outside on trees or fire hydrants is definitely *not* acceptable inside on the carpet and drapes. For those who don't learn, altering always helps and can be an effective cure for the habit of marking.

Norfolks are a small breed and easy to control. A future owner should carefully consider the sex of a puppy when there are other unaltered dogs in the household. Two same-sexed dogs can live in harmony if one has a more dominant personality. However, today, spaying and neutering are such viable options the question of sex merits little importance. The most important question to ask when matching a puppy to a potential owner is not "Male or female?" but "But is it irresistible?"

PUPPY OR ADULT?
*Sheila Foran, **Folklore**, Glastonbury, Connecticut*

Traditionally people in search of a pet Norfolk seek out the youngest they can find. There's no denying that watching a three- or four-months-old youngster gambol on the hearth, blissfully shedding puppy teeth while chewing on Dad's tasseled loafer, is a sight that brings joy to all but the most humorless of souls (and, maybe, Dad). It's easy to understand the attraction of a Norfolk baby, since puppies of this breed are among the most appealing. But it's also important to remember that there *is* life after puppyhood, and there are some compelling arguments to recommend the selection of an older dog as a pet.

While we're extremely fortunate that Norfolks seldom end up unwanted in animal shelters, it could happen. More often, adults become available due to the death or disability of an owner or because of the vagaries of modern life. Sometimes a breeder will decide to place a retired show dog or brood bitch in a loving pet home once the dog's "working" life is over. In each of these situations there may be a perfectly wonderful mature Norfolk searching for folks who will provide a warm bed and plenty of love.

If confronted with the choice between acquiring a puppy or adult consider your situation in life, and consider the dog's. Cute as puppies are, remember their needs make a fairly long list. Housebreaking, multiple

daily meals, training and exercise are involved. That shoe of Dad's may be an attractive target during teething.

Figure 194: **It's easy to understand the attraction of a Norfolk baby.**

While many people are willing to put up with the challenges of raising a puppy, others have neither the time nor the inclination to do so. Consider, then, the joys of bringing home a happy, outgoing (albeit older) Norfolk—one already housebroken, leash trained, and long past the age of destruction.

A natural concern is whether or not an older dog can make the emotional adjustment required to live with a new family. In almost all cases the answer is a resounding "Yes!". They seem only to ask, "Please love me so I can love you back." Ideally, in obtaining an older dog you'll be able to have a trial period so that both dog and family can become acclimated to one another.

Since Norfolks tend to live to a ripe old age, getting a dog who is three or four years old, or even older, gives you the promise of many years together. Finally, there's an unmistakably warm feeling when you know you've given a needy Norfolk a special place in your home. The bond that forms is usually every bit as strong as the one formed with a puppy—in certain cases even stronger.

So, before automatically choosing a youngster, give some thought to establishing a relationship with an older Norfolk. The problems are small and the rewards immense.

"SAFE AND SOUND"
Carolyn Pyle, C and J Kennels, Freeville, New York

Most dog owners start with a puppy. Before bringing home your young Norfolk it's essential to prepare a safe environment for it. "Puppy-proofing" your home involves thinking about all possible dangers and eliminating them.

House
Hazards include all medicines, sprays, glues, and bleaches that can be easily gotten into. Toxic plants and dangling electric cords are also dangerous. Plug up or block all nooks and cracks, such as spaces behind a refrigerator, washer, or dryer.

Figure 195: Toys for young puppies should be examined with safety in mind. "Teddington," a Ch. Dalcroft's Kyrie son, surveys his collection.

Garden and Yard
The most important safety factor is adequate fencing. Like many terrier breeds, Norfolk will stalk or chase anything the moves—including automobiles! Make sure your outdoor area is enclosed, with no holes or gaps for clever escapes.

Freshly sprayed lawns, shrubs and plants, fertilizers on top of all soil or in open bags, and pellet-type snail and grub poisons are all potential dangers to an untrained, inquisitive puppy.

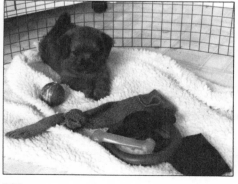

Garage
Antifreeze is deadly to dogs, and unfortunately they love its taste. Oils, gasoline, paint thinner, chlorine for the swimming pool, rat poison, and plugged-in electric tools are also hazardous.

Pool
Norfolks usually love water, and

some, but not all, are excellent swimmers. If you have a swimming pool, make sure your puppy cannot fall into it. And be certain, if your dog does go into the pool, that it understands water and knows how to paddle and stay afloat.

RECOMMENDED EQUIPMENT

1. A fiberglass crate, lightweight and almost indestructible.
2. Portable wire exercise pen (can be used indoors and out).
3. Stainless steel or crockery dishes for food and water.
4. Flat show lead (noose type with sliding safety catch); 5/8 inch Resco "Hyde" lead is excellent for puppy training.
5. Flat web collar and lead, or leather set.
6. "Safe" toys, including marrow, and large rawhide bones. Squeaking rubber toys must be monitored to make sure puppies don't dislodge and eat the "squeakers."

FEEDING AND NUTRITION

There are as many diets and feeding schedules as there are dog breeders. Follow the diet and schedule given you by the breeder from whom you buy your puppy. It shouldn't take long for you to learn how much food is right for your dog. Use the following guidelines as to how often to feed and what to feed:

Age	Meals Per Day
6 weeks – 3 months	4
3 months – 6 months	3
6 months – 1 year	2
1 year	1

For a puppy three to six months old, a balanced diet for a three-meal day is:

Morning: Puppy meal moistened with milk or water.

Afternoon: Meat or canned food with puppy meal

Evening: plus a vitamin supplement.
                Same as afternoon, but no vitamin.

HOUSEBREAKING
Margaret Pugh, Tompkins County SPCA,
Tailbearer, *Fall 1979*

Housebreaking a puppy does not come naturally, but dogs normally do not like to soil their sleeping area. By confining a puppy in a small space when sleeping or unattended, you take advantage of the dog's natural instinct for cleanliness. A crate is excellent for this purpose, as it provides the dog with its own "den."

Establish a regular schedule for feeding, play, and exercise. By feeding your puppy at the same times each day, you'll "train" his digestive system (he'll need to eliminate shortly after each meal). Take him outside as soon as he wakes up in the morning, after eating, play sessions, naps, and always before retiring at night. A Norfolk is small enough to carry out after he's been confined, which is a good idea because many a puppy will eliminate on his way out the door. Be consistent with food. A puppy has a sensitive digestive system, and changing his diet can thwart your housebreaking efforts. For instance, adding too much milk to the diet gives most pups diarrhea.

Always take the pup out the same door, and to the same area. When you take him outside, stay with him until he has relieved himself, praise him, and then bring him in immediately. Keep an eye on him when he is awake in the house; if he begins to sniff, circle, or squat, pick him up and take him out immediately.

Gradually increase the time between trips outside as the puppy gets older. A 10-to-12-week-old pup begins to have better control of urination and fewer bowel movements as meals are cut to three a day. A four-month-old Norfolk should have fairly good control, with only an occasional accident, usually when the routine is upset. But remember that Norfolks are small dogs with small bladders, and Norfolk puppies need to urinate more frequently than larger breeds. Gradually give the pup supervised freedom of more areas of the house, but continue to confine him when unsupervised.

Whenever the puppy has an accident, clean it up immediately and deodorize the area with a solution of white vinegar and water. If you catch him in the act, say"No!", pick him up, and take him outside. Praise him when he is done. Do not punish him for the accident by hitting him or rubbing his nose it it. It is only by mistake that he will really learn. If he is not allowed to make mistakes, you will be the one who is housebroken, not the puppy!

Many young dogs, and some insecure older ones, will urinate when they greet their owners or feel stress; this is called submissive urination. Never punish a dog for this, as it will only add to the problem. Plan to greet the dog calmly, then mop up, remembering to use white vinegar. Submissive urination is a normal response by a subordinate dog to a dominant one or to a pack leader. Most puppies outgrow this phase, and as insecure dogs gain confidence the problem will disappear.

LEAD TRAINING

There are many ways of teaching puppies to lead. It is best to begin with a wide, soft collar or broad slip lead, as young Norfolks have sensitive tracheas which narrow leads can harm. At first let a young puppy run around with a short show lead around its neck to get the feel of it before he is asked to gait. Tasty rewards improve cooperation, and puppies soon learn to pose and follow the "bait" hand.

If you have a stubborn student and an already lead-broken adult dog is available, try walking the two together. The puppy will almost inevitably follow the other dog and forget about the lead around his neck. Lessons should be brief, no more than five to fifteen minutes, and fun, as Norfolk puppies, although intelligent, have short attention spans.

"TABLE MANNERS"

Even if you don't plan to show your puppy, it's useful to train him to stand quietly on a table with a towel or rubber mat underfoot to prevent slipping. All dogs are asked to get on a table at the veterinarian's office, and being table-trained can lessen the stress of a veterinary visit. "Tabling" your puppy is also convenient for weekly grooming sessions, which should include checking the teeth for tartar and retained milk teeth, brushing the coat and removing dead hair, keeping nails nipped, and checking the body and ears for parasites.

PROBLEM EARS

Correctly dropped ears are an important Norfolk characteristic. Due to the Norfolk's mixed heritage, however, and its recent separation from its prick-eared Norwich relative, all ears are not alike in size, placement, or shape.

Some Norfolks carry their ears correctly from birth, while others need gentle massaging to encourage correct ear carriage. Many puppies fool around with their ears when they shed their milk teeth between four to six months of age. They also can carry their ears askew anytime the feel insecure, submissive, or for some special recognition, even if they normally have correct placement and carriage. More than one ring debut or camera pose has been unexpectedly spoiled by a first-time "flying" ear.

The correct pendulous ear is attached to the side of the wide head, forming a line just below the arc of the skull. When relaxed, ears hang skinside inside, parallel to the cheek. When alert, the muscle pivots the ear forward so its long edge rests on the cheek with its blunt tip close to the outside corner of the eye. The correct ear is medium-sized, covered with a short velvety coat, has a marked vertical indentation, and is both pliant and expressive.

Small, highly set ears that break horizontally across the top, like a fox terrier's, or those that merely tip over, like a collie's, lack the typical vertical dip and sometimes become erect with age. Heavy leathers also detract from the true expression.

PRESCRIPTION FOR SETTING DROP EARS

There are a number of methods for setting ears. Taping is safe, easy, and will not damage the ear or coat. The purpose of ear taping is to prevent the ear from flying sideways, because an ear carried sideways throughout puppyhood can encourage the cartilage to break into a crease that can never be corrected.

The following method uses *duct tape* because:

A. It stays on, yet is easy to get off without pain or hair loss.

B. It is the proper weight. Heavier tape or moleskin, or tape that is too light in weight, can actually do harm as it strengthens ear muscles and causes "flyaway" ears when you remove it.

Figure 196:

ILLUS. 1:   Shows correct ear carriage with its slightly vertical indentation.

ILLUS. 2:   For mild cases, cut a piece of duct tape in a shield shape, then trim corners and apply to (clean) inner ear.

ILLUS. 3:   For more stubborn cases, lift the ear and fold it back on the head at the natural break. Then place 1/2 inch-wide duct tape between the edge of the break and the ear tip.

ILLUS. 4:   Flip the ear forward to the natural position. Tape should extend an inch on either side of the ear.

ILLUS. 5:   Now fold the ear fur-side inside, edge-to-edge, and stick the ends of the tape together. If necessary, trim excess tape and leave it on as long as it will stay. Repeat taping until the ears have set or until the permanent teeth are in.

COPING WITH COATS

Puppies from two to four months old need little grooming and lots of fun training. Life is a game. Ten minutes daily teaches them a regular routine. Sit, then stand your puppy on a steady table. Introduce him to a brush and comb. Place one hand lightly under the puppy's chin; with the other gently stroke his nose and raise his upper lip to show his puppy teeth.

Trim his nails by snipping the curved tip off — never too short, for they will bleed if the vein at the end of each nail is cut. Long nails are uncomfortable and impede the gait.

Between four and six months, after brushing and combing, with your forefinger and thumb strip out the dead puppy coat. Always keep your wrist rigid, and pull the hairs out in the direction in which they grow. Begin with the top of the head and continue from side to side until the dog looks neat and tidy.

There are two basic types of coats: hard and soft. The correct hard, double coat is best described as a wiry-textured, broken coat with naturally shorter furnishings on legs and head, slight eyebrows and whiskers, and a full, protective mane around the neck which starts behind the ears.

Very hard-coated dogs are at a disadvantage in the show ring with nothing to hide their outline. Balance, soundness, and expression must excel to appeal to most terrier judges today.

The softer coats grow longer, have full furnishings, a denser undercoat, and can be sculpted into the outline of any clever groomer's choice. Though not correct according to the Standard and more difficult for the pet owner to maintain, these heavier coats are favored by today's exhibitors who promote the breed for Group and all-breed competitions. Some very soft coats never shed and must be trimmed with razor, scissors, or knife for comfort and cleanliness. These appealing "wrong-coated" (Hairy Bears) Norfolks are not for ring competition.

Grooming can start at three to four months, and a litter may have puppies with basically different coats. Some whelps are slow to develop guard hairs. They are smooth red sucklings for their first weeks, turning dingy and growing dark guard hairs by weaning age. Then the hair about the ears, muzzle, and feet starts to change and brighten. Soon the guard hairs, now much longer and darker than the rest, stand away from the body.

Guard hairs can be an indication of future coat density but not of its texture. At between two and three months these long, dark hairs wear off or can be removed by hand. Now is the time to start grooming your pet weekly with a bristle brush and metal comb.

Even with weekly grooming the Norfolk coat can become "blown" (ready to fall out). Now is the time for removing all the dead hair using your fingers as the basic tool. First comb the coat thoroughly before starting to pluck (pull out) the dead hair by hand.

These illustrations demonstrate Norfolk coat maintenance:

Figure 197:

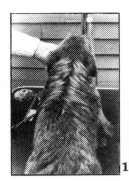

1. A Norfolk with a loose, blown coat. It is ready to pluck when it parts down the back and bands to a lighter color. The new coat has started to grow, so give it room by removing the dead hair by hand.

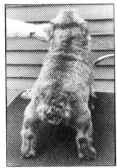

2. This dog shows a coat that has had all the old blown coat removed. The dark color down the back is the soft new undercoat, and the lightcolored hairs you can see mixed in indicate that the new outer coat is starting to grow in.

3. As the coat continues to grow, the darker undercoat will no longer be visible, and the harsh outer coat will now completely cover the dog. This coat will continue to grow longer and thicker until it again resembles Number 1; then it will be time to start again. With combing and brushing in between, this whole process will take the better part of a year.

4. Whether working on the dog's body or head, separate the hairs and pull a few at a time with the thumb and forefinger. Always pluck in the direction the hair grows and keep your wrist rigid. THIS IN NO WAY HURTS THE DOG as the hair that you are removing is dead and often causes itching if left in place.

5   6   7

5, 6, and 7. These three photographs show how to remove and tidy the head. Note the difference in the head of the dog with half of the dead coat removed. The expression of the eye becomes apparent, as well as the set of the ear. The head is the most important single area. When it is cleaned and tidied up your Norfolk takes on the appearance and bearing of its breed.

8

8. This illustration shows the proper use of the fine stainless steel comb in removing almost all loose and dead hair as the coat becomes longer.

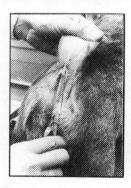

9

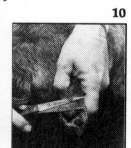

10

9 - 10. The last two photographs demonstrate the only use of scissors occasionally necessary for coat care. Scissor around the feet to keep dirt from being tracked into the house, and around the underside of the tail for sanitary reasons.

GROOMING TERMINOLOGY

Stripping -   Can be done by hand, but implies using a serrated metal tool (knife or comb) and removing the top coat. Same as **Taking Down a Coat.**

Plucking -   Implies removing dead hair by hand. The correct way to prepare a Norfolk for the show ring.

Rolling -	Method of keeping a coat in show shape without removing it all at one time.
Raking -	Taking out undercoat, usually with brush and fine-tooth comb.
Tidying -	To neaten coat and furnishings with thumb and forefinger.
Trimming -	Usually done with thinning shears under body where skin is sensitive.
Scissor -	Clip around anus and bottoms of feet.

Puppies should have dead guard hairs removed by hand by about three months. If coats are soft or silky, strip all over before six months to improve texture. Coats sometimes come in harsher, with successive changes every six to nine months.

Figure 198:
**Bellamy Longtails with
Bee Ege in Cornwall.**

Figure 199:
**Regular veterinarian
visits are a require-
ment for a healthy
Norfolk.**

8

HEALTH AND HAPPINESS

Nat R. LaMar
Reidmar, Brooklyn, New York

It's essential to your Norfolk's health that you have a good relationship with your veterinarian. Even if it means "shopping around," find a veterinarian in whom you have complete confidence and with whom you are comfortable.You'll want to be able to ask "stupid" questions without feeling *totally* stupid, and you'll want to know that your veterinarian can be called on day or night in an emergency.

IMMUNIZATIONS

Besides safety and nutrition, the most important aspect of your Norfolk's health is immunizations.

The most important aspect of your Norfolk's health is immunizations.

D-H-L-P-P
The first and basic immunization is the DHLPP vaccine (Distemper–Hepatitis–Leptospirosis–Parainfluenza–Parvo). This is usually administered as a series of three shots. Some veterinarians start the series at seven or eight weeks, while others begin at ten weeks, with the shots given at three or four week intervals. At six months a booster should be given, and another booster once a year thereafter. Find out from the breeder of your new puppy exactly how many shots, if any, he has had.

Rabies
Whether you live in the city or country, have your dog vaccinated against rabies at anywhere from four to six months of age. Wildlife such as foxes, squirrels, skunks, rats, and raccoons can transmit rabies in the rural environment, but so can feral cats and dogs in the city. Your dog needs a rabies booster at one year and

once a year thereafter, depending on the type of serum used. Some veterinarians give a three-year rabies shot.

Briefly, here are the diseases preventable by immunizations.

Distemper

Common in the United States in unvaccinated dogs. Caused by an airborne virus and present in urine, saliva, and nasal discharge. Symptoms: initially sleepiness, grogginess, fever, with signs of a "cold." Later, fits, convulsions and nerve impairment, and frequently death. Treatment: no sure cure, and recovery slow if at all. Supportive drugs are vitamins and antibiotics. Recovery gives permanent immunity.

Infectious Hepatitis

Viral, highly contagious, and transmitted by direct contact with body fluids: blood, saliva, urine. Affects the liver and blood vessels. Recovered dogs shed the virus in their urine for long periods. Symptoms: high fever and marked depression, with progress so rapid that death can occur within 24 hours from the first symptoms. Treatment: supportive antibiotics, immune serum, and intravenous fluids to prevent dehydration. Recovery gives permanent immunity.

Leptospirosis

Transmitted by urine of infected animals, particularly rats and feral dogs. Caused by spirochete microorganisms, and can be transmitted to humans. Affects the kidneys; and an infected animal's urine contains contagion for many months. Symptoms: fever, depression, grogginess, vomiting, soreness of body parts, and sometimes jaundice. Treatment: intravenous antibiotics and blood transfusions. Kidney damage may be permanent.

Parvo Virus

Highly contagious and frequently fatal. Since death can occur within days or hours, urgent attention is essential. Symptoms: frequent vomiting of small amounts of mucous or clear fluid; inability to keep down food or water; watery diarrhea, listlessness, weakness, sudden weight loss, and dehydration. In young puppies all or none of these symptoms may be accompanied by sudden heart failure and death. Treatment: supportive therapy of antibiotics, vitamins and anti-inflammatory drugs, and subcutaneous injections of glucose to prevent dehydration. Note: CORONA VIRUS is a serious, potentially fatal infection with symptoms extremely similar to Parvo. Laboratory tests of blood and fecal samples can detect the difference between these two diseases. Fortunately, to date (1989) there is a new effective vaccine against Corona. Supportive treatment is the same as for Parvo.

PARASITES

Internal Parasites

These include most worms and infectious protozoa that live in a dog's intestine, where they feed and reproduce. Eggs and protozoan cysts transmitted to the soil via an infected animal's feces pose a threat to other dogs that sniff or walk across the infested ground. After treatment, keep your dog away from feces-contaminated areas. Be alert for signs of internal parasites in your dog.

Be alert for signs of internal parasites in your dog.

ROUNDWORMS: Frequently found in young and newly weaned puppies, and usually transmitted by the nursing dam. Can often be seen in stools, and look like strands of spaghetti. Medication: either Nemex, available from your veterinarian, or Evict (trade name) available at pet supply stores.

HOOKWORMS AND WHIPWORMS: Occur in both puppies and adult dogs. Microscopic examination of fecal samples is the means of detection. Symptoms: jellylike, black stools, sometimes containing traces of blood. Medication: Panacur, which can be prescribed by your veterinarian. (Panacur also eliminates several other types of worms.)

TAPEWORMS: Occur both in puppies and adult dogs. Can sometimes be seen in stools as small, flat, white segments, moving slowly. Also appear as brownish, dried segments resembling rice grains on the coat near the dog's anus. Medication: Droncit, prescribed by your veterinarian, one of the most effective and widely used drugs. Note: Since frequently fleas are the carriers of tapeworm eggs, eliminating fleas is doubly important.

HEARTWORM: Different from other intestinal worms, much more dangerous, and capable of causing shortened life span and/or death. Transmitted by mosquitoes, so first ask your veterinarian whether there have been any cases in your area. If recommended, have your dog tested and use whichever of the two types of preventive medication is prescribed: (1) administered daily or, (2) as recommended more recently, administered once a month. Treatment of an animal already infected is complicated and has dangerous side effects.

GIARDIA: A hard-to-detect microorganism that lives in the digestive tract, causing chronic diarrhea and mucoid stools. Contracted through exposure to feces of wildlife such as beaver, rabbits, squirrels, skunks, and raccoons. Can also be contracted in the city from the feces of infected cats and dogs. Contagious to humans. Medication: Flagyl or Atabrine (commercial names), either of which must be obtained by veterinary prescription. Several courses of one, or both, of these drugs may be needed due to likely recurrences.

COCCIDIA: Like Giardia, a microorganism of the digestive system, causing "inexplicable," chronic diarrhea. Frequently contracted from bird droppings, but also can be contracted from feces of wildlife and infected dogs and cats. Medication: the sulfa drug Albon (Bactrovet) prescribed by your veterinarian and administered according to directions.

External Parasites

External parasites include fleas, ticks, lice, and mites. Insects that live on your dog's skin not only cause irritation but also can infect the animal with disease. Some can also infect humans.

FLEAS: If your Norfolk has fleas, you probably already know it. They are usually easy to see, but a fine-tooth flea comb run through the coat will bring them to the surface. Fleas feed on your dog's blood, cause itching, and, if swallowed, can also transmit tapeworm eggs. If fleas are present, you will also see tiny, black, gritty particles of flea excrement in the coat. Depending on where you live, the "flea season" can last many months, and since these pests spend most of their time *off* the dog, you'll need to treat both your pet and his surround-

If your Norfolk has fleas, you probably already know it.

ings. Wash his bedding in hot water every week or two, thoroughly vacuum all carpets and crevices (throwing away the vacuum-cleaner bags afterward), and treat your Norfolk with a flea powder, spray, or dip recommended by your veterinarian.

TICKS: There are many kinds of ticks, but fortunately in most areas they are not as common as fleas. A tick bite can transmit Rocky Mountain Spotted Fever and Lyme Disease to humans and dogs. When you find a tick on your Norfolk's skin, grasp the insect as near its head as possible with tweezers and pull it out. Dab the spot with alcohol or hydrogen peroxide to prevent infection. Checkpoints for ticks on your dog are the head, insides of the ears, the neck, and the groin. With Lyme Disease, the dog can be lame or stiff and generally acts "old." Fortunately the response to antibiotics is usually effective.

Checkpoints for ticks on your dog are the head, insides of the ears, the neck, and the groin.

MANGE MITES: The two most common mange mites are sarcoptic and demodectic. The mites live in or on the dog's skin or hair follicles and are not visible to the naked eye. Sarcoptic mites lay their eggs under the skin. The dog scratches and rubs, the skin becomes dry, thickened, and wrinkled, the hair falls out, and crusts form. Itching is very severe. Sarcoptic mange is highly contagious to both animals and human beings and must be treated by a veterinarian. Demodectic mites live in the hair follicles and cause skin lesions with bare spots and pustular areas. Either variety of mange mite can spread quickly, but demodectic mange is slower-acting, recurrent, and more difficult to control than sarcoptic. Follow your veterinarian's advice for treatment. Fortunately, mange is not common among Norfolks.

DANDRUFF MITES (CHEYLETIELLA): Cheyletiella mites are relatively large in size and most commonly are found in puppies. Symptoms: itching, scratching, and the appearance of white, scaly dandruff, usually extending from the base of the tail upward along the middle of the puppy's back. Frequently referred to as "walking dandruff," Cheyletiella dandruff can often be seen with the naked eye or a magnifying glass as tiny white specks or flecks moving through the fur. It first appears in two- to three-week-old puppies and is highly contagious among litters. Bathe your puppy two or three times with a flea shampoo to eradicate this condition. (Most of these containing pyrethrins are particularly effective.) Dandruff mites are fairly common among Norfolk litters but are easy to control.

EAR MITES: Ear mites, which dogs often contract from cats, cause an animal to scratch at or paw his ears and shake his head. You can detect these parasites by checking your Norfolk's ears for dark wax or a material resembling coffee grounds or dried blood. Your veterinarian can prescribe an ear-drop medication that can be administered over a specified period until the problem clears up. Remember, ear mites also live outside the ear, so flea powders and medicated flea shampoos are good precautions.

COMMON HEALTH PROBLEMS

Dogs with drop ears are more prone to ear problems.

Eyes and Ears

Your Norfolk's eyes should be clear and bright, and the area around the eyeball should be white. If there are any red spots, discharge, or other abnormal conditions, take him to your veterinarian immediately. The ears should be checked at least once a month. Keep your Norfolk's ears free of long or wispy hair by trimming or plucking. Dogs with drop ears are more prone to ear problems, and any excess hair around the ears prevents air from getting into the ears. Check the ear canal. If it is red, inflamed, and hot, has a foul odor, or is sensitive to the touch, see your veterinarian.

Teeth

Check your Norfolk's teeth regularly. He will gradually lose his temporary or baby teeth, and should have all his 42 permanent teeth by the time he is seven months old. Make sure he does not retain his baby canine teeth. These may need to be extracted if he still has them by the time he is eight months old, as they could affect his overall bite.

Dental care is very important to your Norfolk's good health, and dental examinations should be a part of his regular veterinary checkup. Many veterinarians now recommend brushing your dog's teeth once a week with a soft toothbrush and toothpaste or a mixture of salt and baking soda moistened with warm water. Check for tartar buildup, which can lead to gum disease.

ANESTHETICS AND TEETH: More often than not it's uncalled for and undesirable to send your pet into a stupor for hours just to have his teeth cleaned, or even for the extraction of an already wobbly tooth. Removal of a stubborn baby tooth in puppies can usually be accomplished by the gentle push-pull tactic with thumb and forefinger a few minutes at a time over a day or two. If you're squeamish about any of these do-it-yourself techniques and feel you must rely on a veterinarian, ask that anesthetic *not be used unless it's absolutely essential.* A number of Norfolk breeders have made the wise observation that our dogs seem generally more sensitive, more allergic, and more easily devastated by anesthesia than some other breeds of the same size. If an anesthetic must be administered, by all means make your veterinarian aware of this fact. A mild tranquilizer is usually all that is needed for teeth cleaning and most extractions.

False Pregnancy

There are new veterinary views and approaches to false pregnancies in dogs. It was once thought that high levels of the hormone progesterone caused a bitch to manifest strong maternal symptoms after an estrus when she had not been bred. An obvious "false" pregnancy causes milk production, and the bitch may be nervous, cranky, and protective of an object or toy that she adopts as a substitute whelp. Recent studies have found that the responsible hormone is prolactin, and that the condition is normal and not a disorder.

It is now thought that pseudopregnancy has an evolutionary history, with a survival value for dogs in the wild, and even in rearing puppies today, because nonpregnant females with milk can sometimes suckle orphaned or excess puppies. Now that false pregnancies have finally been recognized as normal, the current emphasis is on letting nature take its course, although a drug, Bromocriptine, can be administered to inhibit the secretion of prolactin. Spaying, as a last resort, will prevent future pseudopregnancies. However, this operation should never be scheduled during a false pregnancy or during the heat cycle.

There are new veterinary views and approaches to false pregnancy in dogs.

Loose Stools and Diarrhea

Young puppies often experience diarrhea or loose stools at weaning time. Yogurt and/or buttermilk are natural foods that often correct this intestinal imbalance by providing *beneficial* bacteria. Older puppies and dogs often suffer from diarrhea due to stress or "travel nerves." The Borden product Bene-Bac is one of several live-bacterial remedies on the market that quickly and safely cure this common problem. Another veterinarian-prescribed product is Biosol-M, which calms the stomach and contains an antibiotic in case the problem is bacterial and not viral.

"Travel Nerves"

Norfolks seem especially prone to nervous diarrhea whenever their routine is changed by unaccustomed travel, a new environment, visiting a new place, or even a different feeding schedule. It is wise to start taking a new puppy with you on brief errands right away and socializing and introducing him to different situations early, so that when he is older and you want to take him on vacation or even visit a friend, he will be comfortable traveling with you. Norfolks are very sensitive to their surroundings, and it's important to build their confidence when they are still young.

No vaccine offers complete immunization against infectious canine cough.

Canine Cough (Kennel Cough)

No vaccine offers complete immunization against infectious canine cough, as it is caused by not one but a number of different viruses and bacteria. Although vaccination is about 90 percent effective, vaccinated dogs can still contract kennel cough. The chief symptom of this ailment is a deep and persistent bronchial hacking, which may also be accompanied by a decrease in appetite. Since kennel cough is highly contagious, dogs that are frequently in shows, boarded at kennels, or exposed to other canines in large numbers are likely to have this problem from time to time. More a "nuisance" illness than life-threatening, canine cough can cause an animal to be sick for from 7 to 20 days and should in all cases be treated by a veterinarian.

Asthmatic Breathing or Reverse Retching

Occasionally a Norfolk suddenly stands still, apparently trying to catch its breath or clear its throat. Standing stretched with head up, neck extended, and rib cage heaving, the dog at first appears to be retching but in fact is spasmodically drawing air into its nostrils (hyperventilating).

These brief episodes tend to occur seasonally—sometimes several times a day—when the dog is shedding its undercoat. They can also be triggered by a lead that is too tight around the neck. Asthmatic breathing is thought to be associated with some restriction of the trachea, or windpipe. These disconcerting attacks are more frightening than threatening and have no apparent aftereffects. However, in the show ring an episode can be disruptive or even unnerving to the uninformed judge or handler. Fortunately, immediate relief can be obtained easily by pressing the palm of your hand over the dog's nostrils, effectively blocking the nasal passage, while massaging the throat and allowing breathing to occur through the mouth.

FIRST AID

No matter how well you take care of your Norfolk, accidents will happen. When they do, try to keep a cool head, act quickly, and get your pet to a veterinarian as soon as possible. *Always* call first to make sure the doctor is there, and alert the office that an emergency case is on its way. In most cities nowadays there are also animal hospitals or medical centers that are open 24 hours a day for emergencies. Make it your business to know the name, telephone number, and location of the animal medical facility nearest you in case your veterinarian is not available.

Even your own pet may bite if he is in pain so he should be muzzled before you attempt to give him first aid. You can use a scarf, a stocking, or a soft dish-towel for this purpose. If he has a serious cut or bite, apply a pressure bandage to stem or stop the bleeding. Place a sterile gauze or a clean handkerchief or washcloth directly over the wound and press. If you suspect a broken bone, try to keep him from moving. If you suspect poi-

Good rapport with your veterinarian is essential to the health and happiness of your Norfolk.

199

soning, tell the veterinarian what your Norfolk has swallowed (if you know), try to describe the symptoms accurately, and take the doctor's advice on first aid or call the Poison Center listed in every local phone directory. Wrap your Norfolk in a heavy towel or blanket and move him carefully—but hurry! Since all this could be as traumatic for you as your dog, it might be best to ask another family member or neighbor to drive you to the veterinarian.

As a precautionary measure, keep a few first-aid items in your Norfolk's "medicine chest." These should include any medications prescribed by your veterinarian; an assortment of sterile dressings, gauze, adhesive tape, cotton swabs and balls; hydrogen peroxide to clean and disinfect *minor* wounds and scratches (not to be used on deep puncture wounds); a rectal thermometer; and tweezers to remove broken glass, splinters, burrs or ticks from the skin. Note: Learning to use the rectal thermometer is a good idea since any elevation in temperature usually means infection, but a warm nose does not necessarily indicate illness. A dog's normal temperature ranges from 101° to 102°.

Unless your dog is of good quality, there is no need to breed him or her at all.

NEUTERING YOUR NORFOLK

While your Norfolk is still young, discuss with your veterinarian and the breeder of your Norfolk the advisability of neutering or spaying. Since these are irrevocable surgical procedures, be sure that you will never want to use your pet for breeding. As Norfolks are a sturdy breed, both operations are relatively safe and simple. Neutered pets live longer, roam less, and so are less likely to be hit by cars. Females are less likely to develop mammary tumors and pyometra, a uterine infection usually only cured by spaying. Altered males are less likely to fight with other males or lift their legs, marking their territory inside as well as outdoors.

When a bitch is spayed, the ovaries and uterus are removed. General anesthesia is required for this surgery, and the hospital stay is approximately one to two days. Recuperation at home takes seven to ten days, after which the sutures, or stitches, are removed. The bitch may seem quiet for the first few days at home, but this may be due to anesthesia more than discomfort from the surgery. The greatest risk in this surgery is the same as in any surgery: the anesthesia.

When a male dog is altered, the testicles are removed and the incision is closed with sutures. As with the female, general anesthesia is used. Recuperation is usually one day in the hospital and seven to ten days at home, after which time the sutures are removed; and there is no physical disfiguation.

Bitches mature a little earlier than males, and most veterinarians agree that spaying can be done anytime after six months of age. Castration of the male puppy is not usually done before six months but can be performed at any age thereafter. However, if you do not intend to use your male for breeding, the sooner the neutering the better.

Bitches mature a little earlier than males.

SENSITIVITY TO ANESTHETICS

In connection with any surgical procedure, remember that many Norfolks are easily and adversely affected by general anesthetics. Exercise due caution in allowing their use under all but the most mandatory conditions, particularly if a local anesthetic can be substituted. You will find your veterinarian cooperative and understanding in taking these precautions.

Figure 200:
**Ch. Mt. Paul
Terracotta**

STANDARDS, CONFORMATION, AND GOALS

BREED STANDARDS: 1933-1987

How often we hear it said that the standard of a breed is the "blueprint" for that breed. Some owners and breeders revere a standard, while others find it either too narrow or too permissive. Does the Norfolk Standard succeed in describing the three-dimensional "model" of the small, hardy, working companion that its name inevitably evokes?

Norfolk were derived from a mixture of terrier types, among them the early working Yorkshires. But perhaps the most important element in their ancestry was the Miniature Irish Terrier, a breed first exhibited at the Dublin Dog Show in 1873 in classes with a 10-pound weight limit. Thanks to the resourcefulness of Henry Bixby, the following description of a pair of 1874 Dublin Show winners, received by the American Kennel Club, was added to the Norwich Terrier Club files in 1945.

MINIATURE IRISH TERRIER 1874

Jacket: Wiry, bright red.
Nose and Nails: Jet black.
Ears: Uncropped, smooth, filbert-shaped. Darker red than coat.
Legs: Straight.
Body: Compact and sturdy, made of tough sinews and hard but flexible muscles.
Tail: Docked, carried erect.
Height: 10 inches.
Weight: 8 to 10 pounds (not more).
Character: Alert, loyal, obedient, intelligent.
Traits: Active with a superabundance of stamina and 35 pounds of pluck. Persistent ratters. Go underground for rabbits. Retrieve land and water. Enjoy being mauled by children.

From file of Henry Bixby, Sect. NTC 1945

Figure 201:
**Photo copy of the
1935 Standard.**

The first Norwich Terrier Club was formed in England in 1932, but it took a year for the Club's 13 original sponsors to approve a breed standard due to dissension over ear carriage and color. Some members owned Norwich prick ears, while others favored the drop ears; and originally there was strong opposition to including black and tans, though white patches and marks were allowed on the throat and chest. Predictions about future problems with ears and color notwithstanding, in England and later in the United States both prick ear and drop ear Norwich were shown in the same classes; and the

NORWICH TERRIER

CH. BIFFIN OF BEAUFIN
First Champion in England
1935

The smallest of the terriers. A game little working terrier. Under the old name of "Jones" terrier many were imported to this country immediately after the World War for use with Foxhounds. Harsh wire coat. Not a fighter, but game and affectionate. An exceptional companion, due both to his size and disposition. Color, red, wheaten, black and tan, or grizzle.

NORWICH TERRIER CLUB

Henry D. Bixby Sec.-Treas.   221 Fourth Ave, N. Y.

STANDARD ADOPTED

Standard of Perfection for Norwich Terriers, as adopted by the Norwich Terrier Club of England, was approved by the Board of Directors of The American Kennel Club, February 12, 1936.

Description and Standard

HEAD. Muzzle, "foxy," yet strong; length about one-third less than a measurement from the occiput to the bottom of the stop, which should be a good one and well defined. Skull wide, slightly rounded with good width between the ears. Ears, if erect, slightly larger than a Cairn's; if dropped, very neat and small, and CORRECTLY dropped.

EYES. Very bright, dark and keen. Full of expression.

TEETH. Strong; rather large; closely fitting.

JAW. Clean, strong, tight lipped.

NECK. Short and strong; well set on clean shoulders.

LEGS. Short; powerful; as straight as is consistent with the short legs at which we aim. Sound bone, feet round, thick pads.

QUARTERS. Strong, with great powers of propulsion.

TAIL. Medium docked, carriage not excessively gay.

Weight. 10 to 14 lbs., 11 lbs. being the ideal.

HEIGHT. 10 to 12 inches at the withers (not to exceed).

COLOR AND COAT. Red (to include red wheaten), black and tan, or grizzle. White is undesirable but shall not disqualify. Coat as hard and wiry as possible, but lies much closer to the body than a Cairn's, and is absolutely straight. It is longer and rougher on the neck and shoulders, in winter forming almost a mane. Hair on the head, ears and muzzle, except slight eyebrows, and slight whisker, is absolutely short and smooth.

GENERAL APPEARANCE. A small, low, keen dog, tremendously active. A perfect demon, yet not quarrelsome, and of a lovable disposition, and with a very hardy constitution.

FAULTS. Long weak back, a mouth badly over or under shot, full eye, soft expression.

DISQUALIFICATIONS. Yellow eyes; soft coat, or wavy, or curly, or silky. A long narrow head; square muzzle, trimming is not desirable, and should be penalized rather than encouraged. Honorable scars from fair wear and tear shall not count against.

drop ears were the first champions of the breed in both countries.

In 1936, with recognition of the Norwich Terrier by the American Kennel Club, the English Standard crossed the ocean and set the pattern for both prick ear and drop ear Norwich for the next decade.

The American Norwich Terrier Club (NTC) was finally recognized in 1947, and there began a succession of changes and so-called innovations to the Standard that proved to be of questionable value because they sometimes obscured or left ambiguous the guidelines that had been straightforward and clear in the original. In 1947 and 1949 certain disqualifications were either deleted entirely or changed to "faults." Minor changes on size, ears, weight, height, and coat type were made in 1952 and 1961; and rephrasings on allowable colors were added.

DESCRIPTION AND STANDARD OF POINTS
(Adopted by The Norwich Terrier Club
and Approved by
The American Kennel Club, February 11, 1949)

Head.—Skull wide, slightly rounded with good width between the ears. Muzzle strong but not long or heavy, with slightly "foxy" appearance. Length about one-third less than the measurement from the occiput to the bottom of the stop, which should be well defined.
Faults.—A long narrow head; over square muzzle; highly rounded dome.
Ears.—Prick or Drop. If pricked: neat, small and erect. If dropped: neat, small and correctly dropped.
Faults.—Oversize; poor carriage.
Eyes.—Very bright, dark and keen. Full of expression.
Faults.—Light or protruding eyes.
Jaw.—Clean, strong, tight lipped, with strong, rather large closely fitting teeth.
Faults.—A mouth badly over or undershot.
Neck.—Short and strong, well set on clean shoulders.
Body.—Moderately short, compact and deep with level top line, ribs well sprung.
Faults.—Long weak back, loaded shoulders.
Legs.—Short and powerful and as straight as is consistent with the short legs for which we aim. Sound bone, round feet, thick pads.
Faults.—Out at elbow, badly bowed, knuckled over.

Too light in bone.

Quarters.—Strong, rounded, with great powers of propulsion.

Faults.—Cow hocks.

Tail.—Medium docked, carriage not excessively gay.

Color.—Red, wheaten, black and tan or grizzle. White markings on the chest, though allowable, are not desirable.

Faults.—White markings elsewhere or to any great extent on the chest.

Coat.—As hard and wiry as possible, lying quite close to the body. Coat absolutely straight but in winter longer and rougher, forming almost a mane on the shoulders and neck. Hair on head, ears and muzzle, except for slight eyebrows and slight whiskers, is absolutely short and smooth. These dogs should be shown with as nearly a natural coat as possible. Excessive trimming shall be heavily penalized.

Faults.—Silky or curly coat.

Weight.—10 to 14 lbs., 11 lbs. being the ideal.

Height.—10 to 12 inches at the withers, not to exceed.

General Appearance.—A small, low, cobby, keen dog, tremendously active. A perfect demon, yet not quarrelsome, and of a lovable disposition, and a very hardy constitution. Honorable scars from fair wear and tear shall not count against.

Disqualifications.—Cropped ears shall disqualify.

In 1964, through the unstinting perseverance of Colonsay Kennel's Marion Sheila Scott Macfie, drop ear Norwich in England officially became Norfolk Terriers. The achievement of breed separation logically necessitated a parent club and a Norfolk Standard, both of which were accomplished with effectiveness and dispatch. In the description of the new breed, besides mandating drop ears of medium size and proper carriage, there is an important change in specifications for head and skull, calling for a "wedge-shaped" rather than "foxy" muzzle now half the length of the skull, with oval eyes and a scissor bite. Also added under Temperament are the words: "alert" and "fearless." Other, more subtle changes can also be noted between this and the earlier English and American Standards for Norwich.

Fourteen years after breed division in England the American Norwich Terrier Club in 1978 petitioned the American Kennel Club's recognition of Norfolk in the United States. This was granted as of January 1979, and it seemed that progress, long overdue, had finally pre-

Standard of the Norfolk Terrier

Characteristics. The Norfolk Terrier is one of the smallest of the Terriers, but a "Demon" for its size. Of a lovable disposition, not quarrelsome, with a hardy constitution. Temperament : Alert and fearless.

General Appearance. A small, low, keen dog, compact and strong with short back, good substance and bone.

Head and Skull. Skull wide and slightly rounded with good width between the ears. Muzzle wedge-shaped and strong; length of muzzle slightly less than half the length of skull. Stop should be well defined.

Eyes. Oval shaped and deep set, in colour dark brown or black. Expression alert, keen and intelligent.

Ears. Size medium 'V'-shaped but slightly rounded at tip, dropping forward close to cheek.

Mouth. Tight lipped, jaw strong; teeth strong and rather large; scissor bite.

Neck. Medium length and strong.

Forequarters. Clean and powerful shoulders with short powerful and straight legs.

Body. Compact with short back and well sprung ribs.

Hindquarters. Well muscled, good turn of stifle, hocks well let down and straight when viewed from rear; with great powers of propulsion.

Feet. Round with thick pads.

Tail. Medium docked, not excessively gay.

Coat. Hard, wiry and straight, lying close to the body. It is longer and rougher on the neck and shoulders. Hair on the head, ears and muzzle short and smooth.

Colour. All shades of red, red wheaten, black and tan or grizzle. White marks or patches are undesirable but shall not disqualify.

Size. Ideal height 10in. at withers.

Faults. Excessive trimming is not desirable. Honourable scars from fair wear and tear shall not count against.

vailed. Through a frustrating blunder, however, the new Standard, already perfunctorily approved by the AKC, had not been ratified by the required two-thirds membership vote of the newly formed Norwich and Norfolk Terrier Club. As a result it was not until 1982 that our present Standard (a revised version of that 1979 "draft") attained legitimate status.

Figure 202: 1964 English Standard.

AMERICAN REVISED NORFOLK TERRIER STANDARD

The Board of Directors of the American Kennel Club approved the following revised Standard for Norfolk Terriers submitted by the Norwich and Norfolk Terrier Club, to be effective January 1, 1982:

General Appearance and Characteristics—The Norfolk Terrier, game and hardy, with expressive dropped ears, is one of the smallest of the working terriers. It is active and compact, free moving, with good substance and bone. With natural, weather-resistant coat and short legs, it is a "perfect demon" in the field. This versatile, agreeable breed can go to ground, bolt a fox and tackle or dispatch other small vermin, working alone or with a pack. Honorable scars from wear and tear are acceptable in the ring.

Head—Skull wide, slightly rounded, with good width between the ears. Muzzle is strong and wedge shaped. Its length is one-third less than a measurement from the occiput to the well-defined stop.

Ears—Neatly dropped, small, with a break at the skull line, carried close to the cheek and not falling lower than the outer corner of the eye. V-shaped, slightly rounded at the tip, smooth and velvety to the touch.

Eyes—Small, dark and oval, with black rims. Placed well apart with a sparkling, keen and intelligent expression.

Mouth—Jaw clean and strong. Tight-lipped with large teeth and a scissor bite.

Forequarters—Neck of medium length, strong and blending into well laid back shoulders—good width of chest, elbows close to ribs, pasterns firm. Short, powerful legs, as straight as is consistent with the digging terrier.

Body—Length of back from point of withers to base of tail should be slightly longer than the height at the withers. Ribs well sprung, chest moderately deep. Strong loins and level topline.

Hindquarters—Broad with strong, muscular thighs. Good turn of stifle. Hocks well let down and straight when viewed from the rear.

Feet—Round, pads thick, with strong, black nails.

Tail—Medium docked of sufficient length to ensure a balanced outline. Straight, set on high, the base level with the topline. Not a squirrel tail.

Coat—The protective coat is hard, wiry and straight, about 1 1/2 to 2 inches long, lying close to the body, with a definite undercoat. The mane on neck and shoulders is longer and also forms a ruff at the base of the ears and the throat. Moderate furnishings of harsh texture on legs. Hair on the head and ears is short and smooth, except for slight eyebrows and whiskers. Some tidying is necessary to keep the dog neat, but shaping should be heavily penalized.

Color—All shades of red, wheaten, black and tan, or grizzle. Dark points permissible. White marks are not desirable.

Gait—Should be true, low and driving. In front, the legs extend forward from the shoulder. Good rear angulation showing great powers of propulsion. Viewed from the side, hind legs follow in the track of the forelegs, moving smoothly from the hip and flexing well at the stifle and hock. Topline remains level.

Size—Height at the withers 9 to 10 inches at maturity. Bitches tend to be smaller than dogs. Weight 11 to 12 pounds or that which is suitable for each individual dog's structure and balance. Fit working condition is a prime consideration.

Temperament—Alert, gregarious, fearless and loyal. Never aggressive.

Since recognition of the Norfolk Terrier in the U.K. in 1964, England has changed its Standard only once—in 1987.

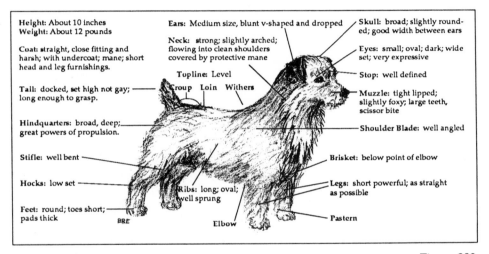

Height: About 10 inches
Weight: About 12 pounds

Coat: straight, close fitting and harsh; with undercoat; mane; short head and leg furnishings.

Tail: docked, set high not gay; long enough to grasp.

Hindquarters: broad, deep; great powers of propulsion.

Stifle: well bent

Hocks: low set

Feet: round; toes short; pads thick

Ears: Medium size, blunt v-shaped and dropped

Neck: strong; slightly arched; flowing into clean shoulders covered by protective mane

Topline: Level

Croup   Loin   Withers

Ribs: long; oval; well sprung

BRE   Elbow

Skull: broad; slightly rounded; good width between ears

Eyes: small; oval; dark; wide set; very expressive

Stop: well defined

Muzzle: tight lipped; slightly foxy; large teeth, scissor bite

Shoulder Blade: well angled

Brisket: below point of elbow

Legs: short powerful; as straight as possible

Pastern

Figure 203: Points of the dog.

ENGLISH STANDARD OF THE NORFOLK TERRIER
(K.C. Revision 1987)

General Appearance: Small, low, keen dog, compact and strong, short back, good substance and bone. Honourable scars from fair wear and tear permissible.

Characteristics: One of the smallest of terriers, a "demon" for its size. Lovable disposition, not quarrelsome, hardy constitution.

Temperament: Alert and fearless.

Head & Skull: Skull broad, only slightly rounded with good width between the ears. Muzzle wedge-shaped and strong; length of muzzle about one-third less than measurement from occiput to bottom of well defined stop.

Eyes: Oval shaped and deep set, dark brown or black. Expression alert, keen and intelligent.

Ears: Medium size, V-shaped, slightly rounded at the

tip, dropping forward close to cheek.

Mouth: Tight lipped, strong jaw, teeth strong and rather large; perfect, regular scissor bite, i.e. upper teeth closely overlapping the lower teeth and set square to the jaws.

Neck: Strong and of medium length.

Forequarters: Clean, well laid back shoulder blade, approximating in length to upper arm. Front legs short, powerful and straight.

Body: Compact, short back, level topline, well sprung ribs.

Hindquarters: Well muscled, good turn of stifle, hocks well let down and straight when viewed from rear; great propulsion.

Feet: Round with thick pads.

Tail: Docking of tails optional. (a) Medium docked, set level with topline and carried erect. (b) Tail of moderate length to give general balance to the dog, thick at the root and tapering towards the tip, as straight as possible, carried jauntily, but not excessively gay.

Gait/Movement: True, low and driving. Moving straight forward from the shoulder. Good rear angulation showing great powers of propulsion. Hindlegs follow track of forelegs, moving smoothly from hips. Flexing well at stifle and hock. Topline remaining level.

Coat: Hard, wiry, straight, lying close to body. Longer and rougher on neck and shoulders. Hair on head and ears short and smooth, except for slight whiskers and eyebrows. Excessive trimming undesirable.

Colour: All shades of red, wheaten, black and tan or grizzle. White marks or patches undesirable but permissible.

Size: Ideal height at withers 25-26 cms (10 ins.).

Faults: Any departure from the foregoing points should be considered a fault and the seriousness with which the fault should be regarded should be in exact proportion to its degree.

Note: Male animals should have two apparently normal testicles fully descended into the scrotum.

The above revisions include a description of movement (as in our own Standard) and an added clause on optional tail docking. Although similar to one another, the American Norfolk Standard and the English Standard, which is used elsewhere throughout the world, are by no means identical. The basic difference between the two may stem from the American view of our first Norwich Terriers derived from Frank "Roughrider" Jones's breed of fox bolters. Unquestionably, this would also influence our requirements for Norfolk size, height, and length. On the other hand, the noted breeder Marjorie Bunting describes English Norwich and Norfolk as indefatigable ratters specifically bred to rid the farmers' hay ricks, barns, and stubble fields of rodents—a job demanding slightly different proportions than those called for by fox hunters.

Differences in terminology and the use of language have also played their part in creating dissimilarities between the English and American Standards. Although disparities exist, if the two are compared intelligently it is clear they are neither "poles apart" nor "hazardously different," as some few breeders on either side of the Atlantic maintain. Since separating from Norwich, Norfolk Terriers have steadily increased in number and are now 107 out of 130 AKC-recognized breeds, with 256 individuals registered in 1987.

As numbers grow and quality continues to improve, judges will become more skilled at interpreting the standards and evaluating the breed on fundamental similarities, no matter what country a dog hails from. There have always been cordial relations among Norfolk owners around the world; and the exchange of knowledge and interbreeding of stock on an international basis continue to remove unimportant differences. Among our current champions are imports from England, Sweden, and Germany; and both Canada and Germany have American-bred and English champions. So finally it can be said although a breed's standard may be its "blueprint," it is the flesh-and-blood stock that creates and shapes the Norfolk Terrier Standard.

CONFORMATION

Tom Horner, Adapted from Dog World
Drawings by Renée Sporee-Willes

BALANCE

Exhibitors and judges must develop an eye for exactly what makes a Norfolk "typical," and the breed balance is certainly a prime ingredient. In the past Norfolk and Norwich were judged as one breed. Today the two have grown apart, so a trained eye can easily discern a

Figure 204:
(Top right) **Too short: outline of a straight-fronted dog with an over-angulated rear.**

Figure 205:
(Top left) **Too tall: outline of a dog showing a straight stifle.**

Figure 206:
(Bottom) **Correctly balanced.**

difference in the balance of each breed. Although similar to Norwich in size, colors, and general requirements, the Norfolk's short back coupled with its good front and rear angulation and overall length from sternum to buttock varies its balance from that of its less angulated, somewhat stuffier kinsman, the Norwich. Adding ears and eyes for expression, and tail for character, to balance this outline, the Norfolk Terrier's type clearly emerges.

TYPE AND QUALITY

Type and quality are quite different. A dog can excel in type but lack quality, just as a dog can have great quality, but lack true type. Type is the sum of those points which make a dog look like its own breed and no other.

A typical or "typey" dog is one which approaches its breed standard very closely, looks capable of carrying out its particular function, is correctly put together, and behaves and moves in a manner described in its standard. It is quite possible for a dog to fulfill the points listed above but be just an ordinary specimen quite lacking in distinction.

On the other hand a dog may be well made, sound moving, the correct size, correct in coat, and so finished that it presents a pleasing overall picture, but if it has the wrong head for its breed, a badly carried tail on an unduly long body, or some other gross fault of type, then it will be quite untypical.

Quality is that subtle overall something that makes one dog look better than its peers. Part of it is the texture and refinement of the materials of which a dog is made; it is not lack of substance, but it is the way the parts flow together without unsightly interruption; and above all it is the dog's bearing and expression. If he feels like an aristocrat he will look like one—quality and merit are not the same.

Quality is a finishing touch, an extra embellishment that lifts one dog above his rivals. It is an indefinable factor but is instantly apparent to the connoisseur. Quality is more than just a measure of how good the dog is; it is an element in itself which adds greatly to the merit of the dog. Quality in a dog can be greatly assisted and improved by skillful presentation.

FORE

A pair of good shoulders is a sovereign virtue in any dog, but is essential in a dog of quality. Almost more than any other point clean, sloping shoulders attached to correctly proportioned upper arms, mark the dog to keep, the bitch to breed, and the stud to seek. These generalizations apply nowhere more forcefully than in breeds with short legs, Norfolks being no exception.

In all the low-to-the-ground breeds, no matter the variety, breeders neglect unsound fronts at their peril–unsound fronts, more often than not, being directly connected with the placement of the shoulders and the placement and length of upper arms. Moreover, well-placed shoulders form the ideal basis for proud head carriage. They take the balance between length of neck and length of back, and prevent those ugly dips in top-

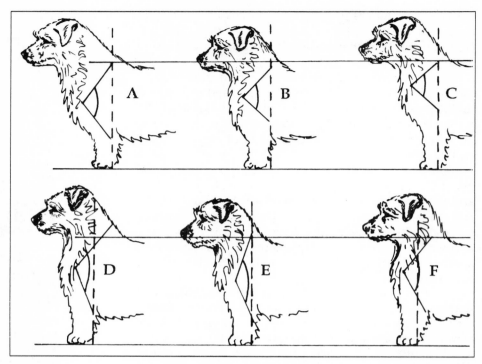

Figure 207:
Shoulder place-
ment and place-
ment and length
of upper arms
decide a sound
front. Drawing
"A" shows a
correct shoulder.

lines. Only when the shoulders and upper arm are of the right length, correctly placed and angled, can a dog achieve the desired length of stride and freedom of front action.

Likewise the balance between length of neck and length of back is influenced by shoulder placement. If set too far forward on the rib cage, the shoulders cause the balance of the dog's outline to appear too short and the back too long. Sloping shoulders are firmly bound to the rib cage, and the line from the withers to elbow will be smooth and clean. The stride will be long and effortless, with the action of the legs almost parallel when viewed from front or back. Conversely, upright shoulders are of-ten loaded with excess bumpy muscle on and under the shoulder blades. This usually causes a dog to move short in front, thereby detracting from its general appearance and overall balance. Such dogs often display loose el-bows, slack pasterns, and feet that turn out or are splayed.

A sound Norfolk Terrier will have an arched neck

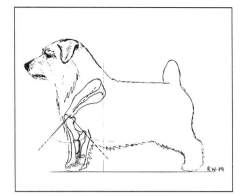

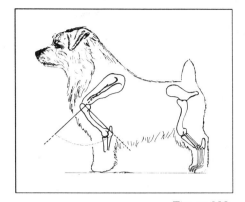

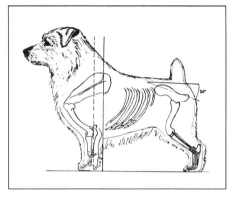

Figure 208:
Upper arm too short, making line from the shoulder blade to the ground too far behind the elbow. Shoulder blade too far up the neck, giving too much width between the tip of the blades.
Figure 209:
Good shoulders, but poor hindquarters. Incorrect angulation at pelvis. Thigh too upright. Second thigh too short, with long hocks.
Figure 210:
Good angulation of both shoulder and hindquaters. The shoulder blade and upper arm nearly equal in length. The correct line from the tip of the shoulder blades, through the elbows to the back of the foot. The correct slope of the pelvis.. The correct balance between the length of thigh and second thigh, giving a good bend to the stifle. The hock joint low to the ground.

fitting into well laid-back shoulders and a short back. On the move, look for a well-balanced Norfolk with proud head carriage, long, low strides, and parallel legs and feet. In essence, clean shoulders give any dog a head start.

AFT

If there is a fore, then there must be an aft, and in any short-legged breed true movers must have equal front and rear angulation. When these angles match, the dog will move smoothly with effortless coordination. Likewise the muscular development at both front and rear is broad and deep rather than thick and bulging. A good mover's powers of propulsion come from the rear and are achieved through angulation. Heavy forefronts

Figure 211:
**Overdevolopment
of certain muscles
caused by bad an-
gulation at front
and/or rear.**

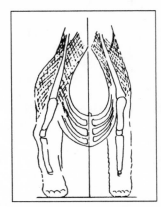

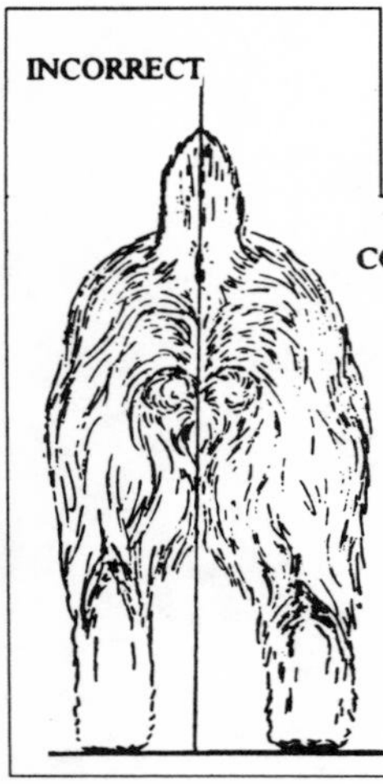

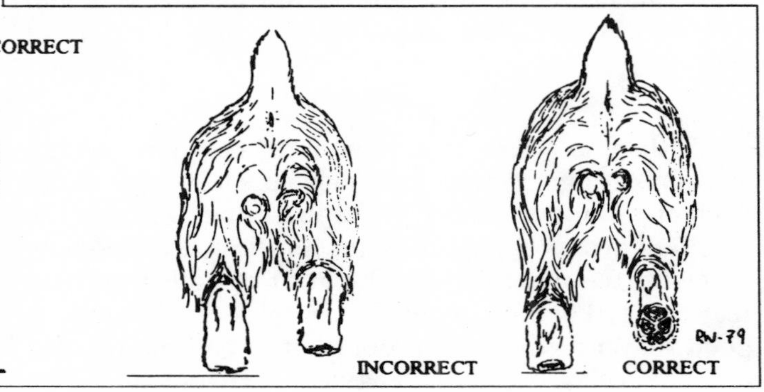

Figure 212:
**(Left)Long hock,
left; short hock on
the right.
(Center) Long
hocks with little
power of propul-
sion.
(Right)
Short hocks,
showing strong
propulsion as the
pad is seen when
moving. If you
can see the pad on
the front foot
when the dog is
moving away
from you, there is
usually better an-
gulation behind.**

tend to distort otherwise sound movement, just as over-angulated rears hamper forward propulsion.

One of the most obvious breed faults easily observed in Norfolks is a topline that runs upward towards the tail, making the shoulders appear too low for the hindquarters. The loin should be very muscular, coupling the ribs to the hindquarters and by its strength adding to the agility of the dog. Pressure with the hand on the back of a well-constructed dog should meet with a strong, springy resistance There is a barely perceptible rise in the loin of a sturdy, well-made dog, although anything in the nature of a "roach" or a dip behind the withers is wrong.

When the pelvis in this breed is too steeply sloped, the rump falls away too much, with a low-set tail as the end result. When the pelvis is too flat, tails are carried too gaily. Overall, the conscientious Norfolk breeder will recognize that balance between hind and forequarters is the key to maintaining the free-moving qualities essential to working terriers.

HIGH-ACTION GAIT

It is the moderate shoulder angulation with a steeply placed short upper arm which prevents an animal from taking a good length of stride with its front legs.

INCORRECT

CORRECT

INCORRECT   CORRECT

When, as is often the case, this type of conformation is combined with well-bent stifles in the dog's hind legs, enabling the dog concerned to take long strides with its hind legs, there is a loss of coordination between the forehand and the hindquarters. The long strides taken by the hind legs take more time to complete their movement than the little short steps taken by the forelegs and the two ends of the dog get out of kilter. The only way the forelegs can take a longer time over each stride, and so keep in time with the hind legs, is to throw the knees up under the chin and the longer the hind legs take to complete their strides the higher those knees will go.

Unfortunately, in extreme cases, shortening the upper arms and placing them at open angles to the shoulder blades, while the latter are placed well back, means that the upper arms move forward on the chest wall with resulting poor attachment to that area, and out go the elbows and in go the pasterns and feet as a result of the forward placement of the upper arms.

The English Norfolk Terrier Club Standard calls for a "clean, well laid back shoulder blade, which should approximate in length the upper arm." And on Movement, "should be true, low and driving. In front, the legs extend forward from the shoulder, good rear angulation showing great powers of propulsion. Hind legs follow in the track of the forelegs, moving smoothly from the hip and flexing well at the stifle and hock. Topline remains level."

Figure 213: (Top) **Sound, correct movement. Good length of stride in front from well-laid-back shoulders with elbows tucked in. Strong propulsion from behind from well-angulated hindquarters.** (Bottom) **Badly made, unsound movement. Upright shoulders give a short, paddling action in front. Upright hindquarters give little propulsion and stilted action behind. This dog would tire easily, especially if he was overweight.**

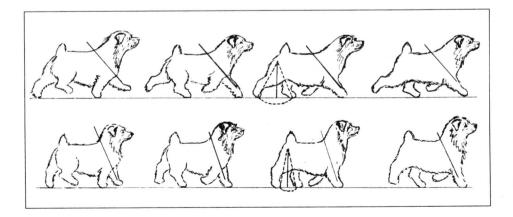

BITES

Figure 214:
(Upper left) **Undershot. The lower jaw protrudes beyond the upper jaw.**
(Upper right) **Level bite, with upper and lower teeth meeting. This is recognized as correct.**
(Lower left) **Overshot. The upper jaw protrudes over the lower.**
(Lower right) **Scissor bite, considered perfect.**

Large, close-fitting teeth are called for by the Standard and are certainly desirable in a ratting terrier. Breeding for the correct scissor bite with the right number of teeth is a challenge, as Norfolk bites can change not only when the second (adult) teeth come in but also much later as well. Overbites can improve until about 18 months, and some "would-be" scissor bites are prevented from closing by the overly large back molars. Missing or crooked incisors are a more common occurrence than missing molars. Untimely tooth loss and bucking out of front teeth, which causes a bite to shift, have accounted for early ring retirement of several notable winners.

Incorrect bites have plagued the breed since recognition, and breeding stock must be carefully assessed. Fortunately some kennel prefixes are noted for their scissor bites, although not having descriptively large teeth. Breeders hope in time this fault may be controlled.

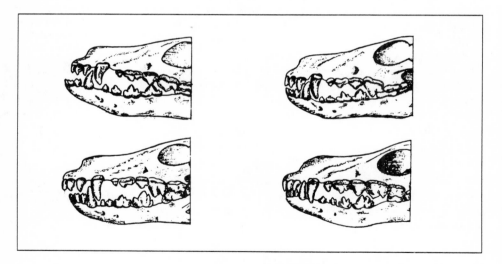

EXPRESSION

It is the ears' shape, carriage, and placement coupled with the set of the eyes and the depth of the muzzle that chiefly create the Norfolk's expression.

Although judicious grooming can be helpful, a Norfolk with high-set ears or ears that break horizontally on a line with, or above, the wide-arced skull are not correct.

The correct velvet-soft drop ear has a modified vee-shape with a slight inside flare, a blunt tip, and a shallow, vertical indentation in the leather. Set back and below the crown of the skull, these small pendant ears fall lengthwise to just below the eye, with the inside leather lying flat against the side of the head. When aroused the ear pivots slightly forward so the curved inside edge rests on the cheek and the tip is drawn up to the level of the eye corner.

Norfolks are derivative of many kinds of cropped, prick-, and drop-eared terriers. Today they are recognized as differing from the Irish, Border, and other hunt terriers not only in type but in ear carriage and expression.

Figure 215: (L to r above) **Incorrect ear placement.**

Figure 216: (Below) **Correct ear placement.**

COATS

Texture
The correct Norfolk coat is dense, harsh, and straight. It is longer on the neck, top of the shoulders, and down the dorsal column. In full coat the protective ruff around the neck makes it appear shorter. The scruff of the neck has a thicker pelt than the body, which should have a close-fitting coat with short furnishings on the eyebrows, whiskers, legs, and feet. The ideal coat is easy to keep, sheds dirt, turns the weather, and displays the outline of the dog.

Color
Although some breeders and judges refer to a dog as being a "good color," they are merely stating a personal preference. The Standard does not value one accepted color over the other. Norfolks may be any whole color: wheaten, all shades of red from sand to mahogany, black

Figure 217:
This series of three photographs of Biffin of Beaufin presents an interesting over-view of how expression changes with the shape, size, and placement of ears.

(Top) Original photo-graph with the fol-lowing comments: "This is the one we want ears retouched to look more or less like the other one. Break should be just above topline of the skull. Ears should come about to outer corner of eye line. This is for use in breed standard."

(Center)
"This one has ears re-touched and they are too small."

(Bottom)
The final retouched version of the photo-graph.

and tan from light to dark, and any shade of grizzle. White marks on the chest are acceptable.

Students of genetics and observant owners and breeders know that red dogs are shaded. Many have darker-tipped topcoats. Some are lighter-colored under their tails, and undercoats can be a mousy black. All are whole-colored, but only the darkest reds come close to being single-toned. The American Kennel Club, which licenses judges and provides and polices dog show rules, states unequivocally that it is a *disqualification* to use any substance that changes a dog's natural color or shade. The Standard also requires eye rims, nose, lips, and nails to be black. Self-colored rims, which occasionally appear in rich reds, alter a Norfolk's typical expression and are therefore undesirable.

GOALS
*Ann H. Winston, **Mt. Paul Kennels**, Gladstone, New Jersey*

Our aim as breeders should be to produce good terrier temperament while striving to improve type and conformation. No terrier can capably perform its job without a good mouth, good clean shoulders, and strong hindquarters and back. The Standard was not drawn up for pure beauty, but for better performance in moving, which enables your dog to handle himself in the field with endurance and strength.

Figure 218:
Judge George Bragaw awarding Best in Show
to Ch. Allright Magic Lamp by
German Ch. Allright Huckleberry Finn
x German Ch. Chidley Magic Carpet (U.S.A.),
1986. Handled by Beth Sweigart.

10

THE DOG SHOW:
SYSTEMS, JUDGING, AND PROFESSIONALS

WHAT IS A DOG SHOW?
George Bragaw, Rockville, Maryland

A dog show is a contest that brings together dogs from a particular area to determine which are best and, in a broader sense, which breeding program is most successful. In form, a dog show is a single elimination tournament. Today competition is generally among individual same-breed entries, first by sex and then by breed. In all-breed shows, this is followed by competitions among similar breeds called a Group and ends with Best in Show. For serious breeders, the dog show also represents an opportunity for exchanging ideas and learning from others with an eye toward maintaining and improving the breed of one's choice. Here, a brood bitch or stud dog can be evaluated firsthand or their children (her *offspring* or his *get*) can be examined and discussed with other equally serious exhibitors or spectators,

Since a judge's opinion on a particular day, time, or place, is only that—an opinion—a series of ratings is necessary to confirm which particular dog or dogs are best. Thus the system of multiple judgings was created before a dog could be declared a *champion*. The American system of dog shows has its roots in English stock show and fair judging. One need only attend a goat, sheep, or cattle show to grasp the similarities. All showing and judging is based on the simple theory that *like produces like;* and when particular qualities are admired in an animal it is the breeding behind the specimen that is being rewarded. The *sport of dogs* consists of purposeful breeding, exhibiting, and appraisal of individual animals. Thus, knowledge of the association of characteristics in dogs is vital in their evaluation because—harking back to the stock shows and fairs—the working abilities and temperament as well as the appearance of an animal

are all judged by eye.

In recent years it has become popular to criticize dog shows as mere "beauty contests" or "ego trips." To a limited extent this is true, but remember that old terrier men, gamekeepers, and shepherds picked their pups by eye, then later confirmed these choices in the field. *An eye for a dog* had the same meaning then as it does now. The system may not be perfect, but thus far a better one has not been developed.

Figure 219:
Ch. Lyndors
Pippin, by Ch.
Castle Point
Iguana x Ch.
Lyndors Paper
Moon, winning
the first Norfolk
Specialty Show
under English
judge Sheila
Monckton (l);
breeder/owner
Doris and Jerome
Gerl (c), and
Ellen Lee
Kennelly (r),
1979.

WORLDWIDE CHAMPIONSHIP SYSTEMS

There are two basic judging systems in the canine world. One is used with variations by the English-speaking countries, the other is a more time-consuming method controlled by the Federation Cynologique Internationale.

The FCI emphasizes the grading of exhibits with a written critique for the owner on every entered dog prior to class judging. This system is used in Scandinavia, Central and South America, and 25 European countries, as well as Japan. The classes offered are divided by sex, and certificates (equivalent to our points) are awarded to dogs over 15 months. The certificate qualifications vary and are either national (CAC) or International (CACIB); and in Scandinavia Norfolks must pass a temperament test to compete for a certificate. No dog can become an International Champion until it has won four CACIBs under three different judges in three countries during a minimum of one year. Champions have their own classes, and judges choose the best dog and bitch before awarding Best of Breed.

From a breeder's point of view, and certainly of greatest spectator interest, are the progeny classes at some FCI events. These consist of five or more dogs all bred by the same person or produced by the same stud or from the same brood bitch. These collections in the Group ring are a most impressive sight and illustrate the importance of breeders and the influence of sires and dams.

In the English-speaking countries a dog is judged on its relative merits compared to others in Class, Breed, or Group, with the emphasis on winning rather than on critiques. In the United Kingdom the system is somewhat confusing to visitors with its profusion of classes and various grades of shows. Champions compete in Open Class and all undefeated dogs compete by sex for the Challenge Certificates, which are awarded to Best Dog and Best Bitch in each breed; then one of the two is made Best of Breed. When three such certificates have been won under three different judges, the dog has earned the title of Champion (Ch.). Norfolks are fortunate to have 17 shows out of a possible 35 a year at which to compete, so winning a Challenge Certificate is a prestigious achievement when the Open Class contains a quota of current champions.

Figure 220: Int. Nordic Ch. Redriff Rambling Rose, by Ch. Cracknor Cute 'N Kissy x Ch. Ragus Betsy Trotwood, shown at 8 1/2 years. Owned by Susann Bjorkfall, Sweden.

Traditionally in breeds with small populations, when championships are won, the dog, if a Norfolk, is usually retired from regular competition. This means more dogs win titles, but the importance of these titles varies widely with the competition at any given show.

Figure 221: Weilheim, Germany, 1987, Norfolk Terrier meeting—two progeny groups: far left, Int. Ch. Allright Firecracker and five of his get; far right, Int. Ch. Cracknor Candidate and five of his get. *Photo by Rolf Wernicke, Germany.*

Figure 222:
First German
specialty show
winner: Ger. Ch.
Allright Magic
Midge by Ger.
Ch. Allright
Huckleberry Finn
x Ger. Ch. Chid-
ley Magic Carpet
(U.S.A.). Ameri-
can breeder/judge
Bárbara Fournier
(l) and owner/
handler Dr.
Frauke Hinsch (r).
*Photo by P. de
Bruiyn.*

Australia combines the English and American systems and requires 100 points for championship. These are offered in the form of "Challenges," each of which is worth 25 points regardless of entry size. Judging rules vary in the different Australian states, at least four shows are required for a title, and champions compete in the regular classes. In Canada 10 points are needed for a title, and in breeds with few Class entries these are usually acquired by placing in the Group ring. In Canada points are awarded for each Group ribbon won.

In the United States there are more than a thousand all-breed shows each year where championship points might be won. Class dogs and bitches are separated by sex, where they can gain points determined by numerical competition without meeting champions. Next they compete in an intersex class against champions for Best of Breed, Best of Winners, and Best of Opposite Sex. Fifteen points are required for a championship, and no more than five points can be awarded at one time.   In addition, two majors (three to five points),each from a different judge, plus at least one additional point from still another judge are necessary for a title. It is possible to achieve up to five points for each Group win.

UNOFFICIAL DOG SHOW SYSTEMS

In the American dog show world the urge to compete has spawned a new crop of point systems. These unofficial systems are confusing to new exhibitors. Various dog-food companies and canine magazines publicize Breed, Group, and Best in Show wins with their own point scores based on public AKC records. Unfortunately, rather than being a measure of merit, most of these advertised point awards are weighted in favor of the extensively campaigned dog.

KENNEL CLUBS

Most countries have their own national organization to record pure-bred activities, and some, like Australia, have more than one. Sweden is acknowledged as providing the most comprehensive and effective canine organization as it combines computer record keeping with sponsored competitions, education, and welfare. Moreover, it firmly denies or deletes stud book entry to dogs with known inheritable diseases.

The nonprofit American Kennel Club presently recognizes and licenses judges for the 130 breeds in its stud book. Like The Kennel Club (England), it approves breed standards submitted by parent member clubs and also is a record-keeping organization.

Figure 223: Eng. Ch. Ragus Boy Blue, by Ch. Jaeva Brown Sauce x Ragus Blue Jay, broke the Ragus tradition and all previous records by winning multiple CCs before his first birthday. Breeder/owners: Marjorie Bunting and Leslie Crawley.

For those who wish to exhibit, breed, or raise a litter your Norfolk must be registered. A registration certificate is your dog's "I.D." and is usually supplied by your dog's breeder or former owner in addition to its pedigree. Registrations contain the information needed for all American Kennel Club–sponsored activities.

The American Kennel Club at 51 Madison Avenue, New York, NY 10010 publishes a monthly calendar of events and supplies entry forms for the 1,000 all-breed shows and the countless Obedience and field competitions it sponsors annually.

JUDGING: AN EYE FOR A DOG

Good judges, like good teachers, need skill in communications, patience with people and puppies, imagination to cope with the unexpected, and an abundance of common sense. A judge shoulders responsibility for ring procedure and all its related consequences. The reward is the pleasure derived from discovering the best qualities in each dog through hands-on experience with one's favorite breeds. Capable judges must understand breed type, the very essence and key characteristics that separate one breed from another. They develop their "perceptions" through the observation and study of correct outline and balance.

In the past, Norwich and Norfolk Terriers were

judged as one breed. Today they have grown apart, and although similar in size and color, both breeds evidence subtle shape differences no matter how they are groomed. Norfolks are longer from point of shoulder to seat bones, though still short-backed. They also have a bit more leg, a deeper brisket, a blunter muzzle, and move with more drive than Norwich.

A judge with an "eye" can see at a glance if a dog has good basic conformation: a good slope of shoulder, compatible length and placement of the upper arm, a correctly sloped croup, and sufficient angulation at the stifle and hock. To achieve the ideal, a dog with sloping shoulders should have an adequate length of neck allied with a short, firm back. The head will be held proudly, with the neck flowing smoothly into the back, and there will be no droop or hollow in the topline. Conversely, when the shoulders are placed too far forward, the dog is liable to be shorter in neck than desirable, longer in back, and the line over the withers often uneven and sometimes marked by a distinct dip. When the shoulders are straight, then the upper arm is either too short or too steep, or both, and the length of front strides will be restricted and choppy. Much the same rule applies to the hindquarters, the angles of which should match those of the forequarters. Well-turned stifles and let-down hocks usually indicate that the dog will move freely and correctly; that is, with a good length of stride in both front and back. Remember that in the Norfolk the forelegs should reach well forward without too much lift, working in unison, with a driving action of the hind legs following in the track of the forelegs. From behind, the pads should be showing.

Figure 224:
Capable judges must understand breed type, the very essence and key characteristics that separate one breed from another.
Photo Ron Willbie.

Knowledge of a breed's standard and close association with good specimens of that breed are essential to successful judging. A judge who observes top-quality stock is much more likely to have a better eye than one limited to dogs of lesser quality. Although other canine sports are timed or scored, conformation judging is based solely on personal opinion. This is aided by an in-depth knowledge and understanding of the breed and by the ability to make decisions. Finally, the key to excellence in judging is the facility to sum up the total merit of a particular dog, irrespective of its condition and training. The judge who can evaluate a dog "in the rough" can truly be said to possess "an eye for a dog," the highest compliment one can receive.

Figure 225: **A judge with an "eye" can see at a glance if a dog has good basic conformation.** *Photo Ron Willbie.*

THE PROFESSIONAL CONNECTION

Three professionals have had significant and lasting influence on the world of drop ear Norwich: Percy Roberts, Leonard Brumby, Jr., and John "Jack" Simm.

Percy Roberts

Percy Roberts was born in England of a gypsy father for whom he was named and by whom he was apprenticed as a teenager in 1905 to the Holegate Variety Kennel for 15 shillings a week. A few years later the transplanted English dog agent, George S. Thomas, hired young Roberts to accompany, on their Atlantic crossing, his 90-dog shipment for American clients. Three of the Fox Terriers aboard went straight from the boat to a Specialty and then to Westminster. Their wins assured young Roberts a kennel position at the Vickery Kennels in Barrington, Illinois, "at $15 a month all found" (bed and board included). The chance to work at a real show kennel under the top conditioner of that era was invaluable. Vickery housed close to 300 champions and retained Thomas as an agent for an annual fee of $5,000 plus a blank check for his buying trips, which were expensive. George Thomas brought more than 3,600 dogs to Ameri-

Figure 226:
The forelegs
should reach
well forward
without too
much lift, work-
ing in unison,
with a driving
action of the
hind legs follow-
ing in the track
of the forelegs.

ca between 1890 and 1925, when he retired and turned to judging.

After two years at the Vickery, Roberts wanted to return home. His chores at the kennel were directed towards maintaining the splendid buildings with brass fittings, while he longed to go to shows and work with the dogs full time. A chance meeting in the railroad station delayed Roberts's return, and he found himself managing a small variety kennel for Mr. Otto Lehmann in Illinois. At that time it was obvious that the center of dog shows was in the East, and Roberts wanted to be where the action was. He soon located suitable acreage in Norton, Connecticut, had plans drawn for a home and kennels, and found a contractor for $22,000. Now married, and with a $1,000 savings account, Percy took the gamble of his life. He withdrew his savings, went steerage to England, and combed the country from Land's End to John O'Groats, returning three months later with 22 dogs to sell and a reputation to establish.

Approaching the owners of the Vickery Kennels, he suggested they host an openhouse party to display their many champions to the canine fraternity. He promised to organize and run the affair for them if he could also show off his own dogs. The dog party was a double success, for it has been said the Connecticut contractor was fully paid in advance the day after the Vickery viewing.

Percy Roberts had by now become a professional handler who made annual buying trips to England, where he relied on two other dog men to spot youngsters with promise. But being more than an agent, Percy Roberts helped build kennels of various breeds, and he studied their stock and pedigrees before going abroad. He also trained kennel managers and other "pros," but no other professional could compete with Roberts in the scope of his influence and the positive effects of his selections.

Details like his impeccable ring attire proved practical, whether handling or judging, setting Percy apart in the crowd. Slim and dapper, with a waxed moustache,

he wore clothes of quality, tailored correctly, and utilitarian for any weather. From jodhpur shoes to wide-brimmed fedoras, Percy's style was dictated by his job: cuffless trousers, belt and suspenders, long, tapered jackets split like riding coats, narrow lapels, button-down collars with double-buttoned cuffs, and always a bow tie.

The influence of Percy Roberts on the entire dog scene is inestimable. Most importantly for Norfolk, he imported a puppy who proved to be the blueprint for type in the U.S. From 1935 to 1939 he continued to provide the breed with sound roots through his selections from English stock. He encouraged the Norwich drop ear cause by his obvious interest, helping to establish breeders first as an agent and then as a judge.

In a letter to Mrs. Warren Thayer following the 1949 Match Show, with 46 drop ear Norwich judged, Roberts stated:

> With all due deference, I thought many of the exhibits were too small and lacked substance, and coats on many were not their fortune. Eyes, I thought were good. Size and carriage of ears in many cases were very good but still in many cases need improvement.

There were very few poor movers behind, but I
thought fronts could have been better. Mouths were
very good; there were only two bad ones, and one of
these would have been much higher in prize list were
it not for this, to my mind, very serious fault. He was
a really nice little dog carrying a really good coat of
grand color.

Roberts admired terrier spirit, expressive ears, and
happy movement. When drop ear exhibits lacked the
sparkle of prick ear rivals he would produce a chunk of
liver from his own pocket to achieve the animation he
desired. Percy Roberts's preference for drop ears never
faltered, and his education of their exhibitors proved
timely. While he admonished the professionals who
propped their dogs in the ring, he was more tolerant toward the squatting amateurs with their squeaky mice.
With patience he explained a judge's difficulty in evaluating show-shy or untrained puppies, and he lived to see
temperaments and show records dramatically improve.

Though the kennel was closed when Percy Roberts
hung up his leads, his annual visits to England continued. These later trips were spiced with searches for canine artifacts to enhance his Norton home, where his devoted family were raised, educated, and surrounded
him when he died at age 86.

Leonard Brumby, Jr.

The second professional handler associated with the
breed was Leonard Brumby, Jr., a third-generation dog
man who went on to become senior vice-president of the
American Kennel Club. He first knew Norwich when his
father exhibited them in the 1930s. Incidentally, it was
Leonard, Sr., a leading professional, who introduced
children's handling classes. Today these classes have
grown to international competitions as Junior Showmanship, with an emphasis rather different from Len, Sr.'s
idea.

In 1948, Len, Jr. exhibited the one-eyed John Paul
Jones of Groton for Alden Blodget, who won his champi-
onship with ease despite his "fair wear and tear" scar.
Soon more prick ear clients gave him dogs which van-
quished their drop ear competitors. This rankled some
Norwich Club officers, who felt professional coat presen-

Figure 228:
Children's
Handling Class
at NTA Match,
Bedford, New
York, 1986.

tation was incorrect and that the breed should be owner-shown. However, Leonard silenced these fears. His restrained ring manners, helpful sporting ways, and endless supply of chewing gum could not be denied.

It was also fortunate that he was given a drop ear, Woodchuck of Wingan, for the 1951 Specialty Show in Massachusetts. "Tich" belonged to David Elliot, the gregarious Scottish retriever trainer, who had acquired his pet from Henry Bixby's daughter. This descendant of the first American champion, Merry of Beaufin, proved to be a winner for Len both in and out of the New England ring. Garnering Specialty points, Woodchuck's trouble-free coat was admired by other exhibitors, and Len Brumby was accepted by the Club hierarchy through his charge's correct ears and natural presentation.

Despite the do-it-yourself preference of Club members, Len was used by clients of both breed types. He set a standard for professional sportsmanship in the Norwich ring that has never been equaled. Ever helpful to newcomers, and accommodating to breeders, he encouraged serious dog lovers to be specialist judges. A calm handler in the ring, Len relied on his dogs to attract the judges' attention and had the ability to seem invisible himself.

Believing he could better serve his favorite sport in a more formal capacity, Len joined the American Kennel

Club as a field representative in 1964. His liaison work between breeders and professionals rapidly changed with the dog-show scene's explosive growth. Similarly, the flavor of the AKC administrative staff changed to accommodate the sport, which blossomed into a business.

Retired now, Len still enjoys recounting incidents about the little brown dogs and some of their eccentric owners which brought him pain and pleasure only yesterday.

John Simm

When the AKC finally amended its judging requirements, our third influential professional, John Simm—"Jack" to all—applied for his judging license. With more than 40 years experience, including breeding, grooming, and handling, the popular Jack has always enjoyed great support from his fellow exhibitors.

As Norfolk owners, few are more loyal to the breed than Jack and his wife, Jenny. Ch. Badgewood Monty Collins was an outstanding drop ear champion who became theirs upon his ring retirement—a gift from his breeders, the P. S. P. Fells.

After decades of helping others with stud work, docking tails, wrapping ears, and tidying coats, Jack was licensed to judge all terrier breeds. Long interested in all phases of animal husbandry, he is a student of pedigrees and breed traits.

While Jack is noted for his infectious laugh and Jenny for her mouth-melting shortbread, both enjoy sharing their home with a champion Norfolk. Besides his busy grooming business Jack has been an NNTC office holder, an AKC consultant for breed video tapes, and a long-time member of the PHA (Professional Handlers Association).

He enjoys picking puppies, is helpful to new owners, encouraging to first-time exhibitors, and tactful and sympathetic with sensitive youngsters. At the first breed seminar in 1980 it was Jack who explained to judges that the table should be used for examination, as swooping down on Norfolk could cause them to back off and stop showing.

The Simmses enjoy the companionship of their pets, and it is obvious that Jack prefers dogs casually handled in natural coat; he has no patience with fakery or propping. He judges the breed as sporting companions, not as fussed-over, "cookie-cutter" competitors. As an owner he appreciates the advantages of rough-coated and sweet-tempered champions.

Figure 229:
Jack Simm with a Badgewood puppy.
Photo ©C.S. Larabee.

Figure 230: NORWICH TERRIER CLASSES FROM THE METROPOLITAN & ESSEX DOG SHOW CATALOGUE 1934

Note: Winner was a full brother of the first American Champion, Merry of Beaufin.

CRUFT'S SUBSCRIPTION PAID NOW COVERS 1935.

NORWICH TERRIERS.   Judge—Mrs. Guy Blewitt.

The Norwich Terrier Club (Hon. Secretary: Mrs. D. N. Rodwell, Many Windows, Aldham, Colchester), offer confined to their members under Club conditions, and guarantee the classification:—

402—Biffin Cup No. 1 for best Norwich Terrier.
403—Comarques Cup for best opposite sex to the Biffin Cup No. 1.
404—Airman Puppy Cup for best Puppy.
405—Biffin Cup No. 2 for best Stud Dog, judged by progeny.
406—Tobit Cup for best Coat and Colour.

To be won outright.

407—The Lapwood Silver Medal for the best natural shower.
408—One 1/- tin of Chienpoo for reserve in Class 552.
409—One 1/- tin of Chienpoo for reserve in Class 553.
410—One 3½ lb. bag of Rawvit for reserve in Open.

Class 552. UNDERGRADUATE, Dog or Bitch.

1835   Mrs. P. V. W. Gell. **Neachley Red Reynard.** d. Born 28/9/33. Breeder, Exhibitor. By Biffin of Beaufin—Neachley Rusty. 20 gns. Entered in Class 553.

R 1836   Mrs. D. N. Rodwell and Mr. R. J. Read. **Horstead Nipper.** d. Born 21/12/33. Breeder, Mrs. Blofeld. By Horstead Mick—Tempest.

1 1840   Major Frank Chambers, O.B.E., F.R.C.V.S. **Joe Buffin.** d. Born 15/5/33. Breeder, Mrs. Mainwaring. By Beaufin of Beaufin—Susan. Entered in Classes 553, 554.

1841   Miss A. C. Moss. **Nicolette of Cynval.** b. Born 25/4/34. Breeder, Exhibitor. By Nick O'Teen of Cynval—Dawn of Cynval. Entered in Class 555.

1844   Mrs. Evelyn Mainwaring. **Littlejane.** b. Born — 7 31. Breeder, Exhibitor. By Car—Susan.

ꝣ 1845   Mrs. Evelyn Mainwaring. **Bunch.** b. Born —/5/33. Breeder, Exhibitor. By Biffin—Littlejane.

1846   Mrs. Evelyn Mainwaring. **Tut Tut.** b. Born 1925. Breeder, Tabuteau. By Norry—Wick.

1848   Mrs. Anthony Lowther. **Lucia.** b. Born —/6/32. Breeder, Lady Maureen Stanley. By George—Jane. Entered in Classes 553. 554.

1849   Mrs. Anthony Lowther. **Sally.** b. Born —/5/34. Breeder, Mr. W. E. West. By Askham Red Ike—Jill.

2 1853   Mr. W. E. West. **Farndon Red Dog.** d. Born 3/7/33. Breeder, Exhibitor. By Toodleums—Too Fresh. Entered in Classes 553, 554, 555.

✓ C 1854   Mr. W. E. West. **Judy.** b. Born 27/9/33. Breeder, Mr. H. Wilford. By Micky—Oh Dear. Entered in Classes 553, 554.

3 1855   Mr. W. E. West. **Russet.** b. Born 5/5/34. Breeder, Exhibitor. By Red Ike—Jill.

Class 553. GRADUATE, Dog or Bitch.

VHC 1837   Mrs. D. N. Rodwell. **Airman's Brown Betty.** b. Born 16/6/33. Breeder, Lady Fairfax. By Tobit—Tiger.

1842   Miss A. C. Moss. **Hazel of Cynval.** b. Born 17/7/33. Breeder, Mrs. G. Blewitt. By Tobit—Neachley Toffee. Entered in Class 554.

1856   Miss Macfie. **Tiny Tim of Beaufin.** d. Born 28/5/33. Breeder, Mrs. Mainwaring. By Beaufin of Beaufin—Little Jane of Beaufin. Entered in Class 554.

R (1835)   Mrs. P. V. W. Gell. **Neachley Red Reynard.** See Class 552.

1 (1840)   Major Frank Chambers, O.B.E., F.R.C.V.S. **Joe Bufin.** See Class 552.

(1848)   Mrs. Anthony Lowther. **Lucia.** See Class 552.

2 (1853)   Mr. W. E. West. **Farndon Red Dog.** See Class 552.

3 (1854)   Mr. W. E. West. **Judy.** See Class 552.

50 BOWLS GIVEN TO CRUFT'S SUBSCRIBERS.

NORWICH TERRIERS—continued.

Class 554. OPEN, Dog or Bitch.

R 1838 Mrs. D. N. Rodwell. **Airman's Sam Browne.** d. Born 17/7/33. Breeder, Mrs. G. Blewitt. By Tobit—Neachley Toffee.

2 1843 Mrs. Evelyn Mainwaring. **Biffin.** d. Born —/5/32. Breeder Hon. Mrs. Hoare. By Kims—Gyp.

/ (1840) Major Frank Chambers, O.B.E., F.R.C.V.S. **Joe Bufin.** See Class 552.

(1842) Miss A. C. Moss. **Hazel of Cynval.** See Class 553.

(1848) Mrs. Anthony Lowther. **Lucia.** See Class 552.

3 (1853) Mr. W. E. West. **Farndon Red Dog.** See Class 552.

(1854) Mr. W. E. West. **Judy.** See Class 552.

(1856) Miss Macfie. **Tiny Tim of Beaufin.** See Class 553.

Class 555. SPECIAL BREEDERS', Dog or Bitch.

1847 Mrs. Evelyn Mainwaring. **Sarah Gamp.** b. Born —/4/34. Breeder, Exhibitor. By Paddy—Binky.

1850 Mrs. Anthony Lowther. **Peter.** d. Born —/5/34. Breeder, Exhibitor. By Biffen—Askham Lucia.

1851 Mrs. Anthony Lowther. **Paul.** d. Born —/5/34. Breeder, Exhibitor. By Biffen—Askham Lucia.

1852 Mrs. Anthony Lowther. **Charles.** d. Born —/5/34. Breeder, Exhibitor. By Biffen—Askham Lucia.

(1841) Miss A. C. Moss. **Nicolette of Cynval.** See Class 552.

/ (1853) Mr. W. E. West. **Farndon Red Dog.** See Class 552.

Class 556b. BRACE.

Miss A. C. Moss's **Brace.**

Mrs. Evelyn Mainwaring's **Brace.**

1 Mr West's brace.

JUDGING PROGRESSION AT AKC DOG SHOWS

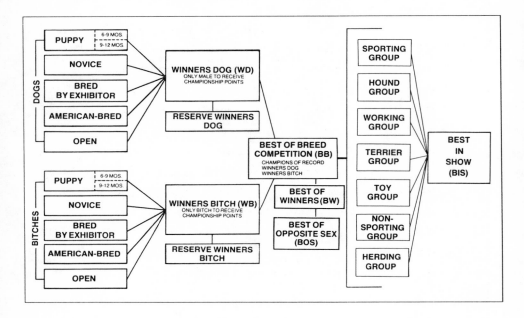

11

THE SHOW DOG:
PROSPECT TO PERFORMANCE

CHOOSING A PUPPY
WITH GOOD BREED TYPE
*Frauke Hinsch (Adapted) **Allright**, Windach, Germany*

Some breeders say that one must look at a puppy on its first day of life to see the balance of its body and other qualities, like horse breeders do with newborn foals. This is very difficult with a five to eight ounce whelp and does not really give one enough information. Eight to twelve weeks is a good time for breeders to evaluate a litter. At this age puppies should be cheerful, adventurous, and coordinated. They are growing independent of their doting dam, who, presumably, has been "playing rough" to toughen her offspring for future terrier tasks. Watching a litter interact with their dam can give an excellent insight into the temperaments the pups will develop. An outgoing, boisterous, happy-go-lucky pup who demands the most of its dam's attention is more likely to be a "show personality" than the more reserved or cautious pup. A good temperament is a must for a youngster to be able to withstand the rigors of the show circuit, as beauty alone is not enough to win the honors.

At this stage you can also start to see body conformation. The most desirable features are a broad skull; low-set ears; a pronounced indentation, or stop, between small dark eyes; a deep, wedge-shaped muzzle just shorter than half the overall length of the head; and a scissor bite. A

Figure 231:
Ch. Surrey
Binnacle at
three months.

Figure 232:
A TIME
TO SHOW:
Ch. Allright
Magic Lamp at
8 months,
15 months,
and 3 1/2 years.

slight overbite should correct to a scissor bite by the time the pup is a year old. If there are missing or misaligned teeth at 12 weeks, it is unlikely the permanent teeth will be correct. The neck should be of ample length, slightly arched, and should blend into close-fitting shoulder blades at the withers. There should be no dip or arch in the topline, and the tail set should be high with its carriage upright. Forelegs should be straight, with the elbows fitting closely to the long ribcage, and the loin should be short.

At 10 to 12 weeks the chest should already be below the elbows, thighs should be broad and deep with parallel hocks close to the ground. In moving, the puppy should track truly; that is, its hind feet step right into its front footprints.

If there is a lot of baby coat on the puppy, this should now be stripped out to see the coat quality beneath. Usually the puppies with less baby coat develop the harsher coats. A slight amount of baby coat is desirable in a potential show dog, as a total absence of guard hairs might mean a very short, smooth adult coat with no furnishings.

Expression is also important to note at this time. Much about the puppy's body shape will change as growth continues. The head especially is likely to change several times. But expression will always be the same, so if you don't like a puppy's expression, don't buy it.

Since Norfolk change quite a bit during their development, the main points to check at 10 to 12 weeks are temperament, a lovely expression, a balanced outline, level topline, and a not overabundant coat. After four months Norfolk Terrier puppies tend to look rangy, leggy, and sometimes long, without depth in chest or brisket. This is normal and shouldn't be cause for worry. This "adolescent" stage can last up to 15 or 20 months in late maturers. Then they start to deepen and look balanced again, as you saw in the 10-to-12-week-old pup. Remember: A promising Norfolk puppy can still be a disappointment after a year or two, but it may also happen that a not-so-promising one matures into a very creditable representative of the breed.

THE SHOW COAT

The Ideal
The Norfolk Terrier Standard is one of the few standards which stresses that these dogs should be shown with as nearly a natural coat as possible. Not all Norfolks are blessed with the coats described in the Standard, and even those that do conform need some preparation for the show ring. Being a ratting terrier with a weatherproof coat, the conformation ring should attract exhibits that are tidy, but look natural and unbarbered. It is best to have an ideal in mind before you work on your dog's coat. To achieve this ideal, do not spend needless hours trimming his coat in a style to which his life is alien. *Train your eyes* to look at the total outline of your dog. It will help you to understand what the end result in grooming should be.

Show careers must be planned three or four months in advance. Even the truest coats should be picked over before a show entry is made. So-called style grooming, e.g. skirts, muttonchops, and backcombing from occiput, all obscure the outline of a working terrier.

SHOW PREPARATION
Lesley Crawley, Ragus, Steeple Aston, England

The following instructions will help you prepare your Norfolk for the show ring.

Head and Neck
As some Norfolks do not have the desired short hair on the top of the skull, they may need this area to be wholly or partially stripped according to the strength of

Figure 233:
A dog with a flat skull and very little stop needs hair left on top of the head to build up the desired slightly rounded look and well-defined stop.
Drawing Leslie Crawley.

Figure 234:
Hair and ruff left on sides of the head improve the width of skull on a small, narrow-headed dog.
Drawing Leslie Crawley.

the head. This needs to be done every few weeks to keep the coat growth coming, otherwise bald spots on the skull will appear.

Ruffs can be left on the dog without creating a stuffy, short-necked appearance by thinning out the coat on each side of the neck from a point behind the base of the ear, down to and over the shoulders to the top of the leg. This is done with a stripping knife, not thinning scissors, and must be blended into the thicker coat behind the shoulders and down the back of the neck. The ruff can also be thinned a little immediately under the chin and halfway down the throat, to prevent a heavy overloaded look to the chest.

Remove all long, straggly hairs from the ears to leave them small and neat.

Toplines

If a dog has a low-set-tail it is advisable to leave as much fur as possible in front of the tail to fill the dip between the spine and root of the tail.

A dip in the topline is improved by the removal of coat from the thick tuft which grows immediately in front of the tail, and also the top of the shoulders. In particularly severe cases the coat needs to be thinned from in front of the tail to along the back over the loin.

Fronts

Many dogs, even ones with good shoulders, carry a tuft of thick hair on the point of the elbow giving an "out at elbow" appearance. This should always be removed.

A. To improve a bandy front, view the dog from the front and remove all the longest hairs from the point of elbow to halfway down the leg, just above the turn in the leg.

B. Cut closely around the outside turn of the foot.

C. Cut around the rest of the foot leaving slightly more hair on the inside of the foot.

D. Remove most of the fur on the protruding joint of the pastern.

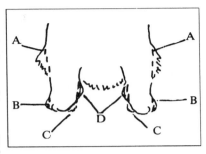

Figure 235: **Grooming to improve fronts.** *Drawing Leslie Crawley.*

Hindquarters

If the stifles are straight it helps to leave the coat much longer in that area, shaping it with the help of thinning scissors to obtain the desired curve of stifle. Brush the hair forward to accentuate this. Cut the hair around the feet into the desired cat-foot shape.

Tails

Smarten the tail by removing all long straggly hairs on the sides and keeping the coat very short up the back of it. Keep the hair short around the anus, for hygiene as well as smartness. Gradually blend from there into the longer coat further down the backside. This is done with thinning scissors as it is a very sensitive area for the dog. It is much less painful than pulling the coat with finger and thumb.

Having gone over the dog completely, place him on the floor and allow him to shake and walk about. Check closely to see if the coat falls into the right shape and that enough has been removed in certain places. Toplines, for instance, can appear OK on the table but once the dog relaxes, moves and stands, more may need to be done.

THE DETAIL
Tony Gabrielli, Domby, Cleveland, Ohio

Ears

The ears take patience, but it is easy to see which hairs to pull. These are usually longer and lighter in color. The outer ear should be kept close (short) and clean looking.

Take the ear gently between your index finger and thumb and hold firmly so that when stripping you are not pulling the dog's head from side to side. After working on the outer ear, move to the outside edge and begin at the base and work your way around the entire ear pulling out those small hairs that you can comfortably grasp with the index finger and thumb of your working hand. The underpart of the ear is tender, and most dogs hate having this done. With difficult dogs use a good pair of curved scissors and carefully clip this area clean. This is a good time to clean your dog's ears with a Q-tip. Just work it around gently, staying close to the top of the ear canal.

Tail

When you are working on your dog's tail, remember that you want the tail to end up thick and neat. It should be carrot-shaped. Begin working on the underside of the tail near the anus and work upward taking almost one hair at a time. When finished, the underside should be smooth. Then proceed to work on sides and top. The tip should also be stripped so that the tail looks proportional to the length that it was originally cropped to be. Don't make the end blunt.

THE ART OF HANDLING

Handling show dogs is a skill that with practice and patience develops into an art. The presentation of a dog looking its best is the handler's role. The well-conditioned, happy dog that shows with no apparent interference is a most compelling sight.

Achieving ring success takes time, planning, and work behind the scenes, for no dog is perfect. Norfolks vary in their conformation and character. Good handlers must first understand their breed, then develop a bond of affection with their show dog. To win, handler and dog must be compatible, with the exhibitor setting the pace as they, heads up, enter the ring and attract the judge's attention.

Examination

Since the introduction of the Examination Table to the show ring, many exhibitors present their dogs to terrier judges who *mistakenly* use the table as the obsolete judging block. The table is in fact merely a convenience for enabling a judge to lay on hands without bending double.

Place the dog on the table in show stance with head and tail held proudly. First impressions are very important when dogs are judged, so don't wave bait or excite a dog being examined except to make it use its ears. Ideally one's dog should be trained to stand for examination. Most judges will use their hands and eyes to check skull width, eye placement, shape and color, ear set and size, teeth alignment, shoulder

Figure 236: Top and tailing on the table: Beth Sweigart with Ch. Chidley Dandelion.

angles, legs and feet, depth of girth with spanned hands, length of rib cage and loin length, tail set, testicles, hindquarters, stifle bend, and hock height. Coat, its texture and presentation so clearly defined in the Standard, is a salient breed characteristic so must be carefully evaluated. Before the examined dog is put on the ground, the judge will want to see its expression and ear use.

Remember you only top and tail on the table, never on the ground where Norfolks show off their good temperaments naturally. Today in terrier judging, the evaluation of the whole dog is the sum of the parts checked on the table and should *always* take place on the ground. As their Latin name implies, terriers are earth dogs who loathe being lifted off their feet.

Gaiting

A judge wants to see how a dog gaits—moving away, from the side, and coming forward. The demonstration of reach—drive and tracking true—is the purpose of moving your dog. A well-trained terrier should possess sufficient temperament to move happily with its nose off the ground and stand alertly when the handler asks for its attention.

Pace your dog correctly so it trots along freely without a hitch, skip or break of stride. This is best accomplished with a slightly tense lead on the move for steady contact and control, a necessity if the judge asks you to move in a triangle or other pattern. Whatever is requested, remember to keep your dog between you and the judge. Practice gives any exhibitor a leading edge.

Posing

In getting your dog to pose, Norfolk exhibitors should never prop, set up, or stack their dogs for conformation judging. Do not on any account continually fiddle with the faulty part of its anatomy. If the dog moves, turn around and walk it into a pose. Be sure your dog is comfortable or it may fidget at just the wrong moment (when the judge is looking.) Much practice is needed to present a dog in the ring looking its best. Resist the temptation to over-handle; a relaxed dog and exhibitor make the best combination. The dog that can be brought to full attention by a word from the handler, or by the sight or sound of bait will be hard to beat. Caution: A Norfolk looking up can fly its ears, so let it focus on a distant object or bait held low to the ground.

Silent Sparring

Norfolks should be shown on a light contact lead which best displays their animation, balance, and confidence in close proximity with one or all their classmates. Sparring shows more than poor manners—it also shows a lack of understanding of the history, purpose, and standard of the breed. Norfolks were developed to destroy small vermin or bolt foxes, so any sign of ill temper should be displayed toward their quarry, not each other.

In the ring, honorable scars from fair wear and tear shall not be penalized unduly, but dogs lacking type or displaying shyness or quarrelsome tendencies should be as severely penalized as dogs with defects of soundness and structure.

Timing

Don't expect too much of your dog. Let him rest when the judge is busy with others. Be gentle and confident so your dog is ready to show when it's his turn. Be relaxed in the ring; nerves travel down the lead, especially a tight one, and can affect the dog. Have confidence that yours is the best dog there, and remember, there is always another day.

Figure 237: Allright Ribot, a Norfolk in natural coat.

THE "NATURAL NORFOLK": AN ENDANGERED SPECIES

Todays professionals—judges, agents, and groomers —have had an impact on the breed's presentation and breeding. The characteristic non-trim coat is being replaced by the cultivation of furnishings; and natural color shadings are often "helped" by dustings of paint, pigment, and color shampoos.

It is an unanticipated fact that our advertised non-trim breed has become influenced by grooming techniques. The Norfolk's unique charm is being threatened by show-ring kudos; however, a good breed representative will reflect quality without coat enhancements and grooming style extremes.

12

OBEDIENCE:
LEARNING HOW TO LEARN

WHY OBEDIENCE?

QUIZ:	TRUE	FALSE
1. Obedience training breaks a dog's spirit.	☐	☐
2. You can't train a terrier.	☐	☐
3. "You can't teach an old dog new tricks."	☐	☐
4. Obedience training ruins a dog the show ring.	☐	☐

If you answered **FALSE** to all of the above questions, take your Norfolk and proceed directly to the Obedience ring. If you answered **TRUE** to any, read on.

Obedience training is one of the best ways to cement a relationship with your dog. Whether it's a local class in the basics or advanced training for a Utility Dog (UD) degree, the interaction between you and your Norfolk will strengthen the dog's innate desire to please you. If done with practice, patience, and persistence, and an all-important sense of perspective, the education of your Norfolk results in pleasure for dog and owner alike.

Aside from the satisfaction realized from a crisply executed Obedience exercise, training has many practical applications. Not only is a well-trained Norfolk a happy Norfolk, he is more likely to be a welcome addition to any social situation in which he's involved. And most importantly, a Norfolk who heeds the command "Come!" or who will "Sit!" and "Stay!" rather than chasing the neighbor's cat, will have a greater chance of living to a ripe old age than his untrained peers.

BASIC TRAINING

Basic Obedience training consists simply of teaching your Norfolk to obey the everyday, practical commands that will serve your convenience and protect his safety. Here they are:

1. Sit
2. Stay
3. Heel
4. Come
5. Down
6. No

One way to teach your dog these basics is by taking him to a beginners' Obedience course. Your veterinarian, local breed club, or county recreation office can usually provide information on when and where these courses are available. If you'd rather teach your Norfolk the basics yourself, there are many excellent books on Obedience training. You may want to consider the benefits, though, of socializing your dog (and yourself) with other people and dogs in a class situation. It may also be useful to go to your library or bookstore and look for a book on Obedience that makes the most sense to you—one that's clearly written and provides the kind of knowledge you'll need for your life-style and that of your dog.

Whichever method you choose, remember that if you aren't an effective teacher your Norfolk will never become an effective learner. Here are some brief pointers:

1. **Never lose your temper when training.** Be patient. Training takes repetition. Learning aptitude in dogs, as in humans, varies from one to another.

2. **Keep training sessions short** (10 to 15 minutes at a time). Gauge your Norfolk's attention span, and don't go beyond it.

3. **Be consistent, firm, and confident.** Always use the same command for the same task, and always use the same tone of voice for that command.

4. **Avoid distractions when teaching a task.** Then, deliberately introduce distractions once that task is learned to insure the command will be

obeyed whether your dog is distracted or not.

5. **Set training goals.** Train every day until these have been reached.

6. **Praise your animal warmly and well for every accomplishment.** Do this the minute it's done.

7. **Always end training sessions positively.** If your Norfolk hasn't mastered the task being taught, end with a task he *has* mastered And praise him for it!

8. **Last, but not least, your Norfolk's motivation should be to please you;** therefore (unless you-have the kind who lives only to eat!) it's best if you avoid food as a reward for obeying.

WHEN SHOULD OBEDIENCE BEGIN?

When to begin training your puppy? There are as many opinions as there are dog owners. One advocate of early training is Mary D. Fine of Storrs, Connecticut, whose Tylwyth Norfolks have broken all records for the highest Obedience degrees.

Figure 238: Raquel Wolf with Mary Fine's champions New Garden Eadith Am. Can. UD and Castle Point Mint Am. Can. UD, CG. *University of Connecticut Research Project photo, Susan Jenks.*

Early Training for Puppies
Mary D. Fine, Tylwyth, Storrs, Connecticut

It seems a shame few people take advantage of the opportunity for early training. Perhaps they are put off by the image of a wobbly puppy being yanked around on a leash or disciplined into cowering submission. Done properly, nothing of the sort is involved and the pup only thinks it has discovered a new game.

Early training is certainly fun. There is nothing more appealing than a five- or six-week-old puppy promptly plopping down on its fat posterior at the command, "Sit!" and then looking up brightly with that "Aren't I wonderful!" expression on its face. This is also the best time to instill the idea that there are times when he may play completely carefree and other times when, even if he thinks he is "playing," he must keep his attention fixed on his owner. This is imprinted during these first brief training sessions—five minutes or maybe a maximum of ten if the pup is really enjoying it. It is not reasonable to expect a puppy's attention to hold for longer than this. To me it is more rewarding to gradually mold a puppy into the sort of dog one wants it to be than to struggle with a half-grown hellion that must be trained quickly just to keep one's sanity.

For openers, it is necessary to shut oneself up with the puppy, preferably in a small room without distractions. With a very young pup it is best to train inside since the outside world with its myriad of sounds, smells, and distractions may prove to be too much. The average puppy will learn to sit on command within 60 seconds, not perfectly, but well enough to demonstrate that he has understood. I have never tried this with a puppy younger than five weeks, but it does seem to work as young as that.

Figure 239:
Mary Fine with
Ch. Castle Point
Mint UD.

The method consists of getting the puppy's attention (the hardest part), saying "Sit!" and gently pushing him into a sitting position. No jerking on the collar. Once "Sit!" has been learned, "Down!" is taught almost the same way. I use food or a toy to encourage the puppy to move into a prone position. If this is done, it is seldom necessary to push hard. Harsh shoving to a down position will scare a very young puppy—and remember, this is a baby that has only been walking a few weeks.

I teach "Stand!" after "Sit!" and "Down!". By then the puppy is accustomed to paying attention to commands, and it is easy to tell if he is responding to the "Stand" or just doing it by accident.

After these commands are taught, I play it by ear. With my small breeds (Norfolks and Pembroke Welsh Corgis) I teach heeling later, as it is often too cold to go outside and my house isn't large enough for heeling inside. If the puppies are interested, I teach the retrieve, but on a strictly voluntary basis—that is, if the puppy doesn't bring the dumbbell back, I don't force him since this seems a bit much for a seven- to eight-week-old.

It is important to make a great fuss over the puppy immediately as soon as he does the right thing—and I do mean a great fuss. Frequently one's most effective reinforcements are administered while crawling on the floor with the puppy, who is usually so intrigued by your behavior that he makes an enormous effort to learn what will produce it again! In a short time you will be amazed to realize that these "play sessions" have resulted in a still very happy but now well-trained puppy. So, if you have the chance to do early training, try it: both you *and* your puppy will like it.

FORMAL OBEDIENCE TRAINING

If you want to go beyond the basics and into the Obedience ring, the American Kennel Club offers a series of increasingly challenging goals. These are the Companion Dog (CD), Companion Dog Excellent (CDX), and Utility Dog (UD) degrees. And, while your Norfolk must be a registered member of the breed, dogs who are spayed, neutered, or are less than perfect physical specimens (flyaway ears? soft coats? gait like a bear?) are still welcome to compete.

Obedience Trial Championship

In 1977 the AKC added another dimension to Obedience tests: the Obedience Trial Championship (OTCH). Unfortunately the pursuit of this title has diminished the friendliness and camaraderie that once characterized this sport by introducing into the Obedience field the competitiveness of professional sports, with emphasis on winning at all costs. Fortunately Obedience competitors can, if they wish, avoid the ultra-competitiveness of the OTCH by concentrating on individual goals and achievements.

Agility Test

A new competition—the Agility Test—introduced at English agricultural shows several years ago has become a drawing card at the famous Crufts Dog Show and, more recently, at American and Canadian shows. An obstacle course patterned after the high, wide, and handsome horse-show jumps in stadium competitions has been adapted for dogs, with the competitors scored on speed, accuracy, and control.

The Norfolk Terrier Club of England added a version of this popular event to its Rallies in 1982, and the American Norfolk Terrier Association (ANTA) has used a variation with often hilarious results. A more complicated form of this activity, which combines jumping with Obedience turns by hand signal, has been submitted for American Kennel Club approval.

Scent Hurdle

Scent Hurdle racing was introduced into the United States in 1965. It is similar to the human hurdle relay race (except for the scent, of course!), and consists of several canine teams competing against one another, two teams at a time. The hurdles are 12 feet apart, and each dog in a team must clear every hurdle and at the end retrieve a small baton (imprinted with the owner-handler's scent). The competitor must then return to the starting point and run the same course again, performing the same retrieve on a second scented baton.

The team whose dogs accurately finish the race first—jumping all hurdles and retrieving the right baton—wins. Dogs must be Obedience-trained to compete, and today there are many Scent Hurdle racing teams in the United States and Canada.

Tracking

Most dogs enjoy using their noses to follow a scent, and with training this instinct can prove useful in finding a lost belonging or even a person or another dog. Basic Tracking, AKC style, offers formal competitions to locate "missing" objects. The formal course, which ends at the "lost" object, must be 440 yards long and have two 45-degree turns. At least 30 minutes before the start the scent is laid, with the "missing" article, a leather item such as a glove, wallet, or belt. A longer, more difficult course leads to an AKC Advanced Tracking degree.

Training for Tracking consists of the handler first stomping out a short track on grass or earth, with the dog staked nearby to observe what's going on. The handler should be wearing leather shoes or boots in order to leave plenty of familiar scent. The dog is then taken along the track on lead to the end, where the bait has been planted for retrieval. One Norfolk breeder and avid tracker we know trains her dogs along a very short track at first, gradually lengthening the course. Praise is given all along the way as the dog correctly follows the scent, on lead, but always by its own initiative. Ultimately, in formal competition, the course itself is laid by someone other than the dog's handler, with both dog and handler out of sight. The object with the handler's scent is at the end. In training, the course is staked with flags to indicate to the handler whether the dog is on scent as the tracking progresses.

Figure 240: **The first Tracking Dog in the breed, Kedron Dappertutto CDX, TD.**

Teaching Norfolks: A Personal Adventure
Nancy Parker, Rye, New York

I started in Obedience in the 1940s, a time when it was so new that many people, including me, had never even heard of it. A friend had a German Shepherd, as I did, and she sparked my interest. I earned a CDX (Companion Dog Excellent) on my Shepherd, but the rules for getting degrees then were quite different than now; and there was as yet none of the fierce competitiveness we see today.

Rearing a family caused me to put Obedience "on the shelf" until 1966. At that time, in addition to an elderly German Shepherd and an aged Cocker Spaniel, I had a 10-month-old Norfolk. This began my second foray into Obedience, and since no one had told me that training a terrier was any different than training a Shepherd, I eventually proceeded to earn a Utility Dog degree (UD) on four Norfolks.

One occasion that I remember most keenly was when I showed my first Norfolk (then Norwich D.E.) in the Open Class in Connecticut. Suddenly, I found myself listening to tremendous applause. It turned out to be for a Norwich Terrier D.E. owned by Mrs. William Dwyer, and she had just gotten the third and final leg in the Utility Class on her River Bend Tory. Tory was the first Norwich dog ever to attain that degree; and my Triscuit's Tuffet was the first Norwich bitch ever to receive it.

The first Obedience degree, of course, is Companion Dog (CD). Based on my own experience, I believe that almost any dog can earn the CD, CDX, and even the UD, given the proper training. The two most important factors are the time and effort. I can think of nothing more frustrating, yet more rewarding, than training your Norfolk to win the Utility Dog degree. Almost every exercise in Utility requires the dog to choose the *correct* article, the *correct* jump, the *correct* glove being pointed to. The dog must think, concentrate, and decide.

Your dog's confidence and enjoyment are vitally important in training for any of the three degrees. In the process, he is constantly shown the correct way to do an exercise and helped to do it that way. The theory here is that dogs do not learn by their mistakes but by doing tasks the right way many, many times. Based on my own experience, I would prefer to train a bitch rather than a dog. (Admittedly, this opinion is limited because I've personally trained only one dog to six bitches.) I prefer the latter, however, because they are less independent than dogs and give you much more of their attention.

Thomas ("Tom-Tom"), my one Norfolk male, was a real character who could invent more different ways to flunk in the Obedience ring than could ever be imagined. He was a charming, lovable, friendly dog — enjoyed by all who watched his performance. I started Tom innocently in Novice, not knowing what I was in for, and in 1968 he breezed through Novice to his CD in three shows with scores in the high 180s. Back to the drawing board, as Tom-Tom and I "studied" for his CDX. I was fresh and confident from getting my Tuffet's

Utility degree, so a CDX for Thomas didn't seem the least bit unattainable. Tom, however, had different ideas. Among his "cute" tricks were bounding out of the ring to help some children eat their lunch and, in Philadelphia, somehow finding a gumdrop in the ring (which the judge and I had to pry out of his mouth). He also once did a very elegant retrieve of a dumbbell, but instead of bringing it back to me he returned it quite smartly to the judge.

By the end of 1969, Tom-Tom had two of the three legs towards his CDX. I started training in earnest during the spring of 1970. At many shows Tom did well but would goof on one exercise—and you must get better than 50 percent on each exercise to score. Finally, however, the magic day arrived when Tom-Tom put every-

Figure 241: Nancy Parker with Tara.

thing together and we got the third leg. I promised him that we would go no further if he would qualify just once more, and I kept that promise. On November 1, 1970, Tom retired with his CDX.

As to the innate learning aptitude of Norfolks, I believe they are no different from any other breed. All seven of the Norfolks I've trained have gotten their CDs quickly — three shows for six of them and four shows for one. Obviously the going gets rougher as you proceed to the higher classes. Norfolks may not have the instinct for being super heelers like the herding dogs, and they may not have the innate aptitude for retrieving like retrievers. What this means to me is that a Norfolk can *learn* just as easily to heel but not with the *precision* of, say, a Sheltie or a Border Collie. A Norfolk can *learn* to retrieve in two weeks, but not with the tremendous *enthusiasm* of a Golden Retriever.

One thing my Norfolks have all done is to sit on one hip with one hind leg out further than the other. This is called a "crooked sit," and because of it points are lost. If I were an absolute perfectionist, every time they sat crookedly I'd get them straightened out. All this is of vital importance to owners of so-called competitive dogs. But to me, points notwithstanding, getting a dog to comprehend and do all the exercises with confidence is the key to everything.

There is also no question that the more a dog learns, the easier it is to teach new accomplishments. For instance, Tara, whom I lost at age 12, did commercials, stills, soap operas, and modeling. About five years ago she did a commercial for Milk Bone in which she had to learn to put her feet up on a bench and push a Milk Bone box over on its side. For this my command was "Push!" In commercials you have no more than a week before going on camera. Tara did the job in that time, although the command "Push!" was completely new to both of us. Another time my agent asked if Tara could "dial" a telephone. I said I could teach her, but I honestly doubted that I could. I placed a phone on the kitchen counter, put Tara on the counter, and had her push at the buttons. At that point I had to go out for about an hour, and when I returned I tried again. This time I put the phone on the floor and told Tara "Push!" To my amazement she walked over to the telephone and pushed at the keys. We did the job four days later!

Tara, particularly, of all my Norfolks most definitely mastered the knack of learning. She could do all sorts of tricks — crawl, sit up, wave, "speak," roll over, dial a phone, push a box, and fetch anything she could carry. This wasn't necessarily because she was smarter than my other three; she simply had more time and effort put into her training and, most important, had *learned how to learn.* The basis of all this is Obedience training.

I've learned from experience that, like children, all dogs differ from one another. Some are more sensitive, some more independent, and some quicker to learn than others. All my dogs have learned to retrieve in about two weeks with no ear-pinching or any other form of punishment. They learn with a food reward until they know what they're doing, and then the food is gradually removed. At that point they realize what they are expected to do. I praise them, reward them, and they re-

Figure 242: Tara did commercials, stills, soap operas, and modeling. This photo was for a calendar.

peat the process — and it works! My Norfolks have always been house dogs, companions on trips, and I'm proud to say they go with me to visit friends who always invite us back! Those not involved in Obedience are invariably amazed at how well behaved and what good houseguests these dogs are. There's no doubt that this can be credited to Obedience training.

There's nothing I can think of that I'm more proud of than having put 22 Obedience degrees on seven Norfolk Terriers. This includes four Utility Dogs, two Bermuda degrees, and three Canadian degrees. I believe earning the Utility degree on four Norfolks is probably a record, but more trainers will achieve this as more Norfolk owners become interested in Obedience.

A few years ago, when I owned six Norfolks, I had them all sit under the Christmas tree for a "formal portrait." Many non-Obedience people have asked me how this amazing feat was accomplished. (To have six dogs lined up in a row, all sitting quietly, seemed quite miraculous to them!) This so-called miracle was of course the direct result of Obedience training. Other things I've done with my dogs that wouldn't be possible without Obedience are Scent-Hurdle racing, flyball, pet therapy (visiting nursing homes, usually once a week), and the modeling business.

Many people have asked me why I don't change breeds since I'm so interested in Obedience. I've been asked many times why I don't work with Goldens, Poodles, or Border Collies — all breeds that have done distinguished work in Obedience. Those who pose this question miss my point completely. I'm interested *first* in Norfolks and *second* in Obedience. The fact that Norfolks don't always get the highest scores in a trial really isn't important to me. What matters most is that through Obedience my dogs are well behaved and marvelous companions — a real joy to live with. And I live with them 24 hours a day!

"Solomon, Heel!"
Prudence B. Read, Sage, Bedford, New York
"Solomon should get his CD this fall."

So spoke Catharine Reiley, founder and director of the Kaeley Obedience School in the spring of 1984. Ten shows and a year and a half later her prediction came true. By that time the value and elusiveness of the Companion Dog degree had become clear to me. To earn the degree owner and dog must qualify with a minimum score of 170 out of a possible 200 points in three shows. Dog and owner are put through patterns of on- and off-lead heeling, the figure eight on lead, a stand for examination, a recall, and all dogs must sit together quietly opposite their owners for one minute and must lie down for three. (Even if you or your dog have been previously disqualified, you are expected to remain and take part in the long sits and downs.)

I've watched friends with Poodles knock off their CDs in a three-day weekend. Norfolks are a different story—independent-minded creatures that they are. Why was I doing this! Rushing off Thursday evenings and practicing diligently at home? I'd sold my dog's brother to Nancy Parker, who has a family of multi-titled Obedience Norfolks, so I felt my puppy deserved the same opportunities his brother was going to have. I began taking "Sol" to school when he was eight months old. We made it through the Beginners' class, although I did hear the comment, "Back for more?" expressed with some surprise when we turned up at the Novice class. Obedience school is habit forming. There's something new to learn about yourself as a handler and about your dog at every session. Fellow students and their dogs are absorbing.

But shows are something else. They combine a high degree of suspense and tension. We were lucky at our first show in the fall of 1984. Solomon had done little off-lead work but, perhaps unnerved by the show environment, followed along quite well. I also think he benefited from being a breed the judge hadn't often seen in the Obedience ring. He qualified with 180 points. I was falsely encouraged by our initial success, however, as a run of disasters followed.

In one show the man next to me, returning to his dog after the long down, tripped on the rubber matting of the gym floor. Sol broke his down and was disqualified. In the next show he sat down during the off-lead heeling; and in the next he wandered loosely along somewhere behind me.

In March of 1985 one judge gave Solomon the "benefit of the doubt" and we qualified in the 170s. We then moved into the outdoor season and found the grass full of distracting scents. We were practicing three times a day. One trainer advised I find something Sol was crazy about and carry it as bait. Cheese? Chocolate? Liver? None of these worked. I labored on, correcting and praising. In my anxiety about heeling I gave repeat commands and got us disqualified in one show.

At Obedience school the teachers conferred. In August of 1985 I was given a linked metal training collar that gave "correction" a new meaning. It only took a few lessons before Solomon was in truth heeling both on and off lead. Oddly, it seemed he enjoyed the work more now that he understood it was serious business.

Figure 243: Prudence Read's Solomon CDX.

I had learned my lesson. I was in no hurry. We waited until October and the Queensboro Show before we tried again. I went through stages of nervousness, pessimism, and optimism to the point of emotional numbness. As we entered the ring, I commented to the judge on the long wait and he told me it would all be over in three minutes. It was. My heart sank during the figure eight when, on the judge's command "Halt!" Solomon greeted one of the stewards, who was a figure-eight post, by standing up and pawing her legs. The judge smiled and told me to continue. Solomon qualified with 184 points. My pleasure and relief were intense. We have framed the AKC certificate.

A CDX? We'll see. We're still going to school, and approaching that possibility with caution and respect.

Jamie, the Hearing-Ear Norfolk
Carole Watson, Ar-Ca Kennels, Lawton, Michigan

"My name is Jamie and I was born in the kennel of Abbedales. My kennel mom was Joanie Eckert, but my real mom is Abbedales Tea & Crumpets and my dad was Ch. Elve Pure Magic. I was born into a family of one brother (Ch. Abbedales American Gigolo) and one sister (Ch. Abbedales Abigail Ray). As you can see, I come from a line of champions and I've done quite well myself, amassing 14 points and both of my majors. But I really hate showing. That sort of game is fine for some guys, but I was meant for something far more special.

"When I was a pup, some very special people came to my kennel and took me home with them. From that day, when Bill and Janalee made me a part of their family, my life took on special meaning.

"Let me tell you just a bit about Bill and Janalee. They are wonderful, intelligent, warm, loving people. They are also hearing-impaired. Deafness sure can make a big difference in a family. For instance they had decided, since they are completely deaf when their hearing aids are not in their ears (such as at night when they are sleeping, or when they take a shower), that it would be best not to have children. Their concern was that they would not hear a baby cry in the night. But these two have been extra special parents to me. Bill loves me; Janalee loves me; I have a special corner to sleep in that is all mine; I get all kinds of treats, my own toys, walks on my leash, car rides, etc. What more could any self-respecting, show-hating Norfolk ask of life? I thought I had it all.

"Then, one day, unbeknownst to me, Joan Eckert called a friend of hers who trains 'Hearing Dogs.' She gave her friend the names of my 'parents.'

"The new term around our house was Hearing Dog—were they really considering bringing another dog into our lives? We were happy just as we were—just the three of us.

"Well, a Hearing Dog trainer, Carole, came to call one day. Carole came with her clipboard, pen, and cookies—COOKIES! She had cookies in her pocket. How could she have known—we became friends immediately! She talked mostly to Bill and Janalee, but I got lots of extra pats and pets and a bite of cookie now and then. We all talked (I listened mostly) about which sounds were necessary for a Hearing Dog to respond to around our home—I was surprised that they didn't mention the sound of a cat or other dogs that visited my property. I guess Carole didn't know about the Great Dane that lives next door.

"Soon after Carole's first visit, new and interesting things began to happen at our house. Every time the phone rang, I got a cookie; every time the doorbell rang, I got a cookie! During the day when Bill and Janalee were at work, I stayed with my Grandma (Bill's mom, Alice). Now, I really like cookies and Grandma really likes me, so I figured that if I told Grandma when her phone was ringing and when someone was at her door, she would give me cookies, too! I was right!

"For the next four months, Carole came to visit nearly every week. I was allowed to show off my skills every time she came. Sometimes Carole would say that I should do something new—like come and get Mom or Dad when the smoke alarm went off. I was certainly eager to do that. What a terrible noise! If Bill knew how badly it sounds, he'd get it fixed. Bill does know how to make it stop ringing; I was sure grateful for that.

Figure 244:
Janalee and Bill
with Hearing Dog
Jamie.

"Each time I told Bill or Janalee something needed their attention, good things happened; not only did I get my cookie, pats, and lots of praise, but something happened inside me. I felt very good about myself because I knew that I was a very important member of this family that I loved so much. They needed me as much as I needed them. These are very important jobs for which I am responsible. Sometimes I am required to leave my food bowl and go and get Bill out of the shower. You see, if someone comes to the door and Bill has his hearing aid off, he can't hear the doorbell. I can't believe the number of times I have had to leave my food bowl or wake up in the middle of a nap. It's a dirty job, but someone has to do it! Besides that, I get extra treats and hugs.

"One day toward the end of my training, I heard a really strange sound that I had never heard before. I was pretty upset because this new and different sound seemed to need attention quickly. I heard this sound for the first time one day when Carole had come to visit us—figures! Boy, these humans! They were all sitting around the living room talking. They didn't even hear this frantic-sounding noise. Well, I just knew I had to get someone to help me fast. I ran to Bill and got his attention; then I ran to Janalee and got her attention and I told Carole that she'd better come, too. They all got up and came running; I was relieved. I heard them say that it was a baby crying—a baby crying? I also heard them say those words that I heard when Carole and I first met—HEARING DOG! I thought again that I was going to have to share my home with another dog. All that time they were talking about me—JAMIE—the 'Working, Certified Hearing Dog'!!"

Note: *In 1975 Master Instructor Agnes McGrath trained six successful hearing-ear dogs, which led the American Humane Society to establish its Training Center in Denver, Colorado. At this writing there are 30 hearing-ear training centers across the United States. There is also legislation in all 48 contiguous states recognizing the usefulness of hearing-ear dogs and allowing them into public places where pets are traditionally banned.*

NORFOLK OBEDIENCE DEGREES
1947-1986

1947 **Kedron Dappertutto CDX, UD.** Breeder: M. McCausland. Owner: Mary Curtis. By Farouk (Imp.) x Ch. Angel's Whisper of Colonsay (Imp.).

1948 **Ch. Tuff CD.** Breeder/Owner: Sylvia Warren. By Bruff x Jenny Pinch.

1949 **Baloo CD.** Breeder: Sylvia Warren. Owner: Elizabeth Copeland. By Ch. Tuff x Muff.

1964 **River Bend Tory CDX** (UD 1966). Breeder: Sylvia Warren. Owner: Mrs. William Dwyer. By Hunston Highflier x River Bend Fleet.

1966   **Ginger Peaches of Eddyshare CDX.** Breeder: Jeanette K. Eddy. Owner: Betty Ann Stokes. By Hunston Highflier x Eddyshare Aconca.

1967   **Bethway's Triscuit CD** (CDX 1970). Breeder: Barbara S. Fournier. Owner: Terry Leith. By Ch. Bethway's Tony x Ch. Bethway's Scarlet.
Triscuit's Tuffet UD, Breeder: Terry Leith. Owner: Nancy Parker. By Newry's My John Anderson x Bethway's Triscuit CDX.

1968   **Triscuit's Tom-Tom CD** (CDX, 1970). Breeder: Terry Leith. Owner: Nancy Parker. By Newry's My John Anderson x Bethway's Triscuit CDX.

1971   **Wendover Talent CDX** (UD 1975). Breeder: Mrs. S.C. Mallory. Owner: Nancy Parker. By Ch. Wendover Foxhunter x Ickworth Moonlight.

1975   **Kinsprit Token CDX** Breeder: Ellen B. Kennelly. Owner: Nancy Parker. By Ch. Castle Point Iguana x Nanfan Nutshell.

1977   **Ch. New Garden Eadith CD** (CDX 1977; UD 1979). Breeder: John Beeler. Owner: Mary D. Fine. By Wymbur Cantata x Castle Point Ely.

1979   **Tylwyth Red Darby CD.** Breeder/Owner: Mary D. Fine. By Ch. Badgewood Monty Collins x Ch. New Garden Eadith UD.
New Garden Swithun CD (CDX 1981). Breeder: John Beeler. Owner: Barbara A. Runquist. By Wymbur Cantata x Castle Point Ely.
Terolin Tara CD (CDX 1982). Breeder: Janis Levanthal. Owner: Nancy Parker. By Ickworth Blacksmith x Osmor Trefil.

Figure 245:
River Bend Tory doing the broad jump exercise.

1980 **Hot Shot CD.** Breeder: Barbara S. Fournier. Owners: Eric and Katharine Bjorklund. By Ch. Bethway's Aramis x Bethway's Chatterbox.

1982 **Ch. Castle Point Mint CD** (CDX 1982; UD 1983). Breeder: Mrs. Stevens Baird. Owner: Mary D. Fine. By Ch. Hatchwood's Creme de Menthe of Cracknor x Wicket of Castle Point.
Castle Point Bark CD. Breeder: Mrs. Stevens Baird. Owner: Barbara A. Runquist. By Castle Point Attila x Maxwell's Betsy Ross.

1983 **Anderscroft Red Rum CD.** Breeder: Jane Anderson. Owner: Sheila Foran. By Ch. Bethway's Joshua x Anderscroft Ruffian.

1984 **Anderscroft Foolish Pleasure CD,** Breeder: Jane Anderson. Owner: Sheila Foran. By Ch. Elve Pure Magic x Anderscroft Ruffian.
Parcott's New Garden Dunstan CD. Breeder: Patricia Adams Lent. Owner: Anne Beeler. By Annursnac Slipper x Branchwood's Autumn.
Terolin's Trinket of CJ CD. Breeder: Carolyn and James Pyle. Owner: Nancy Parker. By Night Hawk of CJ x Aidelweiss of CJ.
Turkhill's Black Top CD. Breeder: Hildegarde Slocum. Owners: Joan Eckert, John Wood, and Nancy Marsman. By Ch. Elve Pure Magic x Ch. Ragus Brown Smudge.
Ch. Trowsnest's Kinsprit Corncob CD. Breeder: Ellen B. Kennelly. Owner: Marjory P. Trowbridge. By Ch. Hatchwood's Creme de Menthe of Cracknor x Ch. Nanfan Cornflower.
Tylwyth Just Chelsea CD (CDX 1985; UD 1986). Breeder/Owner: Mary D. Fine. By Ch. Badgewood Sir Scuff x Castle Point Mint UD.

Figure 246:
Wendover Talent UD competing in Scent Relay Racing.

1986   **Ch. Sage's Solomon Seal CD** (CDX 1988). Breeder/Owner: Prudence B. Read. By Int. Ch. Daffran Dusty x Jasmine Jones' Grey Sage.

Figure 247:
Tylwyth Just Chelsea UD, Can. CDX by Ch. Badgewood Sir Scuff x Ch. Castle Point Mint UD. Chelsea earned her UD at 18 months and currently holds eight titles, five acquired within one year.

13

ABOVE AND BELOW GROUND

THE NORFOLK
AS A WORKING TERRIER

The word *terrier* comes from the Latin *terra*, meaning earth. Norfolk Terriers (drop ear Norwich) were originally bred as ratters and stable dogs, small enough and game enough to enter the den of a fox and bolt the quarry. Furthermore, these little dogs could be carried on horseback, in saddlebags, or in baskets to get them to the spot where needed. Early breeders fashioned this small, short-legged terrier to have plenty of pluck with the hounds as well as for rat catching.

Figure 248: May Marshall, Colonsay Kennel manager, with hunting "terriers" and quarry.

F. Warner Hill wrote in *The Field*, in 1964, that during World War II men could not be spared to kill rats that infested the corn ricks of English farms:

> So in Norfolk they called the Norwich terrier owners, and their dogs saw to it that not a rat escaped. Many show dogs owned by Miss [Marion Shelia Scott] Macfie of the Colonsay prefix put up fantastic rat-killing records. Guts and a good "bite" were the essentials.

WORKING TERRIER TRIALS
Linda Bell, McDonald, Tennessee

There are two ways an owner can learn whether his terrier possesses natural hunting instincts. One is to take his dog

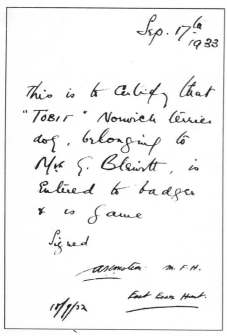

Sep. 17th
1933

This is to certify that
"Tobit" Norwich terrier
dog, belonging to
Mrs G. Blewitt, is
Entered to badger
& is game

Signed

_____ M. F. H.

East Essex Hunt.

18/9/32

Figure 249:
Tobit's Working
Certificate,
September 17,
1933.

Figure 250:
Norfolk ready to
enter the earth,
NNTC Trial, 1986.
Photo G. Siner.

afield to find small vermin. But not eve-ry owner has access to hunting sites—and not every owner enjoys bloodshed, even of vermin. So the American Work-ing Terrier Association (AWTA) has de-veloped a test to determine the hunting instinct of a terrier in a controlled set-ting and without the bloodshed.

Sanctioned AWTA trials are held across the United States and are open to Dachshunds, Jack Russell Terriers, Glen of Imal Terriers, and any AKC recog-nized Terrier Group member able to fit into a nine-inch earth (hole). There are three classes that untitled dogs may en-ter. The Novice class is for inexperi-enced dogs, and is divided into the "A" class for dogs up to one year of age and the "B" class for those over one year. Once a dog earns a score of 100 in the Novice class, or if he has had considera-ble experience in hunting, he is entered in the Open class. A dog that has earned the Certificate of Gameness (CG) title may then be entered in the op-tional Certificate class to compete for its breed's highest score honors.

The Novice earth is much simpler that the Open earth. It is constructed by digging one trench ten feet long and nine inches deep, with one 90 degree corner (Figure 251A-B). It is then lined on the top and sides with boards, but its "floor" is left natural to mimic a real tunnel. The floor is scented with a mixture of rat droppings and water before the liner is set in, and the entrance is re-scented after every five dogs. At the far end of the tunnel, away from where the dog enters, is a section for two male rats. They are caged and further protected from the dogs by iron bars. There is a trap door for the judge to observe the dog working, and from which the dog is removed after his turn is over.

The judge gives a command to each han-dler, one at a time, to release his dog from a des-ignated position about six feet from the en-

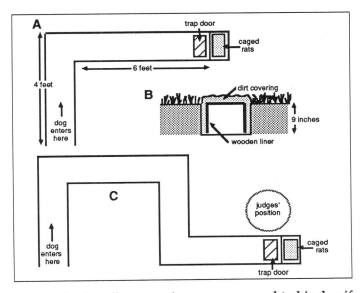

Figure 251:
(A) **Novice earth.**

(B) **Dog's view of earth.**

(C) **Open earth.**

trance. The handler may give one command to his dog if he wishes, and the dog has one minute to get to the rats. In the Novice class the dog may leave and re-enter the earth, but once he reaches the rats he must stay and "work" for 30 seconds. Barking, crying, digging, biting the bars, or any other attempts to get at the rats counts as working. ("Plus scores" are given to those who bark or cry, because in a real working situation a vocal dog is easier to find than a quiet one, thus making it easier to extracate dog or vermin.) A score of 100 is given a dog who reaches the rats within 60 seconds and works for 30 seconds. Four placements are given in the Novice class. Any dogs scoring 100 are eligible to enter the Open class.

Figure 252:
Norfolk reaches the quarry.
Photo G. Siner.

The Open class earth is 30 feet long and has three 90 degree turns (Figure 251C). The dog is allowed 30 seconds to reach the rats (7 to 15 seconds is common). Upon reaching the quarry the dog must work for a full minute. A score of 100 in this class earns a Certificate of Gameness. The Certificate class may use the Open class earth or another, more difficult earth, at the trial chairman's discretion. Strict rules about scoring, earth di-

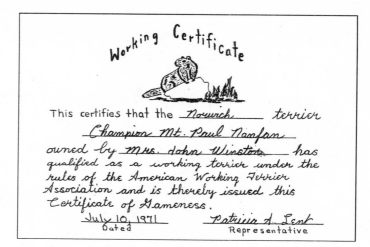

Working Certificate

This certifies that the _Norwich_ terrier _Champion Mt. Paul Nanfan_ owned by _Mrs. John Winston_ has qualified as a working terrier under the rules of the American Working Terrier Association and is thereby issued this Certificate of Gameness.

July 10, 1971
Dated

Patricia A. Lent
Representative

Figure 253: American Working Terrier Association Working Certificate.

mensions, and protection of the rats are outlines in the Trial Rules handbook.

Working trials are not a spectator sport, since only the judge can see the action. But there is excitement in hearing the barking of several enthusiastic dogs hard at "work" and enormous pride in having an entry that places or earns a certificate.

CERTIFICATE HOLDERS

The first Working Terrier Trial was held in 1971. At the second trial, held that same year, Anne Winston's Norwich Terrier Ch. Mt. Paul Nanfan became the first drop ear to earn a Certificate of Gameness. Here is a record of breed certificate holders through 1987:

Year	Dog	Breeder/Owner
1971	Ch. Mt. Paul Nanfan (b.) CG (Tar Heels High Trump x Ch. Nanfan Naiad)	Breeder/Owner: Anne Winston
1972	Nanfan Newsprint (d.) CG Ch. Nanfan Hoppocket x Nanfan Needle)	Breeder: Joy Tayor Owner: James Scharnberg
1979	Ch. Castle Point Indigo (b.) (Nanfan Terrapin x Castle Point Withers)	Breeder: Mary Baird Owner: Doris McGee
1979	Ch. Mt. Paul Viking (d.) CG (Ch. Ickworth Redfox Phillip x Ch. Mt. Paul Tulip)	Breeder: Anne Wins Owner: Doris McGee

1979	Branchwood Autumn Color (b.) WC (Ch. Bethway's Jack x Ch. Bethway's Lilac)	Breeder: Garth Gillan Owner: R.L. Galloway
1979	Branchwood Black-Eyed Susan (b.) WC (Ch. Bethway's Jack x Ch. Bethway's Lilac)	Breeder/Owner: Garth Gillan
1979	Ch. Bethway's Lilac (b.) WC (Ch. Nanfan Ninepin x Bethway's Lilly)	Breeder: Barbara Fournier Owner: Garth Gillan
1979	Ch. Bethway's Jack (d.) WC (Ch. Bethway's Aramis x Ch. Bethway's The Dutchess)	Breeder: Barbara Fournier Owner: Garth Gillan
1980	Annursnac Slipper (b.) CG (Ch. Castle Point Iguana x Annursnac Schnitzel)	Breeder: P. Jewell Owners: P. Lent and R. Galloway
1980	Dolly (b.) CG (Particulars not available)	Owner: William Bakewell
1987	Ch. Castle Point Mint (b.) CG, Am. Can. UD (Ch. Hatchwoods Creme de Menthe x Wicket of Castle Point)	Breeder: Mary Baird Owner: Mary Fine
1987	Ch. Tylwyth Just Chelsea (b.) CG, Am. Can. UD (Ch. Badgewood Sir Scruff x Castle Point Mink)	Breeder/Owner: Mary Fine
1987	Ch. Allright Magic Lamp (d.) CG (Ger. Ch. Allright Huckleberry Finn x Ch. Chidley Magic Carpet)	Breeder: Frauke Hinsch Owner: Joan Read

CG: Certificate of Gameness. Caged game, artificial earth.
WC: Working Certificate. Natural earth.
HC: Hunting Certificate. Above ground, live quarry.

GOTOGROUND TRAINING

Signs of a Good Worker
J. C. Bristow-Noble, **Working Terriers**
By the time a puppy is 12 weeks of age an opinion can be formed as to the kind of dog it is going to make. At this age puppies of the right sort will kill full-grown rats and go to

ground if allowed the opportunity. Indeed, if a 12-week puppy will not kill a rat, the chances are that it will never be more than a third-rate worker. Another sign that a puppy will not turn out as well as desired is timidity — bolting on the appearance of strange people and dogs, and shying and barking at different objects. I have never known a puppy that did these things to make a really good worker. The satisfactory puppy is as a rule, little trouble, his work coming to him almost as naturally as a duckling takes to water. Often it is neither playful nor quarrelsome, but singularly quiet. People will refer to such a puppy as an "old-fashioned sort." Its little head seems as full of good sense as it will hold.

Figure 254: Ch. Yarrow's Jasmine with her first rat at three and a half months. *Photo F. Corman.*

One of the first lessons it must be taught is obedience—to keep at heel and remain where told. A dog that will not obey is a nuisance and a continual source of anxiety. Next it must be taken out as much as possible amongst poultry, sheep, cattle, and vehicle traffic. It will soon learn to avoid motor-cars and not to interfere with domesticated stock. When it has thoroughly grasped its duties in these respects its more serious schooling may begin.

Working-Puppy Training
Carolyn Pyle, Freeville, New York

Very young Norfolk puppies—five weeks and up—can start their "field" training right in the house! To begin, cut doorways in the opposite ends of a cardboard box and lay it on the floor, bottom side up. Pups will use this fascinating "toy" to play "in-and-out" and will thus become accustomed to dark spaces and small openings.

A galvanized stove pipe eight to ten inches in diameter can be hidden behind a couch, and additional tunnels can be built by taping cardboard boxes together. Old socks with knots in them can be left in the cage of pet rats and mice until they've thoroughly absorbed the scent of the rodents. Then these can be used as toys for the puppies, who will play at "killing" them.

At eight to twelve weeks, as pups get stronger and are outside more, you can add to your backyard:

1. Another galvanized stove pipe
2. A 10-inch by 8-inch transit sewer, or drainage, pipe
3. An underground tunnel liner

Pups will play together along with their elders, running in and out of the tunnels.

Be sure that all tunnels have daylight at the end so that puppies will not feel trapped and become scared. They must know they can get out easily. After all, no smart little Norfolk is going to go into a hole it knows it can't get out of. That's survival!

If you live in an area where you can hunt your adult Norfolks, take the puppies along to romp in the woods and fields. As the adults dig up mice, investigate woodpiles, fallen trees, and woodchuck dens, the pups will follow right along, sniffing, digging, getting excited, and helping the adult dogs to "hunt." Always start pups with experienced adults. It's the easiest way to train youngsters, and they will feel safe with Mom and Pop, and other adult Norfolks telling them what to do.

Before teaching your Norfolk to hunt and kill unwanted varmints, decide on two different commands. A command to hunt and kill ("Sic 'em! or "Get it!") given in a high, excited voice is to be used *only* when you want the dog to hunt seriously. A command to be used around small household animals, such as tiny kittens,

Figure 255: **Baby Norfolk and "quarry" meet at an early age.**

hamsters, gerbils, and rabbits, should be delivered in a firm, low, quiet voice. Teaching your puppies "Be good" or "Be gentle" is important from the very beginning if they are to be socialized with your other household "critters." Once in a while, a sharp rap on the hindquarters and a loud "No!" may be necessary if the youngster shows any

aggressive signs while under the gentle command. Continue using the two different commands for the two

Figure 256:
Ch. Nanfan Nine-ty digging in the field, 1972.
Photo © Sally Anne Thompson.

types of behavior throughout your dog's life. And remember to reward each type of correct behavior with praise and love. Most Norfolk have enough common sense to learn the difference between commands without difficulty.

Keeping one or two adult pet rats that have been handled a lot is a good way to teach your pups to follow a rat scent. First the rat is allowed to go through a tunnel, leaving a trail. It is then put into a small cage that fits the end of the tunnel and the pups are turned loose to enter the tunnel and follow the scent. They will "work" or worry their quarry by barking, growling, digging, and so on. In this way they learn to go to ground and work their prey without harm coming to anyone. This is good training procedure for people who do not want their Norfolk to kill anything, ever. Furthermore this behavior is all that is required to compete in American Working Terrier Association (AWTA) trials and earn a Certificate of Gameness.

If you allow your Norfolk to hunt "for real," make sure they have all their vaccinations, including rabies and leptospirosis.

Notes from a Working-Terrier Seminar
Linda Plummer, Warrenton, Virginia

In 1983 Burt Gripton, a noted canine expert, on a visit to the United States from England expressed the following criteria for working terriers:

1. EYES: Should be dark so as not to be seen by quarry at night, and small, not big and bulging. Bulging eyes usually mean an erratic personality and "blind courage."
2. FEET: Liked to see "fox-footed" terriers, on their toes, because they were better climbers.

3. TAILS: Complained about too-short tails, and liked to see a terrier with enough length of tail to grasp in hand with some left over.

4. FRONTS: Very particular about fronts, and emphasized straight front legs. Frowned on "Queen Anne" legs and "Chippendale" fronts. Stressed that a dog without a straight front or that was out-at-the-elbows would be greatly hindered in going to ground.

5. REARS: Called for good angulation, with short hocks. Especially looked for well-muscled hindquarters.

6. COATS: Must have definite undercoat, with no skin showing underneath.

7. DEWCLAWS: Was emphatic about not removing front dewclaws, because terriers needed these for digging.

8. EARS: Preferred drop ears to prick because the drop-eared dog would not get an earful of dirt when going to ground.

9. BODY: Liked to see a well-balanced dog. Strongly emphasized that the chest should be small enough to be spanned by two hands behind the shoulder blades.

10. TEMERAMENT: Disliked a boisterous, aggressive temperament because it usually indicates a lack of intelligence. Liked to see a terrier with plenty of spunk and "pluck" but sensible enough to think first, and then courage enough to get the job done. Example: If an intelligent terrier cannot corner a fox in an earth, it will lie across the opening so that the fox can only smell the dog and not the hunters behind the dog. (Foxes are not afraid of dogs, but they are afraid of people.) This way the fox would smell only the dog and would bolt.

GAME BOOK

Ratting

RAT-PITS

Of all [gambling] sports which have been made illegal, I only regret the passing of rat-pits. I hate rats and anyhow their end was extremely sudden.

Dogs [that have] worked in the rat-pit required a rather specialized technique. And some of the results were astounding. The main thing was to have a dog which could kill rats more quickly than its rivals. As proof of the pudding, a specific number of rats would be loosed in the rat-pit. This was the same pit which was used for cockfighting and similar forms of entertainment. It was a square pit, bits of metal had to be nailed at the top of the corners because the rats were quite capable of climbing up these if not prevented.

A match would be made up between two or more dogs to decide which was the more efficient at vermin destruction. Sometimes the match would be to decide

Figure 257:
**An early
English rat pit.**
*Drawing from
The Field
magazine.*

which dog could kill the most rats in a specified time and sometimes which could kill a specified number in the shortest time. This way was the most popular. When all was ready, the stakes paid up and the bets made, the rats were turned into the pit and the first dog brought along. He was held where he would see the quarry, his handler waited for a favourable opportunity when the rats were placed as he wanted them, and dropped the dog into the pit. The match had now begun and the time-keeper started taking the time. If the pit was square the rats would bunch in a corner but if it was round they

Figure 258:
**French ratting—
gamblers place a
rat under one of
six pots and then
time the dog to
find and kill it.**
*From The Field
magazine.*

would form into smaller groups, one way suiting some dogs and the other way suiting the rest. The moment the dog touched the pit he started killing rats. He did not bother to pick them up and shake them but just gave each one a hard bite and left him for the next. The dog which liked the square pit would slip quietly up to the bunch in the corner and begin to pick off the nearest rats to him. Any which tried to break from the bunch were nipped as they passed and he would not have much running about to do, if he was clever, until all but a few were killed. He would work rather like a sheepdog keeping a flock bunched to be brought out singly for dipping. If the pit was round, the dog would get the rats on the

Figure 259:
**Tiny Tim of
Biffin, 1938.**
*llustration by Joan
Shields.*

move and remain more or less where he was, just picking them off as they passed. This continued until the last rat was caught, when the dog was picked up, which was noted by the timekeeper as the end of the performance for that dog.

Sometimes in the event of any rats remaining alive after the dog had been picked up, that dog was disqualified. At others he merely had to be put back in the pit, where he was re-timed until he had disposed of his quarry. Occasionally it would be stipulated that the dog could only have one bite at any rat and and that if he touched him after once putting him down he lost the match.

That was how the rats were actually killed when a dog was put in the pit with them, and obviously a great many rats would be needed for a match since these specialist dogs could kill at a simply phenomenal rate. For instance, on May 15th, 1985, Billy, a very famous dog of his time, was matched to kill 100 rats at the cockpit in Tufton Street in twelve minutes for £20 and bets. The floor of the pit was whitened, to give him every chance, and he had stopped the last one kicking within 7 minutes 30 seconds.

In addition to straight matches for which dog could kill a certain quantity of rats quickest, irrespective of the weight of the dog, it was common to have handicaps based on weight. The champion Billy, who was white but for a patched head, weighed 27 lbs. As time went on, however, rats became difficult to obtain in such numbers, handicaps were arranged so that the heavier the dog was the more rats he had to kill. Various handicaps were set ranging from one rat being added to a dog's quota for every 3 lbs. additional weight over his rival to a rat for every pound. This was perhaps the favourite, and it was frequent to arrange a handicap where each dog had to kill as many rats as there were pounds in his weight, the dog disposing of his quota the quickest being the winner. For instance, a ten pound dog would only have to kill ten rats. This put a premium on small dogs and breeds that developed specially for this sport. The little smooth black-and-tan terriers of Manchester and the rough Yorkshire terriers were particularly good for this sport. That dogs so small were game enough to kill large rats at all surprises me. That they could kill 20 in less than 3 minutes seems nothing short of miraculous.

Phil Drabble (Adapted)
From Brian Vesey-Fitzgerald,
The Book of the Dog (Borden, 1948)

MUFF ON RATS

My bitch Muff was an inveterate "sportswoman." All game was worth chasing and catching when possible—rats and rabbits, squirrels and woodchuck—but her finest achievement was when she was 17 years old. One day she found that the old chicken run was being dug up, and Oh! Joy! the rats were being dug out! Muff was in her element. First three large rats leapt out, and she quickly stunned them and then went back and finished them off. Her cup was full when at the end of 20 minutes she had accounted for 18 rats!

Sylvia Warren
River Bend, Dover, Massachusetts

Snakes

APPLE AND THE SERPENTS

Wendover Apple would like to go on record as a snake-killing Norfolk. Her first claim to the title came as we walked in the 30-acre field behind our house, where groundhogs, squirrels, and other terrier game are plentiful. Suddenly she came to a "point." The next second she had a snake in the middle, gave it a vicious shake, and dropped it with a delighted expression on her face. During the next two days she accounted for two adults and six young from that nest. After killing one, she would sit patiently at a distance waiting for another to emerge from the hole.

One year, although she was heavy in whelp, the same performance was repeated; and this spring she has already located two holes which she is confident are snake nests and which, when the weather gets warm enough, will provide her with good hunting. I might add that her four Norfolk companions show absolutely no interest in Apple's favorite sport.

Priscilla Mallory
Mendham, New Jersey

Woodchuck

WOODCHUCK-A-DAY

We took Imp when Mr. Eugene Reynal died in 1940. According to all Reynals, she had distinguished herself at one point in her life by depositing a woodchuck at the front door every day for 30 days. Many thought we were foolish to bring such a spunky old lady to the city, but she took one look at New York and realized at once what she had been missing and led a gay and happy life for three more years.

Mrs. Louis Rey
New York, New York

Raccoons

An old score was settled today when two of my Norfolk Terriers did in a raccoon under the pool house. Two years before this writing, Mt. Paul Hades and his granddaughter, Highburn Calypso, had to be dragged out from under the prefab building after they had waged a loud and unsuccessful battle with what was later

Figure 260: Rabbits from Victor Page's Waveney Valley hunt, 1960.

thought to be a raccoon. The total number of stitches they required has been forgotten, but Hades lost his bottom lip on one side, and they both retained several enduring scars. When similar sounds of combat came from there this morning, we ran for shovels, crowbars, hammer and chisel (in case we had to rip up the floor to get to them), and a stick with which to, hopefully, dispatch the coon—there being no gun in house.

For nearly an hour we peered under the building from all angles—only to get puffs of dust in the eyes and no glimpse of what, from the sounds of things, was a fierce battle in the scant 10 inches of space under the floor beams. The "what ifs" were awful! What if the rocks under there shifted and trapped or crushed one of the terriers? What if, in that cramped and dusty space, the coon managed to get one of the dogs by the throat? We dug at the corner nearest to the fracas, but the building is set on rocks and cement, and headway was negligible. The baying of the terriers and the growls of the coon were making us all frantic, when, to our immense relief, out bolted the raccoon with two dogs snapping and snarling on either side. At this point they were joined by our other terrier, Cosy Pinch, who was hopefully in whelp to Ch. Nanfan Terrapin and had therefore been removed from the battle under the building. Damages: one nicked nose, one bitten tongue. A game and clever bit of teamwork, although a bit harrowing for the audience! Hades is now 11 years old, but, as this account suggests, he is still going strong and bringing his get up as true down-to-earth terriers!

Susan M. Ely
Bernardsville, New Jersey

Bear Fact

During the 1920s Dr. Thomas Clark Hinkle, a prolific zoological author, dedicated a book on Kodiak bears to "Woof" his intrepid Jones Terrier companion. Hinkle so honored his canine friend because, in his own words:

> This little fellow was the only dog I could find that was small enough and game enough, and smart enough to enter a Kodiak's den, wake the biggest and grouchiest bear in the world and bring him out alive.

Deer

Ch. Mt. Paul Anderson not only has bolted foxes, but once when I was run by an irate doe protecting her fawn, he grabbed her by the muzzle when she struck at me and hung on as she ran through the woods, swinging her head back and forth. The dog ended up with some broken ribs after he was swung against a tree.

Anne Winston
Gladstone, New Jersey

Foxes

A BOLTED FOX—THURSDAY, 21ST DECEMBER, 1933

The Runnymede [Unionville, Pennsylvania] coverts were drawn blank on Thursday the 21st, and it isn't often that happens, but such was the case. Therefore, a hurry call was sent to the kennels for a brace of Mrs. Plunkett Stewart's Jones Terriers, as the Master was anxious to see whether our artificial earth was holding a fox. Both terriers were put into the one end of the drain, and immediately the fun began. Such a tow-row one never heard, then presently the white tag of a fox's brush appeared from the other end of the pipe, then the forequarters of a fox. Charlie Smith couldn't stand the strain any longer, he took hold of Charles James Fox's hind legs, gave a tremendous pull, and out came fox and terrier together, their jaws locked in one long and continuous snarling embrace. When they struck the ground, both let go and away went Reyard up over the hill with both terriers yapping at his heels.

J. Stanley Reeve,
Further Foxhunting Recollections

CH. FARNDON RED DOG M.F.H.

Farndog Red Dog, whelped in 1933 by Toodleum 5 x Too Fresh, was the first prick ear Norwich dog champion. He carried the black and tan gene, was a prolific sire, and as a result had a significant influence on both Norwich and Norfolk black and tans of today. In a letter from his owner, W.E. West, to the breed club secretary (1934), Red Dog's prowess at working fox is enthusiastically described:

> On last Dec. 1, the Pytchley Hounds met at Clipston—near here—and when the Missus and Monica came home from hunting, they said the hounds had marked a fox to ground in a small land drain not far away and had left him. I at once sent my groom back with Monica [West's little daughter] to securely stop him in for the night. Next morning, Sunday, we set off with part of the pack to try to get some of the younger ones entered (a nice day for the job it was, teeming with rain and had done so all night). When we arrived there we found the fox had nearly gnawed through the stakes during the night which stopped him in. I had learned from an old farm hand who laid the drain 50 years ago, that it was a straight one and so I decided to put my old dog Toodleum in first on a line so I could get him out for the others to have a go. He met him almost immediately and I had a job getting him out without breaking the line. I next put Red Dog to him who has had some experience, but this time he fairly surpassed himself. He was bursting to

get in and after he disappeared all was silent for some minutes when suddenly there was a tremendous scrap on, but a very long way off. I knew he couldn't stay all day as he only just fitted the drain and couldn't turn, so that he would be bound to come out for air. After we got him out we put several of the bitches to the fox who all did remarkably well. I had hoped to put the puppies to him, but it was such a small drain and came to a dead end and was running with water that I decided not to risk them on their first effort although they were keen to have a go.

We afterwards but Red Dog in again on a thin line (binder twine) and I could feel and hear him battling with the "varmint" and he showed very visible signs of it on his return. How far do you think he went into the pitch black drain and then tackled his foe? You couldn't guess. Of course, it is no record for hunt terriers but for our breed, I think it is. We measured it afterwards and found that it was 31 yards (95 feet) and that Red Dog had traveled up this wet, pitchblack drain and tackled at the end of it. I have spoken to several hunting people since and they all think it is a very creditable performance.

W. E. West
Market Harborough, England

"THE LITTLE DOGS"

I first started Fox hunting about 1939 while still in High school. I bought a Black and Tan hound pup from a local foxhunter and trained her myself. I lived at that time in Huntington County (South Central Pennsylvania). All hunting was done on foot with the intention of shooting the fox ahead of the hound or hounds at various crossings. The usual procedure is to go out early in the morning and let the hounds "cold trail" to rout out a fox. If you aren't familiar with this term it means to follow a fox track where he has traveled the previous night.

The Red Fox will usually run all day ahead of the hounds, but the Gray Fox will very often go to ground or will be "holed up" at the very beginning.

In Huntington County there are large open patches of rocks near the tops of the mountains where the Gray Foxes would stay during the day. When my hound cold-trailed one to his sleeping quarters I would leave my brother to stand watch while I went for Mr. Clayton who had a pair of terriers, "Mike" and "Slim." Mike, the older of the two and the more experienced was a cross between a small Foxterrier and Manchester, and Slim was nearly all Manchester.

About the same time there were two Snyder brothers and a son-in-law who were so situated that they could hunt all winter and their annual kill was from 75 to 100 foxes and about 75% were killed when the terriers bolted them. They called them "The little dogs."

My brother and I decided we would like to have a terrier of our own but we soon discovered that it was easier said than done. The good ones just weren't for sale and since they were all crossbreds there weren't many good ones. We first bought a one-year-old male from Mr. Clayton and he would have turned out just right except for one thing. He was for some reason afraid of those rocks and he didn't want to go near them. He would go into a groundhog hole very eagerly and would kill any cat that he could catch but as a fox dog he was useless.

Anther try was a male pup from a pair of dogs that were top notch. They were small Foxterriers and were real terrors when they went after a fox. This pup would have been just like his parents except that he grew too much! As a fighter he was something to watch. If we helped him dig he would reach in, take a groundhog by the face and pull him out and quickly kill him.

After the war and several years in school I decided to try again. I was now living in Williamsport but since there weren't any terriers used for foxes in this area I took a trip to Huntingdon County and bought a small one-year-old bitch that looked promising. That Fall she pulled five opossums out of a groundhog hole one at a time and killed them. I also had her along at a kill ahead of the hounds and she really went at the fox and wouldn't let go. Needless to say I was delighted with her, but sad to say I learned a lesson I shall never forget. I neglected getting her shots right away and she contracted distemper and died.

I next tried a Toy Manchester pup but she turned out to be so fragile, and too much of a family pet to use.

In the meantime I started a study of the Breed Standards of various terriers with hopes of selecting a breed that would be just right without crossing for size, etc. I finally wrote to Dog World magazine describing the type of dog I wanted and they recommended a Norwich.

As for qualifications, I think the two most important are size and temperament, and a very close third is conformation. First a terrier has to be able to get to a fox and a fox can get into a surprisingly small space. The rule that a hunt terrier should be spanned by a large man's hands is a good one provided the hands aren't too large! A fox minus long hair is a very slim animal. Last winter I shot a very large Gray fox and it measured 14" circumference behind the shoulders or 4 1/2" diameter. If the dog is too large or has to dig to get to the fox you usually have to dig both dog and fox out.

As for temperament and conformation a terrier must have the desire to fight and have the strength to punish a fox to the extent that his den becomes a very uncomfortable place to stay.

I have high hopes for the Norwich to fill all qualifications in addition to having a heavy coat to withstand our cold winters.

I believe the Norwich is the only terrier in this country that is small enough to be a practical working terrier and still be within the weight standards for show.

Donald W. Fleming (Adapted),
Letter, January 8, 1961
Williamsport, Pennsylvania

RACING

Go-to-ground competitions are not designed for spectators, as all the real action occurs in the earth, and only the judge is the observer. However, many terrier trials end the competition with flat racing and hurdle racing, which are a great spectator sport as well as fun for the dogs. Whereas many dogs will not enter an earth at their first few trials, and some will never attempt it, most will race or chase after a fox tail or lure on a string. So racing is just plain fun, as the following accounts illustrate.

Races in Illinois

It was probably in the November '71 issue [of *Norwich Terrier News*] that I read about the Norwich Terrier races held at English fox hunts. This caught my fancy because I have long been interested in coursing live on farmland and, along with our own Jones, can field almost a dozen belonging to local friends. None of us ride to hounds, but we all enjoy a Sunday picnic luncheon and some activity thereafter.

The English, it seems, drag a fox tail over a 100-yard course by attaching the other end of a line to the tireless rim of the back wheel of a bicycle that is stationary on its stand. The person who winds the bicycle's pedal is stationed at the finishing slot and can see the course of the race and control the speed of the quarry, which, in our case, is a plastic mouse that squeaks when squeezed. I think anything would do, so long as the person at the starting gate can attract the contestants' attention to it just before the gate is dropped. It is, of course, necessary to have someone operate the gate upon signal from the "motorman" at the finish end of the course. A flag will do, but if you've always wanted an excuse for owning a walkie-talkie set, that's fine too.

The important discovery we've made is to have all owners and spectators behind the finish line. It is becoming more and more evident that many dogs start off trying to catch the quarry but end up trying to be the first to reach the loving arms of "Mama." Our Jolly Good is one of the few who would rather chase the plastic mouse, and has even been known to humiliate his master by getting ahead of it and then stopping until it catches up. But that's because he lives here, knows the mouse and course, and has no feeling of insecurity. Also he is a showoff.

Before the race contestants are "auctioned off" to the highest bidder, who can, of course, sell shares back to others who have a similar faith in their choice of a winner. This "Calcutta" type of wagering is not necessary, but it certainly livens up the picnic luncheon. To date, none of the nine Lake Forest entrants that may be regularly counted upon to compete has established himself or herself as a consistent champ.

With nine dogs, we run three at a time in three heats; then the winners of each heat run a final race. The 100-yard track is about 20 feet wide and is created by clearing a swath in the pasture with a rotary mower. The "finish line" is a slot in a bank of hay bales through which the lure is drawn. Originally we feared some independent, uncooperative competitor might live up to its terrier character and leave the course, but this has never happened. The pack instinct seems to dominate.

F. Newell Childs
Lake Forest, Illinois

Racing Equipment

The materials needed for setting up a race course are simple to construct or easy to obtain. Both the starting box and the racing reel can be conveniently transported and stored. After the apparatus has been assembled, go through a few trial runs to make sure everything works.

Figure 261:
The starting box can be built out of plywood and wire.

MATERIALS CHECK LIST:

1. Lawn of about 50 yards' length
2. No-gear bicycle with wide-rimmed tires
3. Length of 1/2 inch copper tubing to fit into space from the front wheel fork to top of tireless rear wheel.
4. 100 yards of strong, narrow cord for decoy string
5. 2" X 10" block of wood
6. Portion of rubber tire
7. Electrical tape
8. Tennis ball
9. Fur lure and scent (e.g., a piece of fake fur or raccoon tail dipped in an attractively "smelly" substance)
10. In front of the lure apparatus, six hay bales banked with a finish-line opening wide enough for one dog at a time to dash through

INSTRUCTIONS:
1. Remove the rubber tire from the rear wheel of the bicycle you are going to use, leaving just the hollow rim of the wheel.
2. Turn the bicycle upside down and secure its han-

dlebars to its seat with wire.

3. Cut a piece of copper tubing or 1-inch pipe to fit the distance from the front of the empty front-wheel fork to the top of the tireless rear wheel. The string attached to the lure will run through this to the flared mouth of the feeding tube.

5. Position a wedge of 2" X 10" wood with a 1" circular hole drilled to accommodate the decoy string into the empty front-wheel fork. Secure wood block with strong electrical tape or wire.

6. Fit the copper tubing into the hole in wood block.

7. Fit the opposite end of the copper tubing into the rear-wheel cavity at the 11 o'clock position.

8. Leave 1/2" well clearance for cord, and cover the end of feed tube with a portion of the removed rubber tire. Tape wire to tubing with strong electrical tape. (This acts as a guide to avoid any backlash.)

9. Attach and wind the cord onto the rear wheel. Thread the cord through the "mouth" of the copper tube. Anchor a tennis ball as a stopper, leaving

Figure 262:
A no-gear bicycle with wide-rimmed wheels, turned upside down, is the mechanical device that propels the lure for racing.
Photo J. Wood.

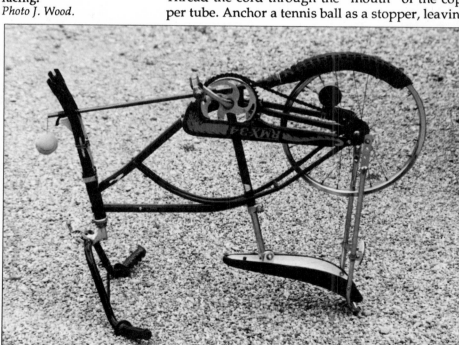

enough cord to attach to the lure.

10. For the starting box, construct a bottomless, rectangular crate out of plywood and wire. Divide the interior into small compartments so that up to four dogs can run at a time. The top of the starting box is hinged so each dog can be placed in a separate compartment. The front wood-framed wire flap of the starting box extends across the stalls and is attached to a lever, allowing all dogs to be released at the same time when the wire flap is raised.

Figure 263: Detail of the feed tube showing the cord, rubber strip, and copper tubing in place in the rear-wheel cavity of the bicycle. *Photo J. Wood.*

Fig. 264: **River Bend Derry.** *Photo © Constance S. Larrabeee.*

14

PHOTOGRAPHY, CHARACTER, AND TRAITS

PHOTOGRAPHING YOUR NORFOLK
Constance S. Larrabee, King's Prevention,
Chestertown, Maryland

Norfolk Terriers are enchanting to photograph. These small sporting terriers, alert and friendly, face the camera with confidence. Spring is the perfect time for photographs. The light is crisp, the dogs and their photographer enjoy the moderate temperatures, and, an important point, coats should be in good condition.

High noon with its deep shadows should be avoided. The light is usually good before 11 a.m. and after 3 p.m. Spare the film and choose a fast exposure. Action shots are revealing as to movement in young animals. Simple backgrounds are best. Be careful that the ears do not fade into the background and that feet do not sink into the grass. (Cut the lawn extra short that day.)

In photographing your new champion, it takes patience and probably more than one person. First, know the Standard and your dog. The dog should stand well on all four feet. The tail need not be at "high mast" but should fit the description, carriage, and not be excessively gay. Neither should it be between his legs! The ears should not be pressed back but, if possible, well forward. The mouth preferably closed, and the expression keen and far from bored. Most photographs are taken in profile to show as many of the dog's good points as possible. Movement and noise attract a dog's attention. Be ready to click the shutter. Your champion should pose as a *champion.*

A litter and their dam, a brace, or a team fall into delightful groups. What is more captivating than the loving expression in the eye of a brood bitch at play with her litter. Your photographs will be a great record for you and for the breed.

Figure 265:
(Upper left) **Ch. Max-Well's Lone Ranger, 1984.** *Photo Margaret Miller.*
Figure 266:
(Upper right) **Norfolks on a farm in Maryland, 1970s.** *Photo © Constance S. Larrabee.*
Figure 267:
(Center) **Out for a stoll.**
Figure 268:
(Bottom left) **King's Prevention, 1950s.** *Photo © Constance S. Larrabee.*
Figure 269:
(Lower right) **Puppies belonging to Jim and Carolyn Pyle.** *Photo © C.H. Brown.*

TRADE SECRETS OF A
PROFESSIONAL PHOTOGRAPHER

Sally Anne Thompson, Painswick, Gloucestershire, England

Sally Anne Thompson, one of the best canine photographers in England, and her husband, Ron Willbie, are the remarkable husband-and-wife team that shine in two fields of communica-tio—through their pictures and by the written word. As editors of the English Club's comprehensive quarterly magazine, they see that every member's interest is served. Their own first dog, Nanfan Sage, arrived in 1972, eight years after Sally first photo-graphed the great Nanfan Heckle. Although establishing the Chalkyfield line has been delayed, veterans of the pack enjoy their spirited walks and continue to inspire Sally toward her innovative goals. Summer rallies complete with scaled agility tests, a placement service, a personal collection of salvaged and new photographs, and historic pedigrees and documents post-ed or published by Sally all serve to enrich breed knowledge.

The trouble with photographing Norfolk and Nor-wich Terriers well is that it is very hard work. Our cho-sen breeds are among the most difficult to photograph but a really good picture is worth working for and al-though, like breeding a champion, it *can* really happen by chance you cannot always count on good luck.

I suppose that the first consideration is "what came-ra?" I have always thought that a long-focus lens was my most important piece of equipment, but Mrs. Larra-bee's beautiful photographs taken with a Rolliflex have

Figure 270:
**Sally Anne
Thompson awards
a prize at the
1986 ANTA
Match.**

disproved that. The point is that to fill the frame you have to move in close and then you are likely to get distortio —large head and small hindquarters—and being so close you may also distract the dog. A long lens eliminates this as you can fill the frame while standing farther back. A two-and-a-quarter or 35 mm camera makes no great difference. It all depends on what you are used to and can use quickly.

Although you are probably using colour you may want the pictures to be reproduced in black and white. As Norfolks and Norwich are the same tone as grass in black and white, you must have a contrasting background. A dark background is usually best; shade beneath trees, dark but not shiny bushes, dark wooden walls are all good. Side lighting can help, but most of my pictures are taken with the sun full on the dog from behind me, as I find this the most flattering. With complete back lighting, if the background is very pale it can merge with the furnishings and chest fur of the dog, giving a false impression of lack of substance in the dog.

We have found that Norfolks look their best for photography when still a little short of coat. If your dog grows a heavy coat it will be accentuated if you photograph him when his coat is on the blow and it can make him look stuffy. If your Norfolk flies an ear stick a lump of chewing gum on the end of the flap inside—everything is legal in photography.

Figure 271: "As Norfolks. . . are the same tone as grass in black and white, you must have a contrasting background." Ch. Delladale Wendy by Ch. Salad Burnet of Vicbrita x Delladale Magna. *Photo © Sally Anne Thompson.*

We'll think now about the problems of the "show pose." Pet owners may think that they don't want their dogs in a show position, but we are not talking about stringing him up on a lead or standing on a table. He is going to be standing on the grass—looking like a king— we hope. Don't forget to cut the grass, no daisies. You must now first decide on the best place to take the photograph, keeping in mind the slope of the ground (it must be level or very slightly uphill) and direction of the light and background. Do all this in an atmosphere of calm, not letting friends overexcite the dog with food or rehearse the attractions you are arranging for him. Remember always to have a low camera position on a level with your dog.

In most photographs in black and white the dog is on a lead, which is later retouched out. When I take colour, which cannot easily be retouched, the problem, if we want our subject to appear to be standing free, is how to restrain him while at the same time exciting him enough to keep his tail up and looking alert. Sometimes a thin collar and fine lead can be used to tether the dog to a handy tree or small stake hammered completely into the ground close to and behind him. Some dogs with show training will stand free looking up at their handler. In both cases, having first gotten your dog standing attractively or correctly, you attract him with his favourite quarr —arch enemy, bitch in season (use sparingly), mock mailman, food, unaccustomed face in upstairs window, squeaky toy, car horn, friendly cat, person in bushes. With these kinds of attractions one dog's meat is another dog's poison, so you must find the right one for yours. Do have the attraction in the right place to get the head angle you require and don't let people shout from all directions. Of course you must all react quickly because he may not repeat a good pose many times. It is hard work!

For the most informal or portrait type of picture, where the background plays a more significant part, you can keep a lookout for places that would suit your dog on all your walks or travels. Norfolk and Norwich Terriers look lovely among the natural things of the countryside. Bracken, fallen logs, pine branches, long grass, ploughed field, and autumn leaves all look good with our dogs' size and colour, and a cut tree stump is always a natural place to sit a dog for a picture. If your dogs are taught to "stay" it will make this kind of picture much easier because you will have time to compose your shot and also get that eager look with a thrown stone or noise, without him running off.

Figure 272: "Remember always to have a low camera position on a level with your dog." *Photo © Sally Anne Thompson.*

A bitch with puppies is something special, and it's worth extra trouble to have a lovely picture to remind you of those happy days of sleepless nights and endless tiny meals. The best age for puppies is just before they become too active—about 6 weeks. Younger than this a picture is quite easy but the pups are very babyish; older pups will be more mature but can be quite a handful.

A more advanced lighting technique than a flash on the camera will improve your picture a lot and stop that "blind eye" look. I use two lights, one close to the camera in a two-foot reflector with a baffle in front of the flash tube; this is similar to an umbrella set up. The second light is at half the power, in a smaller reflector, and it lights the background and the subject with direct light from about six feet high from the back.

Choose a place that your bitch will like—a rug on the floor against a plain wall will do, or you can use the whelping box or her bed if it is attractive and clean. I do not like draped sheets or anything too makeshift that will become untidy as you wrestle with the puppies. Make sure that your bitch will stay put, otherwise you haven't a chance. Feed the pups to get them drowsy and then arrange them around their mother, or whoever else is to be in the picture. An "anchor" in the form of a steady adult is extremely helpful. The pups will wake up and for the next hour your helpers (you'll need one for every two pups) will say it can't be done as they dash about. But patience will be rewarded, and as they become genuinely tired you will get the picture. Sometimes puppies can be "hypnotized" by a very stern and forceful command. This only lasts a second but can be useful if you are in a hurry; the rest of the time of course you must talk very sweetly to them, otherwise they might all get upset.

The most common fault I see in photographs is that the dog is too small in the picture. Unless you can get a selected area of the negative enlarged you must order a bigger print than you eventually want and then trim it down. Usually a slightly different tilt helps, so study your print carefully and be brave enough to cut off all the background that is not important to the picture. You will be surprised by the improvement.

I'll end with a confession. In my work I can go on

photographing a dog all day without losing my patience. However, my own dogs drive me mad within minutes when they don't do as I want, and unless I get the picture straight away I give up and put the camera away.

— AND FROM THE OTHER HALF
Ron Willbie, Painswick, Gloucestershire, England

Having helped Sally on innumerable assignments I will put in my two penny worth of advice, mainly directed to those willing or unwilling helpers. Sally mentions that she does not like voluminous backgrounds when taking bitch and puppies as these may give a fussy look to the result. Also, when the puppies are being constantly put back with mother it is an added complication to see that the background is not disturbed, and if it is, that it is quickly put right. Time is of the essence when setting up these shots as the pups will almost certainly momentarily remain still and a quick photographer may just get a good shot. The chance of this if the helper is straddled across everything readjusting the drapes is very unlikely—keep it as plain as possible. It is necessary to be quick, firm, and kindly when putting pups back; restrain them if need be whilst standing to one side of the set. You must also keep in mind, if flash is being used, that your shadow must not fall on the subject, which means constant checking especially if modeling lights are not being used.

When photographing outside remember that the photographer is in command. Such things as jumping in the air, making noises, or appearing out of the dustbin must be strictly to command. A lot of my work is jumping when Sally says "now!" I well remember standing in a clump of bushes remaining quiet until called, missing the tea that Sally and Joy Taylor were having after finishing the session.

Remember that dogs act dif-

Figure 273: Ron Willbie and Sally Anne Thompson with four of their Norfolks.

ferently to various noises and situations and even your own dogs, that you know intimately, will not necessarily behave in their normal way to a situation that you have created. As a helper you should constantly observe and adjust, bearing in mind that, above all, violent reaction is not wanted. The two rules to observe are keep calm and remain observant. Good Luck!

CHARACTER AND TRAITS

Stance
Alert Norfolks often pose with a front leg off the ground, apparently "pointing" with their bent knee.

Figfure 274: Guestlings Waiki-ki Way by Ch. Gainsay Striking Gold x Guestlings Teatime Tiddles exhibits typical Norfolk stance, Sweden.

Talking, or "Greeting Gargle"
Norfolk puppies start their verbal greetings early. These sound like rolling (guttural) gargles. Such undulating murmur are reserved for human companions, not litter-mates or other dogs. Many Norfolks "talk" to you this way all their lives.

Smiling
This endearing but elusive recessive trait is becoming rare in the breed today. It can vary from a mouth wreathed in smiles to an expression mistaken for a silent snarl. Grinning Norfolks usually curl their lip on only one side, but can be urged to take this action as an expression of happy recognition instead of the usual canine indication of subservience.

Treble Soprano, or "Operatic Bark"
Norfolks from some bloodlines seem to be reaching for E above high C! This vocalizing bark is ear-splitting to some humans and can trigger pack action if the individual is turned out with other unfamiliar dogs. Most Norfolks who have this excited, persistent squeak also have a deeper normal bark that can (and should) be encouraged for the welfare of both dog and master.

"Leather" Nose

"Leather" noses and occasionally "leather" ears are seasonal, with occurrence (usually in winter) most prevalent among the very deep red and hard-coated dogs. The skin on the bridge of the nose gradually goes bare from the nostrils back towards the stop. The exposed skin then turns leathery or shiny, like an extension of the nostrils, and becomes the last place the new coat reappears.

Figure 275: "Leather noses and occasionally leather ears are seasonal."

Doting Dams

Most Norfolks are superior mothers, housekeepers, and "nursery-school" teachers. The dam deserves a quiet, safe, and warm area for her newborns. It often takes a week or more before she will leave the nest unless invited, so be prepared to separate the mother from her whelps so that she can eat, drink, and relieve herself.

After weaning, dams play very roughly to teach their offspring hunting skills. In fact, to the uninitiated it sometimes appears that a dam is determined to hurt her puppies, or, in rural areas, to lose them! Usually brood bitches have a favorite puppy, and often "mother knows best."

Figure 276: Few Norfolks sit squarely.

Hip-sitting

Few Norfolks sit squarely. They prefer a more casual one-hip approach. This informal attitude offers a challenge in the Obedience ring.

Begging and Paw-Waving

Some individuals sit and put their front paws up and play "so big." Some sit with front paws bent down in a nonchalant pose and plead with their eyes. Others, sitting or standing on their hind legs, place their front pads together, then briskly pump their paws up and down. Most Norfolks pick one of the above ways of begging.

Figure 277:
(Left) **Colonsay Gypsy Queen** at three months old, circa 1938.

Figure 278:
(Center) **Mt. Paul Anderson.**

Figure 279:
(Right) **Ch. Daffran Dusty. The "begging" trait is evident for successive generations in Norfolks.**

Figure 280:
Norfolks like larger canine companions.

TV Watching

Many Norfolks are avid TV watchers with a sustained attention span and a preference for sports or nature programs, especially ones with horses, dogs, and birds. Some Norfolk TV viewers race behind the set when a favorite character disappears or is turned off, while others snap at the "star" or try to "catch" the electricity. Others bark at the darkened set to turn it on or race noisily from elsewhere in the house, protesting mightily when the set is turned off.

One Norfolk of our acquaintance, Midge (King's Prevention Belinda), is a TV "addict," with a chair of her own for uninterrupted viewing. When her owner met Midge's grandsire, Ch. Nanfan Ninety, the day of the 1982 Cheltenham Cup, Ninety rejected the color set but not the race. At age 13, he balanced on a kitchen stool in front of an equally ancient black-and-white "telly" for the entire racing card!

"Togetherness"

Norfolks are like peanuts—it's hard to have just one. They also like to live with larger canine companions, preferring those with hunting or working proclivities. They bring joy to a senior dog and in return learn manners by example. Many Norfolks treat big dogs as children treat their teddy bears—they go to sleep together and often are inseparable for years. Norfolks are also particularly good companions for young

Figure 281: **Norfolks are like peanuts—it's hard to have just one.**

children, who prefer a live "teddy bear" to a toy one.

Braving the Elements

Most Norfolks adore water. They trot through the rain, race in the snow, and "skinny dip" in pond, pool, and stream. With only a shake or two the coat that was drenched and dripping is as dry as a rug.

Figure 282: **Most Norfolks adore water.**

Figure 283: **"Water log."** *Photo Roma Baron.*

Figure 284:
Norfolks often exhibit a "talking" trait. Ch. Redriff Sweet Pea, Ch. Guestlings Guess Who, Guestlings Highlight, Ch. Guestlings Waikiki Way and Ch. Redriff Rambling Rose, Sweden.

Figure 285:
The porch railing is an ideal perch to watch for squirrels.

15

MILESTONES, CHAMPIONSHIPS, AND PEDIGREES

SOME MILESTONES

1923 Jones Terriers become fad among fox hunters in Virginia, Pennsylvania, and New York thanks to Louis Reynal, Frederick Warburg, Nancy Harriman Penn-Smith, and Sterling Loop Larrabee.

1930 Mary Stevens Baird buys black and tan drop ear "Aunt" terrier from Mrs. Fagan, later registered.

1932 Breed gains Kennel Club recognition as Norwich Terriers.

1935 Biffin of Beaufin first breed champion, England.

1936 AKC recognizes Norwich Terriers.

1939 Merry of Beaufin first AKC champion.

1940 Colonsay All Kiff first black and tan champion.

1947 Breed Club holds first match, Bedford, New York.

1948 Ch. Cobbler of Boxted wins first Specialty show.

1963 AKC permits ear designation on registration certificates.

1964 England achieves separation. Drop ears recognized as Norfolk Terriers with own club.

1967 Eng. Ch. Colonsay Orderley Dog wins 19 CCs, a record.

Nanfan Nyiad becomes first English American Champion.

1969 Eng. Ch. Ickworth Ready first Group winner.

1970 Ch. Bethway's Ringo first Norwich to win a Group.

1973 Eng. Ch. Ragus Whipcord first black and tan champion.

1974 Ch. Ickworth Nimrod first D.E.Norwich to win a Canadian Championship.

1975 Eng. Ch. Nanfan Sweet Apple wins a Terrier Group.

1976 Canada recognizes Norfolks as a separate breed.

AKC requires ear carriage designation.

1977 Ch. Badgewood the Huntress first bitch to win a Group.

1978 Eng. Am. Ch. El Cid of Tinkinswood wins an all breed Best In Show.

ANTA (American Norfolk Terrier Association) formed.

1979 AKC recognizes drop ear Norwich as Norfolk. Permits Club to submit two standards and change its name while working towards separation.

1986 England adopts optional docking.

1988 Norway bans docking as of July.

1989 Sweden bans docking as of January.

NORFOLK CHAMPIONS OF RECORD
1939 — 1989
Norwich D.E.

1939
Merry of Beaufin (B) *Biffin of Beaufin x Susan*

1940
Colonsay All Kiff (D) *Tiny Tim of Beaufin x Kinmount Pip*
Petter Russet of Ways End (D) *Witherslack Sport x Ch. Merry of Beaufin*

1947
Tuff (D) *Bruff x Jenny Pinch*

1948
Cobbler of Boxted (D) *Bulger of Boxted x Colonsay Canteen Eggs*

FIRST BREED CHAMPIONS

Figure 286:
Ch. Merry of Beaufin, 1935.

A daughter of . . .

Figure 287:
Ch. Biffin of Beaufin, 1935.

FIRST GROUP WINNERS

Figure 288:
Eng. Ch. Ickworth Ready,
a dominant breed influence.

Figure 289:
Ch. Bethways Ringo, 1970.
Judge, Lydia Hutchinson. Owner: Barbara Fournier.

Muffin II (B) *Ch. Tuff x Kedron Dorcas*
Pippet (B) *Ch. Tuff x Kedron Dorcas*

1951
Partree Sparkle (B) *Ch. Cobbler of Boxted x Partree Chance*

1952
River Bend Solo (B) *Ch. Tuff x Kedron Dorcas*

1953
Brigham Young (D) *Ch. Tuff x Kedron Cobbler's Biscuit*
Colonsay Flap (B) *Red Scarlett x Polly Flinders*
Colonsay Harkers (D) *Colonsay Fag Wagger x Kandy Koe*
Partree Cobbler (D) *Ch. Cobbler of Boxted x Corry Pinch*
Rednor Red Rufus (D) *Red Wraith x Colonsay Caulk*

1954
Waveney Valley Honey (B) *Elel Spruce x Reddy of Waveney Valley*

1955
Colonsay Kelly's Eye (B) *Colonsay Fag Wagger x Colonsay Granny*
Rivets (D) *Ch. Brigham Young x River Bend Riff-Raff*

1956
Bethway's Kelly's Blinkin (D) *Ch. Brigham Young x Ch. Colonsay Kelly's Eye*
Bethway's Lady Winston (B) *Ch. Rivets x Jackie-Lynn*
Newry's McAleenan (D) *Ch. Brigham Young x Newry's Finnegan*

1957
Bethway's Portia (B) *Ch. Brigham Young x Ch. Colonsay Kelly's Eye*

NOTABLE BITCHES

Figure 290:
Ch. Badgewood The Huntress, 1977. A Group and two time National Specialty winner. Mrs. Potter Wear, judge. Jack Simm, judge.

Figure 291:
1967 Nanfan Nyiad, first Eng. Am. Champion and dam of a champion with an AWTA Working Certificate.

Castle Point Simon (D) *Ch. Tuff x Ch. Partree Sparkle*
Colonsay Griffin (D) *Dimbols Nutmeg x Charmar Georgette*
Newry's McShane (D) *Ch. Brigham Young x Newry's Finnegan*
Ragus Jimmy Joe (D) *Ragus Sweetwilliam x Waveney Valley Pandy*

1958
Bethway's Pound (D) *Ch. Ragus Jimmy Joe x Ch. Colonsay Kelly's Eye*
Newry's McGilly (D) *Ch. Brigham Young x Newry's Finnegan*

1959
Bethway's Pence (D) *Ch. Ragus Jimmy Joe x Ch. Colonsay Kelly's Eye*
Mt. Paul Anderson (D) *George Pinch x Castle Point Trivet*
Ragus Vanity (B) *Red Duster of Redlawn x Veracity*

1960
Bethway's Mr. Chips (D) *Ch. Bethway's Pence x Ch. Bethway's Portia*

1961
Bethway's Colonsay Fee Fee (B) *Ch. Ragus Jimmy Joe x Ch. Colonsay Kelly's Eye*
Bethway's Cricket (B) *Ragus Solomon Grundy x Ragus Brandysnap*
Bethway's Fritz (D) *Ch. Brigham Young x Ch. Ragus Vanity*
Bethway's Lil' Brigham (D) *Ch. Brigham Young x Ragus Brandysnap*
Bethway's Scarlet (B) *Ch. Bethway's Pence x Ch. Bethway's Portia*
Gambler (D) *Ch. Bethway's Pound x Gee-Gee*

1962
Bethway's Tony (D) *Hunston Highflier x Ch. Colonsay Kelly's Eye*
The O"Doul's Seal (B) *Newry's Lefty O'Doul x Newry's Miss Tiggy Winkle*

1963
Bethway's Mr. Kennedy (D) *Ch. Bethway's Pence x Ch. Bethway's Portia*

1964
Bethway's Miss Itch (B) *Ch. Bethway's Tony x Ch. Bethway's Scarlet*
Bethway's Pensum (D) *Ch. Bethway's Pence x Wensum Tinker Bell*

1965
Bethway's Little Tinker Bell (B) *Ch. Bethway's Tony x Wensum Tinker Bell*
Castle Point Alfalfa (B) *Ch. Bethway's Mr. Chips x Castle Point Twig*
Newry's Mrs. McThing (B) *Ch. Newry's McAleenan x Bethway's Chess*

1966
Bethway's John (D) *Ch. Bethway's Pence x Bethway's Mandy*
Bethway's Little Mister (D) *Bethway's Pensum x Bethway's Little Miss*
Bethway's The Duke (D) *Ch. Bethway's Tony x Ch. Bethway's Scarlet*
Colonsay's Quimp (B) *Raughmere Wanderer x Colonsay Plush*

1967
Bethway's Aramis (D) *Nanfan Nugget x Ch. Bethway's Little Tinker Bell*
Bethway's Mr. Cricket (D) *Ch. Bethway's John x Ch. Bethway's Cricket*
Bethway's The Dutchess (B) *Ch. Bethway's Tony x Ch. Bethway's Scarlet*
Nanfan Hoppocket (D) *Nanfan Nimble x Nanfan Hayseed*
Nanfan Nyiad (B) *Nanfan Heckle x Nanfan Needle*

1968
Bethway's Bitter Sweet (B) *Ch. Bethway's Tony x Ch. Bethway's Scarlet*
Bethway's Little Girl (B) *Ch. Bethway's Mr. Chips x Ch. Bethway's Scarlet*

1969
Bethway's Penny Kenny (B) *Ch. Bethway's Mr. Kennedy x Bethway's Penny*
Bethway's Ringo (D) *Ch. Bethway's John x Colonsay Aring*

1970
Bethway's Miss Chop (B) *Ch. Bethway's Mr. Cricket x Ch. Bethway's Little Tinker Bell*
Bethway's Sister Scarlet (B) *Ch. Bethway's Aramis x Bethway's Little Scarlet*
Bethway's Tramis (D) *Ch. Bethway's Aramis x Bethway's Miss Trinket*
Newry's Red Fox (D) *Ch. Bethway's John x Ch. Bethway's Miss Itch*

1971
Badgewood Bonnie (B) *Nanfan Heckle x Badgewood Miss Poppet*
Bethway's Trampet (B) *Ch. Bethway's Aramis x Bethway's Miss Trinket*
Bethway's Willow (B) *Ch. Bethway's John x Bethway's Dixy*
Castle Point Iguana (D) *Nanfan Terrapin x Castle Point Withers*
Castle Point Indigo (B) *Nanfan Terrapin x Castle Point Withers*
Ickworth Nimrod (D) *Hanleycastle Brock x Nanfan Nymph*
Mt. Paul Nanfan (B) *Tarheel's High Trump x Ch. Nanfan Nyiad*
Nanfan Hayrake (D) *Nanfan Nimble x Nanfan Hayseed*
Nanfan Ninepin (D) *Nanfan Halleluia x Nanfan Needle*
Nanfan Nogbad The Bad (D) *Nanfan Heckle x Nanfan Needle*
1972
Badgewood King's Lynn (B) *Ickworth Ready x Ch. Badgewood Bonnie*
Bethway's Abbie (B) *Ch. Bethway's Mr. Cricket x Ch. Bethway's Little Tinker Bell*
Bethway's Lilac (B) *Ch. Nanfan Ninepin x Bethway's Lilly*
Bethway's Red Baron (D) *Ch. Nanfan Ninepin x Bethway's Penny*
Bethway's Willow (B) *Ch. Bethway's John x Bethway's Dixy*
Castle Point Tantrum (B) *Ch. Mt. Paul Anderson x Castle Point Sickle*
Mt. Paul Piccadilly Rose (B) *Ch. Wendover Foxhunter x Ch. Mt. Paul Nanfan*
Mt. Paul Terracotta (B) *Ch. Castle Point Iguana x Nanfan Tilly Tally*

1973
Badgewood Blakeney (D) *Ickworth Ready x Badgewood Bonnie*
Badgewood Miss Alice (B) *Ch. Ickworth Nimrod x Ch. Badgewood King's Lynn*
Badgewood Monty Collins (D) *Ch. Ickworth Nimrod x Ch. Badgewood King's Lynn*
Bethway's Honeybun (B) *Ch. Bethway's John x Ch. Bethway's Bitter Sweet*
Bethway's Jill (B) *Ch. Bethway's Aramis x Ch. Bethway's The Dutchess*
Bethway's Sassafras (B) *Ch. Bethway's Aramis x Ch. Bethway's The Dutchess*
Ickworth Red Fox Phillip (D) *Ickworth Juniper x Ickworth Penelope*
Madroof's Trinket (B) *Ch. Nanfan Hayrake x Twiggy*
Nanfan Mustard (D) *Nanfan Heckle x Minton Mary Anne*

1974
Badgewood Bluemarking Saffron (B) *Nanfan Nimble x Gotoground Cuckoo*
Badgewood Duchess of Norfolk (B) *Ch. Ickworth Nimrod x Ch. Badgewood King's Lynn*
Dorland's Miss Aladdin (B) *Ch. Nanfan Mustard x Nanfan Fresco*
Lyndors Flower Power (B) *Ch. Bethway's Aramis x Bethway's Bell*
Mt. Paul Rowdy (D) *Ch. Nanfan Nogbad The Bad x Ch. Mt. Paul Nanfan*
Mt. Paul Tulip (B) *Ch. Castle Point Iguana x Nanfan Tilly Tally*
Nanfan Fracas (B) *Nanfan Ninety x Nanfan Fiddlesticks*

Nanfan Mint (B) *Nanfan Heckle x Minton Mary Anne*
Ravenswing Foxfire (D) *Ravenswing Fleet Leader x Ravenswing Fay Royal*

1975
Aladdin's Scheherazade (B) *Ch. Nanfan Nogbad The Bad x Mt. Paul Piccadilly Rose*
Badgewood Moreston (D) *Ch. Badgewood Blakeney x Ch. Badgewood Miss Alice*
Badgewood Windmill Girl (B) *Ch. Badgewood Blakeney x Ch. Badgewood Miss Alice*
Bethway's Fagin (D) *Ch. Newry's Red Fox x Bethway's Baby Cricket*
Bethway's John Boy (D) *Ch. Bethway's John x Ch. Bethway's Miss Chop*
Bethway's Miss Fancy Pants (B) *Ch. Ravenswing Foxfire x Bethway's Miss Nancy Dee*
Kinsprit Nutcracker (D) *Ch. Castle Point Iguana x Nanfan Nutshell*
Lyndors Ring-O-Round (D) *Ch. Bethway's Ringo x Ch. Lyndors Flower Power*
Mt. Paul Viking (D) *Ch. Ickworth Red Fox Phillip x Ch. Mt. Paul Tulip*
Panda Bear of Bethway (B) *Bethway's Teddybear x Ch. Bethway's Willow*
Willow 's Whisper of Bethway (B) *Ch. Bethway's Pensum x Ch. Bethway's Willow*

1976
Badgewood Woodpecker Trail (B) *Tarheel's High Trump x Ch. Badgewood King's Lynn*
Bethway's Hush Hush (B) *Ch. Bethway's John Boy x Bethway's Chatterbox*
Bethway's Jack (D) *Ch. Bethway's Aramis x Ch. Bethway's The Dutchess*
Lyndors Cricket (B) *Ch. Wendover Half Pound x Ch. Lyndors Flower Power*
Lyndors Mister (D) *Ch. Mt. Paul Rowdy x Ch. Lyndors Paper Moon*
Lyndors Paper Moon (B) *Ch. Bethway's Ringo x Ch. Lyndors Flower Power*
Nanfan Corricle (B) *Nanfan Ninety x Cinnamon of Nanfan*
Nanfan Stormcock (D) *Nanfan Thistle x Nanfan Sickle*
Wendover Torrent (D) *Ch. Nanfan Stormcock x Ch. Mt. Paul Terracotta*

1977
Badgewood Basil (D) *Ch. Badgewood Blakeney x Ch. Badgewood Bluemarking Saffron*
Badgewood The Huntress (B) *Ch. Ickworth Nimrod x Ch. Badgewood King's Lynn*
El Cid of Tinkinswood (D) *Leddington Diplomat x Tinkinswood Cariad*
New Garden Eadith CD (B) *Wymbur Cantata x Castle Point Ely*
Ragus Brown Smudge (B) *Ragus Whipcord x Ragus Brown Sugar*
Redfox Halleluiah (D) *Ch. Ickworth Redfox Phillip x Ickworth Bluemarking Briar*
Wigan of Blacksmith (B) *Ickworth Blacksmith x Osmor Trefil*

1978
Badgewood Rowdy Duke (D) *Ch. Mt. Paul Rowdy x Ch. Badgewood Duchess of Norfolk*
Bethway's Joshua (D) *Ch. Bethway's Aramis x Ch. Bethway's The Dutchess*
Bethway's Limey of Calabra (D) *Ch. Nanfan Ninepin x Bethway's Vixen*
Elve Pure Magic (D) *Ragus Bitterman x Ragus Brown Cider*
King's Prevention Ahoy (B) *Ch. Wendover Torrent x Ch. Nanfan Corricle*
Lenclare's Ladybug (B) *Ch. Redfox Halleluiah x Lime Tree Trifle*
Max-Well's Lady Chatterly (B) *Ch. Ickworth Nimrod x Ch. Max-Well's Liberty Bell*
Max-Well's Liberty Bell (B) *Ch. Badgewood Moreston x Max-Well's Rum Raison*
Max-Well's William Penn (D) *Ch. Badgewood Moreston x Max-Well's Rum Raison*
Todwil's Gentle On My Mind (B) *Ch. Culswood Chipwood x Ch. Todwil's Burnt Cork*
Turkshill Brown Nectar (B) *Ch. Ickworth Nimrod x Ragus Brown Smudge*

Norfolk

1979
Badgewood Queen of Hearts (B) *Ch. Badgewood Blakeney x Ch. Badgewood Looking Glass*
Glori's J & B of Bethway (D) *Ch. Bethways John Boy x Bethway's Lexa*
Lyndors Pippin (D) *Ch. Castle Point Iguana x Ch. Lyndors Paper Moon*

SOME BEST IN SHOW WINNERS

Figure 292:
Eng. Am.. Ch. El Cid of Tinkinswood. First to win a Best in Show, 1978. Owner: Ruth Cooper

Figure 293:
Ch. Greenfields The Hustler, 1984. Breeder/owners: Gaynor E. Green and Ruth Cooper.

Figure 294:
Ch. Rightly So Original Sin, 1986. Breeder: J. F. Rumpf and D. Augustus. Owner: Virginia L. Hedges and J. F. Rumpf.

Figure 295:
Eng. Am. Ch. Clockwise of Jaeva, 1985. First Norfolk bitch to win an all breed Best in Show. Owner: Barbara Miller.

Max-Well's O'Henry (D) *Ch. Ickworth Nimrod x Ch. Max-Well's Liberty Bell*
Nanfan Cornflower (B) *Nanfan Sugar Lump x Nanfan Corndolly*
New Garden Godiva (B) *Wymbur Cantata x Castle Point Ely*
Tamerlane's Butter Crunch (B) *Ch. Castle Point Iguana x Max-Well's Bunker Hill*

1980
Annursnac Major Yeats (D) *Ch. Castle Point Iguana x Annursnac's Schnitzel*
Badgewood Looking Glass (B) *Ch. Nanfan Nogbad The Bad x Ch. Badgewood Miss Alice*
Gustylea's Farrah Of Devon (B) *Ch. Ickworth Nimrod x Max-Well's Beekman Place*
Hartleigh Chipping Norton (D) *Ch. El Cid of Tinkinswood x Harttleigh Bubblin Brown Sugar*

1981
Abbedale's American Gigolo (D) *Ch. Elve Pure Magic x Abbedale's Tea and Crumpets*
Badgewood Hunter's Moon (B) *Ch. Max-Well's O'Henry x Ch. Badgewood The Huntress*
Glenelg Tuff Too (D) *Ch. Castle Point Iguana x Glenelg Thimble*
Hartleigh Bovey Tracey (B) *Ch. El Cid of Tinkinswood x Hartleigh Bublyn Brown Sugar*
Hatchwoods Creme De Menthe of Cracknor (D) *Cracknor Capricorn x Hatchwoods Peppermint*
Lyndors Mez-A-Mez (B) *Ch. Lyndors Mister x Ch. Lyndors Cricket*
Lyndors Pippa (B) *Ch. Lyndors Mister x Lyndors Papya*
Max-Well's Lone Ranger (D) *Ch. Ickworth Nimrod x Ch. Max-Well's Liberty Bell*
Max-Well's Scarlet Letter (B) *Ch. Ickworth Nimrod x Ch. Max-Well's Liberty Bell*
Max-Well's The Buckeye Sting (D) *Ch. Badgewood Rowdy Duke x Max-Well's Liberty Bell*
Raggedge Are You Ready (B) *Ch. Elve Pure Magic x Mt. Paul Vesper*
Raggedge Best Bet (B) *Ch. Elve Pure Magic x Mt. Paul Vesper*
Turkshill Brown Buccaneer (D) *Ickworth Peter's Pence x Ch. Ragus Brown Smudge*

1982
Abbedale's Abbegail Ray (B) *Ch. Elve Pure Magic x Abbedale's Tea and Crumpets*
Anderscroft Tylwyth Trollop (B) *Ch. Wendover Torrent x Ch. New Garden Eadith UD*
Badgewood Good Hunting (D) *Badgewood Mighty Hunter x Ch. Ickworth Pretty Piece*
Bethway's Cup Cake (B) *Ch. Turkhill's Brown Buccaneer x Bethway's Scarlet O'Fisty*
Bethway's Just Plain Bill (D) *Ch. Elve Pire Magic x Bethway's Scarlet O'Fisty*
Chidley Jinx (B) *Ch. Elve Pure Magic x Shenanigans of Chidley*
Ickworth Pretty Piece (B) *Ickworth Kythe of Ryslip x Ickworth Penny Piece*
Max-Well's Simon Says (D) *Ch. Ickworth Nimrod x Max-Well's Liberty Bell*
Max-Well's Tinker Toy (B) *Ch. Ickworth Nimrod x Max-Well's Liberty Bell*
Neverdone's Jazz (B) *Ch. Lyndors Mister x Neverdone's Echo*
Surry Skiff (B) *King's Prevention Jolly Roger x Lyndors Kizzy*
Surry Sta'Board (D) *King's Prevention Jolly Roger x Lyndors Kizzy*
Todwil's R To D To of Whitehall (D) *Ch. Bethway's Jack x Ch. Todwil's Gentle On My Mine*
Wonderwood Wensday Addams (B) *Leddington Captain Cook x Leddington Folly*

1983
Abbedale's Egotist (D) *Castle Point Nugget x Ch. Abbedale's Abbegail Ray*
Badgewood Mirror On The Wall (B) *Ch. Elve Pure Magic x Ch. Badgewood Looking Glass*
Badgewood Sir Scuff (D) *Ickworth Pathfinder x Ch. Gustylea's Farrah of Devon*
Badgewood Trophy (B) *Badgewood Mighty Hunter x Ch. Ickworth Pretty Piece*
Castle Point Mint UD (B) *Ch. Hatchwoods Creme de Menthe of Cracknor x Wicket of Castle Point*
Cybele's Sir Turner (D) *Ickworth Pennywise x Ch. Turkhill's Brown Nectar*
Daffran Dusty (D) *Ickworth Bacardi x Daffran Dallus*
Greenfield's Abigail (B) *Ch. Surry Sink or Swim x Ch. Raggedge Best Bet*
Greenfield's Tea and Crumpets (B) *Ch. Surry Sink or Swim x Ch. Raggedge Best Bet*
Hartleigh Peppermint Patty (B) *Ch. Max-Well's Lone Ranger x Ch. Hartleigh Bovey Tracey*
Knollwood's Prince Igor (D) *Ch. Lyndors Pippin x Fiddle Dee Dee of Knollwood*
Lyndors Meiko (B) *Lyndors Pence x Ch. Lyndors Paper Moon*
Max-Well's Saturday Nite Fever (D) *Ch. Badgewood Monty Collins x Ch. Max-Well's Scarlet Letter*

Nanfan Summer Sweet (B) *Nanfan Summer Storm x Nanfan Sweet Apple*
Surry Port (D) *King's Prevention Jolly Roger x Lyndors Kizzy*
Surry Sailor's Delight (B) *King's Prevention Jolly Roger x Ch. King's Prevention Ahoy*
Surry Sink or Swim (D) *King's Prevention Jolly Roger x Ch. King's Prevention Ahoy*
Todwil's Bluegrass Belle (B) *Ch. Bethway's Jack x Ch. Todwil's Gentle On My Mind*
Todwil's E T of Whitehall (B) *Ch. Elve Pure Magic x Ch. Todwil's Gentle On My Mind*
Todwil's Pacman of Whitehall (D) *Ch. Elve Pure Magic x Ch. Todwil's Gentle On My Mind*
Trowsnest's Kinsprit of Corncob (D) *Ch. Hatchwoods Creme de Menthe of Cracknor x Ch. Nanfan Cornflower*
Turkhills Creme of Abbedale (B) *Ch. Hatchwoods Creme de Menthe of Cracknor x Turkhills Patty*

1984
Abbedale's Two Potatoe (D) *Nanfan Sweet Potato x Daffran Donatella*
Barwoods Lord Darby (D) *Ch. Hatchwoods Creme de Menthe of Cracknor x Castle Point Bark CD*
Chidley Magic Marker (D) *Ch. Daffran Dusty x Chidley Pooka*
Chidley Mumbo Jumbo (D) *Ch. Elve Pure Magic x Shenanigans of Chidley*
Hartleigh Butter Toffee (B) *Ch. Max-Well's Lone Ranger x Ch. Hartleigh Bovey Tracey*
Hastings Lord Robert (D) *Ch. Daffran Dusty x Ch. Max-Well's Tinker Toy*
Lyndors Bewitched (B) *Ch. Lyndors Pippin x Ch. Lyndors Mez-a-Mez*
Max-Well's Christmas Cracker (D) *Ch. Max-Well's Lone Ranger x White Star Alice Max-Well*
Norvik Rightly So (B) *Ch. Surry Sink or Swim x Ch. Surry Skiff*
Norvik The Witch (B) *Ch. Surry Sink or Swim x Ch. Surry Skiff*
Surry Spinnaker (D) *King's Prevention Jolly Roger x Surry Dory*
Theodore Bear CD (D) *Ch. Lyndors Mister x Lyndors Daisy May*
Todwil's Six Pack (D) *Ch. Elve Pure Magic x Ch. Todwil's Gentle On My Mind*
Yarrow's Ruff And Ready (B) *Ch. Daffran Dusty x Ch. Raggedge Are You Ready*

1985
Abbedale's Six Gun (D) *Ch. Daffran Dusty x Ch. Abbedale's Abbegail Ray*
Anderscroft P S Of Chidley (B) *Ch. Elve Pure Magic x Bethway's Short Cake*
Chidley Bold Dust (D) *Ch. Daffran Dusty x Ch. Chidley Jinx*
Chidley Charm (B) *Ch. Daffran Dusty x Ch. Chidley Jinx*
Chidley Daphne (B) *Ch. Daffran Dusty x Ch. Chidley Jinx*
Chidley Flip (B) *Ch. Daffran Dusty x Shenanigans of Chidley*
Elve Black Shadow (D) *Ragus Browned Off x Elve Belladonna*
Greenfield's Cinnamon Bear (B) *Ch. Surry Sink or Swim x Ch. Raggedge Best Bet*
Greenfield's The Gambler (D) *Ch. Surry Sink or Swim x Ch. Raggedge Best Bet*
Greenfield's The Hustler (D) *Ch. Surry Sink or Swim x Ch. Raggedge Best Bet*
Lyndors Tag Along (D) *Ch. Bethway's Just My Bill x Lyndors Sabrina Fair*
Max-Well's Winter Wind (B) *Ch. Nanfan Crunch x White Star Alice Max-Well*
Max-Well's Wintersport (D) *Ch. Nanfan Crunch x White Star Alice Max-Well*
Nanfan Crunch (D) *Nanfan Sweet Potato x Nanfan Copycat*
Nanfan Sunshade of Hoheit (B) *Nanfan Sugar Lump x Nanfan Solar*
Paprika of Whitehall (D) *Ch. Surry Sink or Swim x Ch. Todwil's E T of Whitehall*
Poole's Ide Mayflower Madam (B) *Kilwinning Copperhead x Chidley Taboo*
Rightly So What (D) *Max-Well's Lone Ranger x Ch. Norvik Rightly So*
Surry Ship To Shore (B) *Ch. Surry Port x King's Prevention Cotswold*
Todwil's Dapper Dan (D) *Ch. Surry Sink or Swim x Ch. Todwil's Gentle On My Mind*
Todwil's Ellen Lee (B) *Ch. Elve Pure Magic x Ch. Todwil's Gentle On My Mind*
Todwil's Jamie (B) *Ch. Surry Sink or Swim x Ch. Todwil's Gentle On My Mind*
Turkshill Pistol (B) *Ch. Hatchwoods Creme de Menthe of Cracknor x Turkhills Patty*
Wonderwood Barnburner (D) *Ch. Surry Sink or Swim x Ch. Wonderwood Wensday Addams*
Wonderwood Microchip (B) *Ch. Hatchwoods Creme de Menthe of Cracknor x Ch. Wonderwood Wensday Addams*

Wonderwood The Rose (B) *Leddington Captain Cook x Leddington Folly*
Wonderwood Watch Her Strut (B) *Ch. Hatchwoods Creme de Menthe of Cracknor x Ch. Wonderwood Wensday Addams*

1986

Allright Magic Lamp (D) *Allright Huckleberry Finn x Chidley Magic Carpet*
Barwoods Lady Anne (B) *Ch. Hatchwoods Creme de Menthe of Cracknor x Castle Point Bark*
Chidley Dandelion (D) *Ch. Chidley Mumbo Jumbo x Ch. Chidley Daphne*
Everready (D) *Ch. Chidley Margic Marker x Ch. Raggedge Are You Ready*
Greenfield's Kibbles 'N Bits (B) *Ch. Chidley Magic Marker x Ch. Greenfield's Tea and Crumpets*
Lyndors Sabrina Fair (B) *Ch. Lyndors Pippin x Ch. Lyndors Mez-a-Mez*
Max-Well's Ruby Thuesday (B) *Ickworth Pathfinder x Ch. Max-Well's Scarlet Letter*
Max-Well's Sandpiper (D) *Ch. Max-Well's Saturday Nite Fever x Ch. Max-Well's Liberty Bell*
Max-Well's Winter Chill (B) *Ch. Nanfan Crunch x White Star Alice Max-Well*
Norvik The Warlock (D) *Ch. Surrey Sink or Swim x Ch. Surrey Skiff*
Pennywhistle Razzle Dazzle (D) *Nanfan Whistle x Ch. Nanfan Sunshade of Hoheit*
Rightly So Henbit (B) *Ragus Bantum Cock x Rightly So Argue Not*
Rightly So Right Now (D) *Ch. Nanfan Crunch x Ch. Norvik Rightly So*
Sage's Solomon Seal (D) *Ch. Daffran Dusty x Jasmine Jones' Grey Sage*
Spike of Whitehall (D) *Ch. Todwil's Pac Man x Ch. Todwil's E.T. of Whitehall*
Tylwyth Just Chelsea UD (B) *Ch. Badgewood Sir Scuff x Ch. Castle Point Mint UD*
Wonderwood Lo Commotion Lu (B) *Ch. Surrey Sink or Swim x Ch. Wonderwood Wensday Addams*
Wonderwood Motor Scooter (D) *Ch. Hatchwoods Creme de Menthe of Cracknor x Ch. Wonderwood Wensday Addams*
Yarrow's Re-Markable (B) *Ch. Chidley Magic Marker x Ch. Raggedge Are You Ready*
Yarrow's Whizz-Bang (B) *Ch. Abbedale's Six Gun x Ch. Raggedge Are You Ready*

1987

Abbedale's American Hilary (B) *Ch. Abbedale's American Gigolo x Turkshill Black Top CD*
Abbedale's Fox Shadow (D) *Ch. Elve Black Shadow x Ch. Abbedale's Six Pence*
Abbedale's Six Pence (B) *Ch. Daffran Dusty x Ch. Abbedale's Abbegail Ray*
Bear Hill's Mr. Pip (D) *Ragus Bantum Cock x Ch. Greenfield's Cinnamon Bear*
Bear Hill's Miss Crisparkle (B) *Ch. Chidley Magic Marker x Ch. Greenfield's Abigail*
Caper of Whitehall (B) *Ch. Surrey Sink or Swim x Ch. Todwil's E. T. of Whitehall*
Chidley Badness (D) *Ch. Allright Magic Lamp x Ch. Chidley Flip*
Greenfield's It Must Be Magic (B) *Ch. Chidley Magic Marker x Ch. Greenfield's Tea and Crumpets*
Greenfield's Jovial Jasper (D) *Ch. Chidley Magic Marker x Ch. Greenfield's Tea and Crumpets*
Heathjul Christmas Robin (D) *Salad Burnet of Vicbrita x Elve Pure Joy*
Hobbitshire Anne of Abbedale (B) *Nanfan Whistle x Abbedale's Taters and Tea*
Jaeva Matti Brown (D) *Crackshill Hardy x Jaeva Bobby Socks*
Kristl's Mr. T. Beardsley (D) *Ch. Abbedale's Six Gun x Donkeytown Wren*
Lyndors Raz-Ma-Raz (D) *Ch. Surrey Sink or Swim x Ch. Lyndors Bewitched*
Max-Well's Father Time (D) *Ch. Max-Well's Wintersport x Max-Well's April First*
Nanfan Coughdrop (D) *Nanfan Catmint x Nanfan Cribbage*
Nanfan Sandpiper (B) *Nanfan Catmint x Nanfan Sunbeam*
Norvik The Instigator (D) *Ch. Surrey Ship to Shore x Ch. Norvik The Witch*
Poole's Ide's Beach Blanket Bingo (B) *Ch. Hatchwoods Creme de Menthe of Cracknor x Chidley Taboo*
Poole's Ide's Big Chill (D) *Kilwinning Copperhead x Chidley Taboo*
Ragus Pass The Buck (D) *Ragus Blacksmith x Priestess of Ragus*
Rightly So Sherlock (D) *Ch. Nanfan Crunch x Ch. Norvik Rightly So*
Rightly So What Now (B) *Ragus Bantum Cock x Rightly So Argue Not*
Silverstone Bookmaker's Bet (D) *Ch. Wonderwood Motor Scooter x Ch. Wonderwood The Rose*
Surrey Frigate (B) *Ch. Greenfield's The Hustler x Surrey Dory*
Surrey Shore Leave (D) *Ch. Freenfield's The Hustler x Surrey Binnacle*

Surrey Gig (B) *Ch. Greenfield's The Hustler x Surrey Dory*
Surrey Stem To Stern (B) *Ch. Greenfield's The Hustler x Surrey Luff*
Skyline's Max-Well Sundae (B) *Ch. Max-Well's Wintersport x Skyline Tigerlily*
Skyline's Sherlock of Maxwell (D) *Ch. Nanfan Crunch x Max-Well's Meadowlark Lucy*
White Rose Allspice (B) *Ch. Surrrey Sink or Swim x Ch. Lowmita Nutshell*
Wonderwood Turbo Plus (D) *Ch. Hatchwoods Creme de Menthe of Cracknor x Ch. Wonderwood Wensday Addams*
Yarrow's Jasmine (B) *Ch. Allright Magic Lamp x Ch. Yarrow's Ruff and Ready*
Yarrow's Top 'O The Mark (B) *Ch. Chidley Magic Marker x Ch. Raggedge Are You Ready*

1988

Abbedale's Road To Heaven (B) *Ch. Elve Black Shadow x Ch. Abbedale's Abbegail Ray*
Abbedale's Road To Victory (B) *Ch. Elve Black Shadow x Ch. Abbedale's Abbegail Ray*
Aruru's Sticky Wicket (D) *Ch. Allright Magic Lamp x Sage's Sumerian Aruru Tertius*
Bear Hill's Paprika (D) *Ch. Paprika Of Whitehall x Ch. Greenfield's Cinnamon Bear*
Bear Hill's Toby Crackit (D) *Ch. Ragus Pass The Buck x Ch. Bear Hill's Miss Crisparkle*
Chidley Blue Moon (B) *Ch. Allright Magic Lamp x Ch. Anderscroft P.S. of Chidley*
Chidley Magic Aim (B) *Ch. Abbedale's Six Gun x Chidley Magic Circle*
Chidley Magic Moon (D) *Ch. Allright Magic Lamp x Ch. Anderscroft P.S. of Chidley*
Chidley Talisman (D) *Ch. Allright Magic Lamp x Chidley Pooka*
Clockwise of Jaeva (B) *Ch. Jaeva Matti Brown x Nanfan Cherry Tart*
Domby's Mrs. Corneila Pipchin (B) *Ch. Elve Black Shadow x Ch. Poole's Ide Beach Blanket Bingo*
Glori's Terrence (D) *Nanfan Spartan of Hoheit x Ch. Bethway's Cup Cake*
Hobbitshire Allyson (B) *Nanfan Whistle x Abbedale's Taters and Tea*
Landmark Magic Imprint (D) *Ch. Chidley Magic Marker x Ch. Yarrow's Jasmine*
Landmark Magic Legacy (B) *Ch. Chidley Magic Marker x Ch. Yarrow's Jasmine*
Lime Tree Magic Mariner (D) *Ch. Allright Magic Lamp x Surrey Spanker*
Lowmita Skylark of Shanandi (D) *And Harry of Titanium x Lowmita Wren*
Lyndors Music Man (D) *Ch. Lyndors Mister x Lyndors Hello Dolly*
Max-Well's New Years Eve (B) *Ch. Max-Well's Wintersport x Max-Well's April First*
Neverdone Five Oakes A Okay (D) *Ch. Surrey Port x Neverdone Jazz*
Neverdone Prime Time (D) *Lyndors Pence x Lyndors Hello Dolly*
Norvik Miss Fricket (B) *Ch. Norvik The Warlock x Surrey Small Craft*
Pennywhistle Buttercup (B) *Nanfan Whistle x Ch. Nanfan Sunshade of Hoheit*
Rightly So My Sin (B) *Ch. Surrey Sink or Swim x Ch. Rightly So Henbit*
Rightly So Carbon Copy (D) *Ch. Rightly So Right Now x Rightly So Argue Not*
Rightly So Original Sin (D) *Ch. Surrey Sink or Swim x Ch. Rightly So Henbit*
Skyline's Agatha of Max-Well (B) *Ch. Nanfan Crunch x Max-Well's Meadowlark Lucy*
Skyline's Beam of Max-Well (B) *Ch. Max-well's Wintersport x Skyline Tigerlily*
Skyline's Raggle Taggle (B) *Ch. Max-well's Wintersport x Skyline Tigerlily*
Starcyl Wagtail of Saredon (B) *Starcyl Pop x Starcyl Rice Crispy*
Sue-Dan Copper Penny (B) *Ch. Max-Well's Sandpiper x Ch. Max-Well's Ruby Tuesday*
Sunoak's Dick Tracy (D) *Ch. Chidley Magic Marker x Ch. Caper of Whitehall*
Sunoak's Foz of Whitehall (D) *Ch. Chidley Magic Marker x Ch. Caper of Whitehall*
Tickatee Catchascatchcan (D) *Stall Mascot Baloo x Guestlings Toddlertootsie*
Wenwagon Fergie (B) *Ch. Chidley Dandelion x Chidley Lark*
White Rose Nutmeg (B) *Ch. Surrey Sink or Swim x Ch. Lowmita Nutshell*
Wonderwood Calliope (B) *Ragus Bantum Cock x Wonderwood Microchip*
Wonderwood Megabyte (B) *Ragus Bantum Cock x Ch. Wonderwood Microchip*
Yarrow's Gee-Whizz (B) *Yarrow's Benchmark x Ch. Yarrow's Whizz-Bang*

PEDIGREES

The following article was written in 1926 by the Rev. Rosslyn Bruce and was quoted in an article by his daughter, Mrs. Kirkby-Peace, in the *Norfolk Newsletter*, England.

"A pedigree may be a help and a hindrance to a breeder. Wisely used, with a knowledge of what the names in it really represented in faults and merits during their lifetime, a pedigree is a star of guidance to wise men; but if relied on merely because it consists of numbers of champion dogs and bitches, it becomes a mere will-o-the-wisp to lead the thoughtless to despair. Each name should suggest to the breeder some points of established value, and some tendency to avoid carefully. Moreover, a good pedigree is of little value unless it reflects itself to some extent in it's owner's appearance. 'A bad dog with a good pedigree is like a dead crocodile in a silk wedding dress'.

"**The Chief Parts of a Pedigree.** Experts have differed about the relative value of the different places in a pedigree. Galton taught that the two parents together represented half the whole; four grandparents to a quarter, eight to an eighth, and so on in exact mathematical proportion; and his theory was accepted for a long time. Sir Everett Millais assumed it to hold, but sought for something to explain inefficiency. Mendelism discards it completely, and reveals the method heredity by which qualities and groups of qualities descend wholly or in part from a line consisting of but one ancestor (male or female) in each generation; Mendelism explains, but at present hardly guides, the methods of stock breeders. The 'line and family' system holds the field today; Bruce Lowe was its pioneer, and C. J. Davies and Rosslyn Bruce are its convinced exponents; the former wrote of British thoroughbred race horses, the latter two of Scottish Terriers and Fox Terriers respectively. The books of each of these writers are difficult to procure, but the system can be briefly outlined thus: In all pedigrees the most important part is the bottom line, that is the dam, then her dam, then her Granddam, or what is called in heredity the 'tail female'; after that comes the sire, and his sire and his sire again, or the 'tail male'; the remainder or inside of a pedigree will generally cancel itself out and prove of little importance."

ON READING PEDIGREES:

- The Sire is always above the Dam.
- The Male is always above the paired Bitch. Fold the pedigree in half horizontally and the Sire's family is always in the top half.
- Ch. = champion, and though desirable, it is not insurance that its offspring are of extra value.
- Extensive campaigning of certain dogs may give a false impression of their breeding worth, since there is a tendency to believe all champions are of equal value in a breeding program.

INFLUENTIAL ENGLISH SIRES AND DAMS

- Ch. Rednor Red Wraith, 1946
- Ch. Waveney Valley Alder, 1952
- Ch. Widgeon Bunny, 1958
- Ch. Hunston Hedge Betty (bitch), 1957
- Ch. Nanfan Heckle, 1963 (see pedigree Chpt. 5, pg. 137)
- Ch. Ickworth Ready, 1967
- Ch. Ragus Whipcord, 1971
- Ch. Salad Burnet of Vicbrita, 1973
- Ch. Ragus Browned Off, 1973
- Ch. And Harry of Titanium, 1977

...considered "a lovely dog and to my mind a perfect type, excels in head with neat correctly carried drop-ears. A gorgeous rich red coat and looks like tackling any job he is asked to do." Judge: Mrs. A.F. Mirrllees, December 1947.

```
                                         Colonsay Bonfire
                         Colonsay War Scar
                                         Colonsay Flaming Onion
                 Wymondley Grenadier
                                         Ch. Farndon Red Dog
                         Southmore Red Pippin
                                         Southmore Bantum
         CH. REDNOR RED WRAITH (DOG)
                                         Tim
                         Snelston Rogue
                                         Dawn of Cynval
                 Colonsay Golden Arrow
                                         Ch. Biffin of Beaufin
                         Colonsay Birdseed
                                         Kinmount Pip
```

```
                         Colonsay Hudson
         Colonsay Bimp
                         Colonsay Flaming Onion
 Elel Spruce
                         Bulger of Boxted
         Sparkie
                         Colonsay Bunderbust
CH. WAVENEY VALLEY ALDER (DOG)
                         Colonsay Thumbs Up
         Colonsay Cady
                         Colonsay Brahma
 Pennie of Waveney Valley
                         Snelston Rogue
         Tanner of Waveney Valley
                         Congham Penny
```

"Ch. Waveney Valley Alder—Most famous offspring of Elel Spruce. Not the first post-war drop ear champion, but was the one to make the biggest mark in that first decade. He was a bigger dog than his sire, with a little more leg and a dark red, harsh coat—the sort of coat seldom seen today. He had quality unusual in drop-ears at that time. Known as 'Skipper' he was the one who put the Waveney Valleys to the top as he won eight CCs. His first when he was 15 months and his last at six years. Unfortunately, he did not inherit his sire's lovely temperament and could be very sharp. The prepotent Alder and his sire, Elel Spruce, have influenced all of today's winners chiefly through Gotoground, Nanfan, and Bethway descendents.

"Elel Spruce—The foundation sire of the modern Norfolk. The main stud of the Waveney Valley Kennel and the dog to whom both the Gotogrounds and Nanfans were line-bred. His breeder was Mrs. L.L. Lambert of the Elel drop ears, but he was owned from a puppy by Mr. Victor Page. He was line-bred to a famous pair of the '30s, Tiny Tim of Biffin and Kinmount Pip, and it was from Tiny Tim he inherited his lovely type which he passed down to the present day.

He was small, but masculine, with good bone and substance, short back, good head, and a good light red coat. His temperament was typical of that which the early breeders aimed for, easy going and equable but a demon at work.

He was awarded one CC by Miss Macfie and also won a Reserve CC from Mrs. Kirkby-Peace's famous father, Dr. Rev. Rosslyn Bruce. He was the leading sire for both types for many years, the sire of four champions, but his influence was infinite and every one of today's winners descends from him. Of course, there always has to be an "if" and Spruce had doubtful mouth breeding. " —*Marjorie Bunting*.

<pre>
                                        Ch. Waveney Valley Alder
                          Ragus Solomon Grundy
                                        Ragus Sweet Sue
                    Gotoground Foxhunter
                                        Ch. Waveney Valley Alder
                          Gotoground Tiddy Winks
                                        Ragus Merry Maid
     CH. GOTOGROUND WIDGEON BUNNY (DOG)
                                        Elel Spruce
                          Ch. Waveney Valley Alder
                                        Pennie of Waveney Valley
                    Ragus Merry Maid
                                        Colonsay Didlum Buck
                          Congham Merry Moth
                                        Congham Lizzie
</pre>

"Although Nanfan Nimble is in every pedigree, it is through his grandsire, **Gotoground Widgeon Bunny,** that the excellent type is coming. Some worry that the breed should be so strongly influenced by one dog, but others consider this to be a good, not a bad thing. His influence has come by linebreeding to five of his descendents--Ch. Nanfan Nimbus, Ch. Gotoground True Blue, Nanfan Nimrod, Gotoground Diana and Gotoground Cuckoo, not by close inbreeding. When one looks at early pedigrees and sees the odd breeding to nothing in particular which went on, one can only be thankful that one breeder, Esmée O'Hanlon, started breeding on a more scientific basis and gave us all a foundation to start with. " —*Marjorie Bunting.*

"O'Hanlon's **Eng. Ch. Gotoground Widgeon Bunny**--One of the finest drop-eared . . . he moved like a machine, deep in the rib, with his shoulders narrow enough and of proper slope to do a good job of digging in a confined space with length of back to be able to turn around and come out if necessasary."

<pre>
                    Colonsay Bimp
          Elel Spruce
                    Sparkie
     Ch. Waveney Valley Alder
                    Colonsay Cady
          Pennie of Waveney Valley
                    Tanner of Waveney Valley
CH. HUNSTON HEDGE BETTY (BITCH)
                    Colonsay Fag Wagger
          Hunston Herald
                    Colonsay Dizzy
     Hunston Heralda
                    Colonsay Griffin
          Hunston Ha'Penny
                    Polly Flinders
</pre>

Hunston Hedge Betty (left) and Gotoground Vixen (right). Betty bred to Ch. Gotoground Widgeon Bunny produced Gotoground Cuckoo, one of the breeds most influential dams, and her sister, Diana, a granddam of Ch. Ickworth Ready.

Photo © Sally Anne Thompson.

<pre>
                                        Gotoground Moley
                          Nanfan Nimble
                                        Ch. Nanfan Nimbus
                    Kirkby Freddy
                                        Hunston Hooch
                          Nanfan Hannah
                                        Fluellen Readymade
          CH. ICKWORTH READY (DOG)
                                        Nanfan Nimble
                          Kirkby Freddy
                                        Nanfan Hannah
                    Kirkby Tresarden Curvet
                                        Ch. Gotoground Widgeon Bunny
                          Gotoground Diana
                                        Ch. Hunston Hedge Bunny
</pre>

Ch. Ickworth Ready—Of his backgound Mrs. Southwick wrote, "Nanfan Hannah I bred and kept her sister, 'a better one'." A descendant of Hunston Heralda who had "almost prick ears" which occured regularly in Hunston Herald's strain. Their harsh red wheaten coats and dark eyes were useful virtues. Another ancestor, Hunston Holy Smoke, she found less cooperative, less keen on sport, and just not as much fun as her Herald line. Kay liked her Norfolk small and Smoker at five years old weighed 18 lbs. "Too cloddy to be very active." Alder may have been nearly the same size, "but he had better shoulders."

Gotoground Moley
Nanfan Nimble
Ch. Nanfan Nimbus
Ragus Humprey Bear
Ch. Nanfan Heckle
Ch. Edburton Hilarity
Ragus Penny Wise
CH. RAGUS WHIPCORD
Withalder We Winjam
Ragus Sir Bear
Withalder We Stout
Ragus Who Dat
Nanfan Earwig
Ragus Winnie the Pooh
Ch. Withalder We Wingding

Ch. Ragus Whipcord—the first black back Norfolk to gain his title. Undoubtedly, his color descends from Red Duster of Redlawn, Elel Spruce, and Hunston Holy Smoke, himself a black and tan of the 50s back to Red Wraith, Tiny Tim of Beaufin, and prick-ear, Ch. Farndon Red Dog and Smudge. Whipcord sired 16 champions.

Photo © Sally Anne Thompson
Ch. Salad Burnet of Vicbrita—A well-made wheaten who can really move. Attractive head, dark eye of the right shape, lovely front, short body, strong quarters, great little showman.

Ch. Nanfan Heckle
Eng. Am. Ch. Nanfan Nogbad The Bad
Nanfan Needle
Ch. Nanfan Nobleman
Ch. NanfanHeckle
Ch. Nanfan Noctis
Nanfan Nobility
CH. SALAD BURNET OF VICBRITA (DOG)
Nanfan Nimble
Ch. Nanfan Heckle
Nanfan Hayseed
Ch. Vicbrita Costmary
Gotoground Mouser
Vicbrita Nanfan Nutmeg
Ch. Nanfan Nimbus

Nanfan Nimble
Ragus Humphrey Bear
Ch. Edbutton Hilarity
Ch. Ragus Whipcord
Ragus Sir Bear
Ragus Who Dat
Ragus Winnie the Pooh
CH. RAGUS BROWNED OFF
Kirkby Freddy
Ch. Ickworth Ready
Kirkby Tresarden Curvet
Ch. Ragus Brown Sugar
Ragus Sir Bear
Ch. Ragus Bewitched
Ragus Baby Doll

Photo © Anne Roslin-Williams.
Ch. Ragus Browned Off—"Looked all over the winner, being in tremendous form. His eye is outstanding, as is his topline, great hams and movement." Judge: P. Whittaker.

Ch. Ragus Browned off is the most prolific of the combination that produced him and his many winning brothers and sisters which include six champions, three with international titles. See Chaper 5, page 152, for additional information.

Photo © Sally Anne Thompson.
A consistant winner and a prolific producer for linebred and outcross bitches.

Ch. Nanfan Heckle
Ch. Nanfan Nogbad The Bad
Nanfan Needle
Ch. Nanfan Nobleman
Ch. Nanfan Heckle
Ch. Nanfan Noctis
Nanfan Nobility
CH. AND HARRY OF TITANIUM (DOG)
Nanfan Nimble
Ch. Nanfan Heckle
Nanfan Hayseed
Nanfan Semble
Ch. Nanfan Nobleman
Nanfan Sickle
Ch. Nanfan Snapshot

HISTORIC IMPORTED STUD DOGS
- Ch. Cobbler of Boxted, 1947
- Gotoground Foxhunter, 1957
- Eng. Am. Ch. Daffran Dusty, 1982-1983
- Am. Eng. Ch. Jaeva Matti Brown, 1987-89

A dog of great substance, type and character. He always won at shows and did much to overcome the reticence so prevalent among post War drop ears.

```
                                          Colonsay Bonfire
                          Colonsay War Scar
                                          Colonsay Flaming Onion
              Bulger of Boxted
                                          Colonsay George
                          Dimbols Georgina
                                          Colonsay Bob Tack
CH. COBBLER OF BOXTED (DOG)
                                          Colonsay Bonfire
                          Colonsay Thumbs Up
                                          Colonsay Bonza
              Colonsay Canteen Eggs
                                          Colonsay Hudson
                          Colonsay Sky Rocket
                                          Colonsay Flaming Onion
```

```
                          Elel Spruce
              Eng. Ch. Waveney Valley Alder
                          Pennie of Waveney Valley
      Ragus Solomon Grundy
                          Congham Binder
      Ragus Sweet Sue
                          Ragus Shandygaff
GOTOGROUND FOXHUNTER (DOG)
                          Elel Spruce
              Eng. Ch. Waveney Valley Alder
                          Pennie of Waveney Valley
      Gotoground Tiddly Winks
                          Eng. Ch. Waveney Valley Alder
              Ragus Merry Maid
                          Congham Merry Moth
```

Sired Ch. Gotoground Widgeon Bunny before coming to America. He was small, compact, straight legged, with a hard red coat. A bored showman but a great exterminator.

Spent a fruitful eight months which resulted in ten American champions and one in Germany. His most successful mates were sired by Ch. Elve Pure Magic.

```
                                          Int. Ch. Ickworth Kythe of Ryslip
                          Ickworth Pennywise
                                          Ickworth Penny Piece
              Ickworth Bacardi
                                          Ch. Ragus Whipcord
                          Ragus Bristol Cream
                                          Ch. Ragus Brown Sugar
CH. DAFFRAN DUSTY (DOG)
                                          Ch. Ickworth Ready
                          Int. Ch. Ickworth Kythe of Ryslip
                                          Ickworth Bluemarking Katriona
              Ch. Daffran Dallus
                                          Int. Ch. Ragus Buttermilk
                          Ch. Daffran Dana
                                          Ragus Belladonna
```

```
                        Ragus Humphrey Bear
            Ch. Ragus Whipcord
                        Ragus Who Dat
        Ch. Crackshill Hardy
                        Nanfan Ninety
            Nanfan Nightcap of Crackshill
                        Ch. Nanfan Noctis
AM. ENG. CH. JAEVA MATTI BROWN (DOG)
                        Ch. Ragus Whipcord
            Ch. Ragus Browned Off
                        Ch. Ragus Brown Sugar
        Jaeva Bobby Sox
                        Ch. Ragus Song Book
            Jaeva Bizzi Lizzi
                        Ragus Chaffy
```

Has been an exceptionally popular stud. Cobby, with the most charming ways, his success as an Eng. Stock getter and show dog are remarkable.

AMERICAN BROOD BITCHES

- Ch. Partree Sparkle, 1950
- Colonsay Kelly's Eye, imported 1953
- Ch. Lyndor's Paper Moon, 1973
- Shenanigans of Chidley, 1974
- Bethway's Scarlet O'Fisty, 1975
- Ch. Max-Well's Liberty Bell, 1976
- Ch. Wonderwood Wensday Addams, 1979
- Ch. Raggedge Are You Ready, 1979
- Ch. Abbedale Abigail Ray, 1980
- Ch. Norvik Rightly So, 1982

```
                        Colonsay War Scar
            Bulger of Boxted
                        Dimbols Georgina
        Ch.Cobbler of Boxted
                        Colonsay Thumbs Up
            Colonsay Canteen Eggs
                        Colonsay Sky Rocket
CH. PARTREE SPARKLE
                        Tobit
            Trump of Boxted
                        Neachley Toffee
        Partree Chance
                        Colonsay Berry
            Mollycoddle of Down East
                        Colonsay Do-one's-bit
```

A Castle Point foundation bitch.

Bethways founding dam with six champion offspring.

```
                        Colonsay Dabster
            Colonsay Dicky Flutter
                        Wymondley Flirt
        Colonsay Fag Wagger
                        Woe Begone
            Colonsay Coppa Dah
                        Colonsay Kola
CH. COLONSAY KELLY'S EYE
                        Red Scarlett
            Colonsay Flip
                        Polly Flinders
        Colonsay Granny
                        Colonsay Guerilla
            Marpet March Past
                        Shermish
```

Ch. Bethway's Pence
Ch. Bethway's John
Ch. Bethway's Mandy
Ch. Bethway's Ringo
Eng. Ch. Colonsay Orderley Dog
Colonsay A Ring
Colonsay Bluemarking Lady Jane

Ch. Lyndor's Paper Moon: Dam of champions and two winning stud dogs, Ch. Lyndo'rs Mister and Ch. Lyndor's Pippin.

CH. LYNDOR'S PAPER MOON
Nanfan Nugget
Ch. Bethway's Aramis
Ch. Bethway's Little Tinker Bell
Ch. Lyndors Flower Power
Ch. Bethway's Ringo
Bethway's Bell
Bethway's Little Scarlet

Dam of three Chidley champions and many more in succeeding generations. She excels in coat, topline, movement, and eyes.

Ch. Newry's Red Fox
Ch. Bethway's Fagan
Bethway's Baby Cricket
Newry's Mr. Fargo
Ch. Bethway's Little Mister
Bethway's Dixie
Bethway's Miss Nancy Dee
SHENANIGANS OF CHIDLEY
Ch. Bethway's Aramis
Ch. Bethway's Tramis
Bethway's Trinket
Newry's Hey You
Ch. Bethway's Tony
Ch. Bethway's Miss Itch
Ch. Bethway's Scarlet

Eng. Ch. Ickworth Ready
Ch. Badgewood Blakeney
Eng. Am. Ch. Badgewood Bonnie
Ch. Badgewood Moreston
Can. Am. Ch. Ickworth Nimrod
Ch. Badgewood Miss Alice
Ch. Badgewood King's Lynn
CH. MAX-WELL'S LIBERTY BELL
Can. Am. Ch. Ickworth Nimrod
Ch. Badgewood Monty Collins
Ch. Badgewood King's Lynn
Max-Well's Rum Raison
Ch. Bethway's Cricket
Bethway's Miss Susie
Bethway's Chatham Twiggy

The foundation dam for Max-Wells, and dam of six champions and other winning get.

Gotoground Mouser
Nanfan Nugget
Nanfan Nimbus
Ch. Bethway's Aramis
Ch. Bethway's Tony
Ch. Bethway's Little Tinker Bell
Wensum Tinker Bell
BETHWAY'S SCARLET O'FISTY
Ch. Bethway's Pence
Ch. Bethway's Pensum
Wensum Tinker Bell
Bethway's Pecan
Ch. Bethway's Mr. Kennedy
Bethway's Walnut
Bethway's Bridget

This small, rich and harsh coated "perfect demon" endowed all her offspring with her type, color, non-trim "jacket," and exceptionally happy personality.

Ch. Nanfan Heckle
Ch. Nanfan Thistle
Foxhunter Tally Ho
Leddington Captain Cook
Ch. Gotoground Widgeon Bunny
Gotoground Cuckoo
Ch. Hunston Hedge Betty
CH. WONDERWOOD WENSDAY ADDAMS
Tinkinswood Appolo
Leddington Diplomat
Bluemarking Bracken
Leddington Folly
Ch. Ickworth Ready
Bluemarking Bracken
Nanfan Nymph

Pioneered for Norfolk in California. Her worthy champion offspring have also won in tough eastern competition like their dam.

Compact, short-legged, and sound, she endows her descendants with her type and outgoing temperament. Her younger, full sister, Ch. Raggedge Best Bet, is larger with an appealing head.

Ch. Ickworth Pathfinder
Ragus Bitterman
Ch. Ragus Brown Smudge
Ch. Elve Pure Magic
Ch. Ragus Whipcord
Ch. Ragus Brown Cider
Ch. Ragus Brown Sugar
CH. RAGGEDGE ARE YOU READY
Ickworth Juniper
Ch. Ickworth Bluemarking Phillip
Ickworth Penelope
Mt. Paul Vesper
Ch. Castle Point Iguana
Ch. Mt. Paul Tulip
Nanfan Tilly Tally

Eng. Ch. Ickworth Pathfinder
Ragus Bitterman
Eng. Ch. Ragus Brown Smudge
Ch. Elve Pure Magic
Ch. Ragus Whipcord
Eng. Ch. Ragus Brown Cider
Ch. Ragus Brown Sugar
CH. ABBEDALE ABIGAIL RAY
Ch. Bethway's Aramis
Bethway's Popover
Bethway's Robin
Abbedales Tea and Crumpets
Ch. Bethway's John
Bethway's Muffin II
Bethway's Dixy

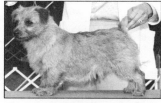

Has four champion get among her many offspring. A fantastic dam, she helped rear orphan Chesapeake puppies along with her own quintet. She excels in correct size, coat, hunting and swimming.

The foundation dam for the Rightly So's. This small, extra-cobby bitch has many top winning Breed, Group, and Best in Show relatives.

Ch. Elve Pure Magic
King's Prevention Jolly Roger
King's Prevention Belinda
Ch. Surrey Sink or Swim
Ch. Wendover Torrent
Ch. King's Prevention Ahoy
Ch. Nanfan Corricle
CH. NORVIK RIGHTLY SO
Ch. Elve Pure Magic
King's Prevention Jolly Roger
King's Prevention Belinda
Ch. Surrey Skiff
Ch. Lyndor's Mister
Lyndor's Kizzy
Ch. Lyndor's Cricket

RECENT INFLUENTIAL IMPORTS

- Am. Can. Ch. Ickworth Nimrod, 1968
- Ch. Elve Pure Magic, 1977
- Ch. Hatchwood's Creme de Menthe, 1978
- Ch. Allright Magic Lamp, 1984

```
                                    Eng. Ch. Gotoground Widgeon Bunny
                   Eng. Ch. Gotoground True Blue
                            Gotoground Vixen
       Hanleycastle Brock
                            Waveney Valley Ditcher
                   Nanfan Nectar
                            Nanfan Bramble
AM. CAN. CH. ICKWORTH NIMROD (DOG)
                            Nanfan Nimble
                   Eng. Ch. Nanfan Heckle
                            Nanfan Hayseed
       Nanfan Nymph
                            Gotogound Moley
                   Nanfan Needle
                            Eng. Ch. Nanfan Nimbus
```

Am. Can. Ch. Ickworth Nimrod—Nimrod was selected by Philip S. P. Fell at a show in England and went on to become Badgewood Kennel's leading stud dog with 12 champion get.

The four Badgewood champions by Nimrod were out of Ch. Badgewood Kings Lynn, a Ch. Ickworth Ready daughter. Two of these have show records with specialty, Montgomery County, and Group wins.

Another champion daughter, is a brood bitch for Badgewood while Nimrod's daughter, Ch. Turkhill's Brown Nectar, is a founding dam for Cybele Kennels in Massachusetts.

The remaining six champions are from Suzann Bobley and Barbara Miller's Ch. Max-Well's Liberty Bell, a Nimrod descendant on both her sire and dam's side.

```
                                              Int. Ch. Ragus Buttermilk
                            Eng. Ch. Ickworth Pathfinder
                                              Eng. Ch. Ickworth Proper
                                              Pretty
                   Ragus Bitterman
                                              Eng. Ch. Ragus Whipcord
                            Int. Ch. Ragus Brown Smudge
                                              Eng. Ch. Ragus Brown Sugar
CH. ELVE PURE MAGIC (DOG)
                                              Ragus Humphrey Bear
                            Eng. Ch. Ragus Whipcord
                                              Ragus Who Dat
                   Eng. Ch. Ragus Brown Cider
                                              Eng. Ch. Ickworth Ready
                            Eng. Ch. Ragus Brown Sugar
                                              Eng. Ch. Ragus Bewitched
```

Ch. Elve Pure Magic—Was a cobby intensly masculine dog with hugh teeth, a scissor bite, black eyes well-dropped ears, a straight front, and long low strides. Balanced and well-proportioned, he could have used more backskull width and a deeper stop. His character was strong, he adored puppies and posing, had a broad smile, tight feet, and begot 13 champions and many black and tans. His accidental death at six was a blow to breeding plans at several kennels.

```
                                    Eng. Ch. Nanfan Ninety
                          Nanfan Tangle
                                    Foxhunters Tallyho
                Int. Nordic Ch. Cracknor Capricorn
                                    Int. Nordic Sh. Ch. Withalder We
                                    Westrum
                          Sandemars Wee Cornflake
                                    Swed. Sh. Ch. Cracknor Corncockle
CH. HATCHWOODS CREME DE MENTHE OF CRACKNOR (DOG)
                                    Eng. Ch. Nanfan Nogbad The Bad
                          Eng. Ch. Nanfan Nobleman
                                    Eng. Ch. Nanfan Noctis
                Hatchwoods Peppermint
                                    Eng. Ch. Nanfan Thistle
                          Leddington Biscuit
                                    Bluemarking Bracken
```

Mrs. Steven Baird's young **Hatch-woods Creme de Menthe** arrived at Castle Point, Bernardsville, New Jersey in early January after winning his second CC at the Norfolk Club Specialty Show in England under Mrs. "Nanfan" Taylor. Now a champion, he made his ring debut here, winning major points under British authority Ferelith Hamilton and continued his winning ways at the NNTC Specialty Show by topping the champions to win Best Norfolk. Small, compact, and extroverted, he has a nice head, correctly dropped ears, a grand coat, super rear drive, and enjoys exhibiting. His sire, Swed. Ch. Cracknor Capricorn, also an English CC winner, and his dam, Hatchwoods Peppermint are both multiple descendants of Ch. Nanfan Heckle or his brothers and most fittingly Foxhunters Tallyho who was reared at Castle Point before joining the Nanfans (1981).

Photo © Sally Anne thompson.

```
                          Int. Ch. Cracknor Sweetcorn
                Int. Ch. Cracknor Candidate
                          Nanfan Country Cousin
          Allright Huckleberry Finn
                          Ickworth Sandstorm
                Allright Chillcotin Girl
                          Ickworth Penny Ha'Penny
CH. ALLRIGHT MAGIC LAMP (DOG)
                          Ickworth Bacardi
                Eng. Am. Ch. Daffran Dusty
                          Eng. Ch. Daffran Dallus
          Ger. Ch. Allright Magic Carpet
                          Ch. Elve Pure Magic
                Chidley Pooka
                          Shennanigans of Chidley
```

Ch. Allright Magic Lamp— (1984) Was slow to mature, but at 18 months was Best of Winners at the breed's 50th Anniversary Show under Joy Taylor. A born showman, "Bronco" can cover ground maintaining his topline. He is an excellent excavator, has his Working Certificate, and eight champion get. He has defeated every important winner he has met.

LEADING AMERICAN BRED SIRES

- Chs. Bethway's Pound and Pence, 1957.
- Ch. Bethway's Aramis, 1967.
- Ch. Castle Point Iguana, 1969.
- Ch. Surrey Sink or Swim, 1980.
- Ch. Max-Wells Winter Sport, 1984.

At eight months of age.

```
                                    Colonsay Didlum Buck
                          Ragus Sweet William
                                    Ragus Sweet Sue
                Ch. Ragus Jimmy Joe
                                    Elel Spruce
                          Waveney Valley Pandy
                                    Tanner of Waveney Valley
CH. BETHWAY'S POUND
CH. BETHWAY'S PENCE
                                    Colonsay Dicky Flutter
                          Colonsay Fag Wagger
                                    Colonsay Coppa Dah
                Ch. Colonsay Kelly's Eye
                                    Colonsay Flip
                          Colonsay Granny
                                    Marpet March Past
```

```
                        Gotoground Moley
                 Gotoground Mouser
                        Gotoground Vixen
        Nanfan Nugget
                        Ch. Gotogound Widgeon Bunny
                 Ch. Nanfan Nimbus
                        Nanfan Nettle
CH. BETHWAY'S ARAMIS
                        Hunston High Flier
                 Ch. Bethway's Tony
                        Ch. Colonsay Kelly's Eye
        Ch. Bethway's Little Tinker Bell
                        Ch. Waveney Valley Alder
                 Wensum Tinker Bell
                        Robincott Tango
```

```
                              Nanfan Nimble
                       Ch. Nanfan Heckle
                              Nanfan Hayseed
                 Nanfan Terrapin
                              Gotoground Foxhunter
                       Foxhunters Tally Ho
                              Gumdrop
        CH. CASTLE POINT IGUANA
                              Gotoground Foxhunter
                       Ch. Wendover Foxhunter
                              Wendover Apple
                 Castle Point Withers
                              Ch. Rednor Red Rufus
                       Castle Point Twining
                              Castle Point Ultra
```

```
                        Ragus Bitterman
                 Ch. Elve Pure Magic
                        Ragus Brown Cider
        King's Prevention Jolly Roger
                        Ch. Ickworth Peter's Pence
                 King's Prevention Belinda
                        Ch. Nanfan Corricle
CH. SURREY SINK OR SWIM
                        Ch. Nanfan Storm
                 Ch. Wendover Torrent
                        Ch. Mt. Paul Terracotta
        Ch. King's Prevention Ahoy
                        Eng. Ch. Nanfan Ninety
                 Ch. Nanfan Corricle
                        Eng. Ch. Cinnamon of Nanfan
```

Sire of 16 champions of record.

```
                              Eng. Ch. Nanfan Ninety
                       Eng. Ch. Nanfan Sweet Potato
                              Eng. Ch. Nanfan Sweet Apple
                 Ch. Nanfan Crunch (Eng. import)
                              Eng. Ch. Nanfan Ninety
                       Eng. Ch. Nanfan Copycat
                              Eng. Ch. Cinnamon of Nanfan
        CH. MAX-WELL'S WINTER SPORT
                              Am. Can. Ch. Ickworth Nimrod
                       Ch. Max-Well's O'Henry
                              Ch. Max-Well's Liberty Bell
                 White Star Alice Max-Well
                              Ickworth Pennywise
                       Ickworth Topaz
                              Daffran Twinkle Toes
```

INFLUENTIAL PAIRS

- **Leddington Captain Cook, 1971**
- **Cinnamon of Nanfan, 1971**

- **Int. Ch. Ragus Buttermilk, 1972**
- **Ch. Ragus Brown Sugar, 1972**

- **Ch. Mt. Paul Vesper, 1974**
- **Ch. Mt. Paul Viking, CG, 1974**

- **Int. Ch. Nanfan Sweetcorn, 1974**
- **Ch. Nanfan Sweet Apple, 1974**

- **Ch. Chidley Magic Marker, 1983**
- **Ger. Ch. Chidley Magic Carpet, 1983**

```
                              Nanfan Nimble
                 Eng. Ch. Nanfan Heckle
                              Nanfan Hayseed
        Eng. Ch. Nanfan Thistle
                              Gotoground Foxhunter
                 Foxhunter's Tally Ho
                              Gum Drop
ENG. CH. CINNAMON OF NANFAN (BITCH)
LEDDINGTON CAPTAIN COOK (DOG)
                              Gotoground Foxhunter
                 Ch. Gotogound Widgeon Bunny
                              Ragus Merry Maid
        Gotoground Cuckoo
                              Ch. Waveney Valley Alder
                 Ch. Hunston Hedge Betty
                              Hunston Heralda
```

Photo © Sally Anne Thompson.

Eng. Ch. Cinnamon of Nanfan —(pictured) Taylor's Cinnamon of Nanfan. "Another topliner, short body which is the hallmark of this famous kennel." Judge: Les Atkinson. Cinnamon is the foundation of the Nanfan "C" line. **Leddington Captain Cook**—Blanford's Leddington Captain Cook. "Needs to let down in body, in excellent coat, nice head and expression, alert outlook, moves well." Judge: Les Atkinson. This sparingly exhibited dog won fame as an exceptional sire at home and abroad.

```
                              Nanfan Nimble
                 Kirkby Freddy
                              Nanfan Hannah
        Eng. Ch. Ickworth Ready
                              Kirkby Freddy
                 Kirkby Tresarden Curvet
                              Gotoground Diana
INT. CH. RAGUS BUTTERMILK (DOG)
ENG. CH. RAGUS BROWN SUGAR (BITCH)
                              Withalder We Winjam
                 Ragus Sir Bear
                              Withalder We Stout
        Eng. Ch. Ragus Bewitched
                              Eng. Ch. Edburton Jackeroo
                 Ragus Baby Doll
                              Ragus Bumble Bee
```

Pictured—**Eng. Ch. Ragus Brown Sugar,** dam of seven champions, all by Ch. Ragus Whipcord.
Drawing by Lesley Crawley.

Int. Ch. Ragus Buttermilk—"Another I liked a lot, built on the same lines and very like his famous father I judged at about the same age. They must both have a brilliant future." Judge: Mrs. J. de Casembroot. Sired English champions before a successful Scandinavian career.

```
                      Eng. Ch. Ickworth Ready
              Ickworth Juniper
                      Eng. Ch. Colonsay Bluemarking
                      Lady Jane
       Eng. Ch. Ickworth Redfox Phillip
                      Colonsay Red Tabs
              Ickworth Penelope
                      Colonsay Pretty Pretties
CH. MT. PAUL VESPER (BITCH)
CH. MT. PAUL VIKING, CG (DOG)
                      Nanfan Terrapin
              Ch. Castle Point Iguana
                      Castle Point Withers
       Ch. Mt. Paul Tulip
                      Eng. Ch. Nafan Heckle
              Nanfan Tilly Tally
                      Foxhunter's Tally Ho
```

Pictured, **Ch. Mt. Paul Viking**—An able competitor at Working Terrier Trials and holder of a Certificate of Gameness.

Ch. Mt. Paul Vesper—Dam of founding bitches for Annunsnac, Greenfield, and Yarrow.

```
                      Gotoground Moley
              Nanfan Nimble
                      Eng. Ch. Nanfan Nimbus
       Eng. Ch. Nanfan Heckle
                      Nanfan Nimrod
              Nanfan Hayseed
                      Hunston Hedge Warbler
SWED. NOR. CH. NANFAN SWEETCORN (DOG)
ENG. CH. NANFAN SWEET APPLE (BITCH)
                      Eng. Ch. Nafan Nogbad The Bad
              Eng. Ch. Nanfan Nobleman
                      Eng. Ch. Nanfan Noctis
       Nanfan Sickel
                      Eng. Ch. Nanfan Heckle
              Eng. Ch. Nanfan Snapshot
                      Gayrunor Golden Spangle
```

Pictured, **Swed. and Nor. Ch. Nanfan Sweetcorn**—"Here was the king, an outstanding dog who could not be denied. Gave me exactly the same feeling of excitement when I looked at him as I had when I first saw him in Sweden, has so much to give to the breed in this country. His coat and presentation were tremendous, his movement correct, he just oozes breed type and character and I very much hope he will quickly gain his title for he deserves it." Judge: Gilean White. He was Cracknors leading sire for 12 years.

Eng. Ch. Nafan Sweet Apple—"By the time he (Heckle) was approaching old age and that we thought, was that. But no, at the age of 10 1/2 he sired another daughter who was to become his most famous child of all. Ch. Nanfan Sweet Apple, who qualified for her title at three straight shows before she was 13 months old, on the day she qualified winning the Terrier Group at Bath Championship Show, the first bitch in the breed to do so and the first Norfolk to win such an award in England. " —*Marjorie Bunting.*

```
                      Ickworth Penny Wise
              Ickworth Bacardi
                      Eng. Ch. Ragus Bristol Cream
       Ch. Daffran Dusty
                      Int. Ch. Ickworth Kythe
              Eng. Ch. Daffran Dallus
                      Eng. Ch. Daffran Dana
CH. CHIDLEY MAGIC MARKER (DOG)
GER. CH. CHIDLEY MAGIC CARPET (BITCH)
                      Ragus Bitterman
              Ch. Elve Pure Magic
                      Ch. Ragus Brown Cider
       Chidley Pooka
                      Newry Mr. Fagan
              Shenanigans of Chidley
                      Newry Hey You
```

Top, **Ch. Chidley Magic Marker.**
Left, **Ger. Ch. Chidley Magic Carpet** . *Photo © Sally Anne Thompson.*

ADDITIONAL BREED INFLUENCES OVERSEAS

- Int. & World Ch. Cracknor Candidate, Germany, 1981
- Int. Ch. Cracknor Canterbury, Sweden, 1977
- Ch. Redriff Rambling Rose, Sweden, 1980
- Int. Nordic Ch. Guestlings Catch A Star, Sweden, 1984
- Ch. Stall Mascot's Air Mail, Finland, 1981
- Ch. Northsea Dunval Half-A-Bob, Canada, 1978

"A great dog. Excels in head and expression, has a lovely top-line and is very sound both ends and really looks a winner." *Siv Jernhake.*

```
                                          Nanfan Nimble
                              Ch. Nanfan Heckle
                                          Nanfan Hayseed
                  Eng. & Int. Ch. Nanfan Sweetcorn
                                          Ch. Nanfan Nobleman
                              Nanfan Sickle
                                          Ch. Nanfan Snapshot
INT. CH. & WORLD CH. CRACKNOR CANDIDATE (DOG)
                                          Nanfan Halleluia
                              Nanfan Ninety
                                          Nanfan Needle
                  Nanfan Country Cousin
                                          Nanfan Thistle
                              Cinnamon of Nanfan
                                          Gotoground Cuckoo
```

```
                              Nanfan Nimble
                  Ch. Nanfan Heckle
                              Nanfan Hayseed
      Ch. Nanfan Sweetcorn
                              Ch. Nanfan Nobleman
                  Nanfan Sickle
                              Ch. Nanfan Snapshot
INT. & NORD. CH. CRACKNOR CANTERBURY (DOG)
                              Gotoground Moley
                  Nanfan Nimble
                              Ch. Nanfan Nimbus
      Ch. Bluemarking Santolina
                              Ch. Gotoground Widgeon Bunnie
                  Gotoground Cuckoo
                              Ch. Hunston Hedge Betty
```

"Excellent size with all the essentials. He has excellent feet, nice expression, well-placed ears, very short-coupled, good dog." *M. Micklewaite.*

Sweden's outstanding winning bitch and producer at eight years.

```
                                          Ch. Nanfan Heckle
                              Eng. & Int. Ch. Nanfan Sweetcorn
                                          Nanfan Sickle
                  Ch. Cracknor Cute 'N Kissy
                                          Nanfan Nimble
                              Ch. Bluemarking Santolina
                                          Gotoground Cuckoo
INT. & NORD. CH. REDRIFF RAMBLING ROSE (BITCH)
                                          Ragus Humphrey Bear
                              Ch. Ragus Whipcord
                                          Ragus Who Dat
                  Ch. Ragus Betsy Trotwood
                                          Ch. Ickworth Ready
                              Ch. Ragus Brown Sugar
                                          Ch. Ragus Bewitched
```

```
                        Ch. Nanfan Ninety
              Ch. Nanfan Sweet Potato
                        Ch. Nanfan Sweet Apple
        Ch. Nanfan Category
                        Ch. Nanfan Ninety
              Ch. Nanfan Copycat
                        Ch. Cinnamon of Nanfan
INT. NORDIC CH. GUESTLINGS CATCH A STAR (DOG)
                        Ch. Nanfan Sweetcorn
              Ch. Cracknor Cute 'N Kissy
                        Ch. Bluemarking Santolina
        Ch. Redriff Rambling Rose
                        Ch. Ragus Whipcord
              Ch. Ragus Betsy Trotwood
                        Ch. Ragus Brown Sugar
```

"Very stylish type. Very good head and neck. Very firm frame. Good quarters. Nice, harsh coat. Showing a lot of quality. Very keen in action." *G. Corish*.

"Typical Norfolk Terrier dog. Nice broad skull, good ears, nice size, good coat, moves well." *Wm. Green*.

```
                              Ragus Humphrey Bear
              Ch. Ragus Whipcord
                              Ragus Who Dat
        Lady Killer
                              Ch. Ickworth Pathfinder
              Ch. Ragus Shady Lady
                              Ragus Scandal
CH. STALL MASCOT'S AIR MAIL (DOG)
                              Ch. Ragus Buttermilk
              Ch. Rough 'N Ready
                              Ch. Sandemars Wee Flame
        Ch. Black Velvet
                              Ch. Ragus Browned Off
              Ragus Wineberry
                              Ragus Wild Honey
```

```
                        Kirkby Freddie
              Eng. Ch. Ickworth Ready
                        Kirkby Tresarden Curvet
        Am. Ch. Badgewood Blakeny
                        Eng. Ch. Nanfan Heckle
              Eng. Am. Ch. Badgewood Bonnie
                        Badgewood Miss Poppet
CH. NORTHSEA DUNVAL HALF-A-BOB (BITCH)
                        Withalder We Winjam
              Ragus Sir Bear
                        Withalder We Stout
        Marmalade of Ragus
                        Robincott Tymothy
              Ortonhill Misty
                        Ortonhill Sherry
```

"Grounder" is the dam of Ch. Dalcroft Kyrie by Am. Can. Ch. Chidley Mumbo Jumbo, and many other winners.

**INT. & SCANDINAVIAN CH RAGUS
BETSY TROTWOOD**
(Ch. Ragus Whipcord x Ch. Ragus Brown Sugar)
Dam of Int. Ch. Redriff Rambling Rose and other Scandinavian champions.

The Kennel Club.
84 PICCADILLY, LONDON, W.1.
Registration Certificate №48404/33

This is to Certify that ~~Norwich Terrier~~ ~~(ANY OTHER BREED OR VARIETY OF BRITISH, COLONIAL OR FOREIGN DOG NOT CLASSIFIED.)~~ has been registered at the Kennel Club by the name of

Tinker Bell

Sex Bitch

The Registration fee has been paid by the owner,

Mrs. G. Blewitt

who has supplied the particulars of Pedigree, and same are duly recorded in the Kennel Club Registers.

Sire Tobit   Dam Neachley Toffee

Breeder Owner   Date of Birth 17 July '33

Date 11 DEC 1933 1933.   H. T. W. BOWELL, Secretary.

NOTE.— If any of the above particulars are incorrect please return this Certificate at once.

This Registration will be published in No. 546 of "The Kennel Gazette" which will be issued on the Third Saturday in Jany 34. Post free, 1s. 2d.

TERMINOLOGY

Almond eye - Eye of almond shape instead of round.

Angulation - Angles formed by a meeting of the bones; mainly the shoulder, upper arm, stifle, and hock.

Apple-headed- Skull round instead of flat on top.

Balanced - Symmetrical; typically proportioned as a whole.

Bench show - A show at which the dogs competing for prizes are "benched" or leashed on benches when not in the show ring.

Bitch - A female dog.

Bite - The relative position of the upper and lower teeth when the mouth is closed.

Bodied up - Mature; well-developed.

Bolt - To drive or "start" an animal from its earth, burrow, or den.

Bone - Refers to the relative girth or thickness of a dog's leg bones.

Brisket - The forepart of the body below the chest, between the forelegs, closest to the ribs. Sometimes called "keel."

Broken-haired - A roughed-up, wiry coat.

Brood bitch - Female used for breeding purposes.

Canines - The two upper and two lower large, sharp-pointed teeth next to the incisors. The "fangs."

Castrate - To remove the testicles of a male dog.

Cat foot - Compact, round foot like that of a cat.

Ch. (Champion) - A dog that has been recorded a champion by the American Kennel Club as the result of defeating a specified number of dogs in specific competition at a series of dog shows.

Character - Expression, individuality, general appearance, and deportment as typical of a breed.

Chest - The part of the body or trunk that is enclosed by the ribs.

Chiseled - Clean-cut in head, particularly beneath the eyes.

Close-coupled - Comparatively short from withers to hipbones.

Cobby - Short-bodied and compact.

Condition - The health as shown by the coat, state of flesh, muscle tone, and deportment.

Conformation - The form and structure, make, and shape of a dog. Arrangement of parts in accord with breed standard.

Corky - Active; lively; alert.

Coupling - The part of the body between the ribs and pelvis; the loin.

Covering ground - The distance covered with each flexion (stride) of a moving dog.

Cow-hocked - When the hocks turn toward each other.

Cropping - The cutting or trimming of the ear leather to a point to make the ears stand erect.

Croup - Portionof the back directly behind the set-on or root of tail.

Cryptorchid - A male dog with neither testicle descended or visible.

Dam - The female parent.

Dewclaw - The extra toe or claw on the inside of the leg.

Distemper teeth - Teeth discolored or pitted due to distemper or some other enervating disease or deficiency.

Dock - To shorten the tail by cropping.

Dog - Male dog.

Dog show - A competitive exhibition at which dogs are judged in accordance with the established standard of perfection for each breed.

Domed - Evenly rounded in topskull; convex instead of flat.

Double coat - An outer coat, resistant to weather and protective against brush and brambles, together with an undercoat of softer hair for warmth and waterproofing.

Drop ear - Ears hanging close and flat to the sides of the cheeks.

Elbow - The joint at the top of the foreleg next to the body.

Estrus or Estrum - The period during which a bitch is receptive to a dog and ready to breed.

Expression - General appearance of all features of the head as viewed from the front and as typical of the breed.

Fancier - A person especially interested and usually active in some phase of the sport of dogs.

Fiddle front - Forelegs out at elbows, pasterns close, and feet turned out. (Sometimes called "Chippendale front.")

Flank - Either side of the body between the last rib and the hip.

Flat-sided - Ribs insufficiently rounded as they approach the sternum or breastbone.

Fluffy - A coat of extreme length with exaggerated feathering on ears, chest, legs and feet, underparts, and hindquarters. (Trimming such a coat does not make it more acceptable.)

Flying ears - Any characteristic drop ears or semi-prick ears that stand out from the sides of the head, or "fly."

Forearm - The part of the foreleg between the elbow and the pastern.

Foreface - The part of the head before the eye. The muzzle.

Front - The forepart of the body as viewed head on; i.e., forelegs, chest, brisket, and shoulder line.

Gait - Coordinated leg action, when the dog moves correctly.

Game - Hunted animals. Also, a dog's attitude of enthu-siasm for hunting.

Gay tail - Tail carried over the back line.

Get - Progeny of a male dog.

Going to ground - A terrier going or being sent into an earth, den, or hole for the purpose of bolting a fox or other animal; or to be of assistance when such an animal is being dug out.

Grizzle - Bluish-gray coat color.

Groups - The canine breeds as divided into seven divisions or varieties to facilitate judging.

Hackles - Coat on neck and back raised involuntarily in fright or anger.

Handler - A person who exhibits a dog in the show ring.

Heat - Common term for season, or estrus, in the bitch.

Height - Measurement from withers to ground; referred to as shoulder height.

Hock - The tarsus or collection of bones of the hind leg forming the joint between the second thigh and the metatarsus. The dog's true heel.

Hocks well let down - When the distance from the hock joint to the ground is comparatively short. Hocks close to the ground.

Honorable scars - Scars from injuries sustained as a result of work.

Inbreeding - The mating of closely related dogs, as father to daughter, mother to son, brother to sister.

Incisors - The upper and lower frontmost teeth between the canines.

Leather - The skin of the external ear.

Level bite - Meeting of front teeth (incisors) edge-to-edge, with no overlap between upper and lower teeth.

Line breeding - A theory of calling for dogs within a line or family to be bred to a common ancestor; for example, a dog to his granddam or a bitch to her grandsire.

Loaded shoulders - When the shoulder blades are shoved out from the body by overdevelopment of the muscles.

Loin - The region of the body on either side of the vertebral column between the last rib and the hindquarters.

Mane - Profuse hair growth on the sides of the neck, shoulders, and down the middle of the back.

Match show - Usually an informal dog show at which no championship points are awarded.

Mate - To breed a dog or a bitch.

Monorchid - A male dog with only one testicle descended.

Muzzle - The head in front of the eyes: nasal bone, nostrils, and jaws. Foreface.

Occiput - The upper, back point of the skull.

Offspring - The progeny or whelps of a female dog.

Open Class - A class at dog shows in which all dogs of the same breed and sex may compete.

Outcross - The mating of dogs of the same breed but of entirely unrelated ancestry.

Overshot - The front teeth of the upper jaw protruding over those of the lower jaw.

Pace - A gait that tends to promote a rolling motion of the body. The left foreleg and left hindleg advance in unison, then the right foreleg and hindleg. Speed of movement.

Paddling - A gaiting fault named for canoeists' swing-and-dip action.

	Can be caused by tied-in elbows or shoulders.
Pads -	The tough, shock-absorbing soles of the feet.
Pastern -	Area below the knee on the front leg or below the hock on the hind leg.
Pedigree -	A dog's "family tree," or genealogy.
Points -	Color on face, ears, legs, and tail when correlated—usually white, black, or tan.
Prefix -	Usually the first part of a dog's registered name, identifying the strain or line from which it has been bred. A kennel name.
Premium list -	An advance-notice entry form for exhibitors containing show details.
Prick ear -	Ear carried erect and usually pointed at the tip.
Purebred -	A dog whose sire and dam belong to the same breed.
Roach back -	A convex curvature of the back toward the loin.
Ruff -	The thick, longer hair surrounding the neck below the ears.
Saddle -	A black marking over the back, like a saddle on a horse.
Scissors bite -	A bite in which the inner surface of the upper incisors touches the outer surface of the lower incisors like the blades of a pair of scissors.
Second thigh -	The part of the hindquarter from the stifle to the hock.
Self color -	One color or whole color except for lighter shadings.
Shelly -	A narrow or "weedy" body.
Shoulder -	The muscle and skin covering the shoulder blade.
Sire -	The male parent.
Sloping shoulder -	The shoulder blade set obliquely and laid back.
Smooth coat -	Short hair, close-lying.
Snipey -	A pointed, thin muzzle, giving a foxy appearance.
Soundness -	State of mental and physical health when all organs and faculties are complete and functioning normally, each in its rightful relation to the other.
Spay -	To surgically remove certain of the bitch's reproductive organs to prevent conception.
Splay foot -	A flat foot with spreading toes.
Spring of ribs -	Degree of rib roundedness.
Squirrel tail -	A tail carried up and curving forward over the back.
Stance -	Manner of standing.
Standard -	A description of the ideal of each recognized breed, to serve as a pattern by which dogs are judged at shows.
Staring coat -	The hair dry, harsh, and sometimes curling at the tip.
Sternum -	Breastbone.
Stifle -	The joint in the dog's hind leg equivalent to the knee in humans.
Stilted -	The choppy, up-and-down gait of a straight-hocked dog.
Stop -	The indentation between the nose and forehead between the eyes.
Straight-hocked -	Lacking appreciable angulation at the hock joints, giving a straight-legged appearance behind.
Straight shoulders-	The shoulder blades rather straight up and down, as op-

posed to sloping or well laid back.

Stud book -	A record of the breeding particulars of dogs of recognized breeds.
Stud dog -	Male used for breeding purposes.
Substance -	Bone.
Thigh -	The hindquarters from hip to stifle.
Tulip ear -	An upright ear with turned-down tip.
Undershot -	The lower teeth projecting beyond the upper.
Upper arm -	Humerus or bone of the foreleg, between the shoulder blade and the forearm.
Varminty -	A keen, very bright, or piercing expression.
Weaving -	When in action, the crossing of the forefeet or the hindfeet.
Well-sprung -	Well-formed, rounded ribs.
Wheaten -	Pale yellow, fawn.
Whelping -	Giving birth to puppies.
Whelps -	Unweaned puppies.
Whiskers -	Longer hairs on muzzle sides and underjaw.
Wire-haired -	A harsh, crisp coat.
Withers -	The highest point of the shoulder blade immediately behind the neck.

INDEX OF ILLUSTRATIONS

lonsay Kelly's Eye; Shenanigans of Chidley; Ch. Max-Well's Liberty Bell; Bethway's Scarlet O'Fisty; Ch. Wonderwood Wensday Addams; Ch. Raggedge Are You Ready; Ch. Abbedale Abigail Ray; Ch. Norvik Rightly So; Am. Can. Ch. Ickworth Nimrod; Ch. Elve Pure Magic; Ch. Hatchwoods Creme de Menthe of Cracknor; Ch. Allright Magic Lamp; Chs. Bethway's Pound and Pence; Ch. Bethway's Aramis; Ch. Castle Point Iguana; Ch. Surrey Sink or Swim; Ch. Max-Well's Winter Sport; Eng. Ch. Cinnamon of Nanfan; Eng. Ch. Ragus Brown Sugar; Ch. Mt. Paul Viking, CG; Swed. Nor. Ch. Nanfan Sweetcorn; Ch. Chidley Magic Marker & Chidley Magic Carpet; Int. Ch. & World Ch. Cracknor Candidate; Int. & Nord. Ch. Cracknor Canterbury; Int. & Nord. Ch. Redriff Rambling Rose; Int. Ch. Guestlings Catch A Star; Ch. Stall Mascot's Air Mail; Ch. Northsea Dunval Half-A-Bob; Int. Swed. Ch. Ragus Betsy Trotwood.

COLOR INSERT

Little Dickens of C and J; Ch. Allright Magic Midge; Neverdone's Quick Pickwick; Two dogs in water; Ch. Wendover Half Pound; Ch. Biffin of Beaufin; painting of early terriers; Three colors of Norfolks; Ch. Nanfan Crunch; Golden and Norfolk; Poole's Ide Pachysandra; Allright Magic Bee and Allright Julie Bee; Ch. Dalcroft's Kyrie; Wally.

PENNIE OF L...

COLONSAY CADY

COLONSAY THUMBS UP

COLONSAY BRAMAH

KINMOUNT PIP

LITTLE JANE OF BEAUFIN

CH BEAUFIN

JANE OF BEAUFIN

TINY TIM OF BIFFIN

CH TINKER BELL (DE) 17.7.33

COLONSAY BONZA 1.5.39

COLONSAY ACK DUM

COLONSAY MIDDY

COLONSAY BONFIRE 21.9.39

COLONSAY ATTABOY

COLONSAY FLAMING ONION

KINMOUNT PIP 11.9.35

TINY TIM OF BIFFIN

DAWN OF CYNVAL

SNELSTON ROGUE

TIM

COLONSAY BOB JACK

DIMBOLS GEORGINA

COLONSAY GEORGE 7.11.38

COLONSAY FLAMING ONION

BUNDERBUST

COLONSAY

BCH BROWN AIRMANS AIRMANS EVER READY AIRMANS SMUDGE

KINMOUNT PIP

TINY TIM OF BIFFIN

CH BIFFIN OF BEAUFIN

LITTLE JANE OF BEAUFIN

KINMOUNT JACK

KINMOUNT DUMPTY

SMUDGE (P.E.)

SMUDGE (P.E.)

PETO

PEGGOTTY

TWINKLE OF PETO

RED IKE

PINCHERS

COLONSAY PETBOX

FLAME

TRUMPINGTON TOWSER

JANE (II)

GEORGE

JILL

HORSTED MICK

JANE (II)

KIEN

GYP

CARR

SUSAN

KIEN

LITTLE JANE

CH BIFFIN OF BEAUFIN

LITTLE JANE

TINY TIM OF BIFFIN

KINMOUNT PIP

KINMOUNT DUMPTY

KINMOUNT JACK

AIRMANS SAM BROWNE

AIRMANS JACK

GYP

KIEN

SUSAN

CARR

GYP

KIEN

LITTLE JANE

PINCHUS

HORSTED MICK

FLAME

CH FARNDON RED DOG 1933

JUDY

BABBLING BINKS

MIDGE OF BOXTED

TINY TIM OF BIFFIN

PINCHUS

BOXTED SOVEREIGN

NEACHLEY

TEASEL OF BOXTED

CH BIFFIN OF BEAUFIN

LITTLE JANE

HORSTED MICK

FLAME

RUFUS

MIDGE

HORSTED MICK

NEACHLEY RUSTY

KY

POL

PEPPER

TOBIT

NEACHLEY TOFFEE

APRIL 1928

KIEN

TOBIT

FRERE

SCAMP

SUSAN

CARR

GYP

KIEN

NEACHLEY TOFFEE

TOBIT

TOP FRED

MICKY

OH DEAR

CRUMPET

JUMBLE

AYLSHAM

MINK

TOODLUMS

SCAMP

FRERE

SUSAN

CARR

GYP

KIEN

HORSTED TEMPEST

NEACHLEY

TOBIT

MIDGE

PEPPER

POL

KY

TUT TUT

BABBLING BINKS

POL

JACK

MIDGE

PEPPER

POL

KY

TUT TUT

BABBLING BINKS

1921

DORCAS

PEPPER

AYLSHAM

MINK

SCAMP

FRERE

SUSAN

CARR

GYP

KIEN

HORSTED MICK

NEACHLEY RUSTY

KY

POL

MIDGE

JACK

PEPPER

POL

MIDGE

JACK

BABBLING BINKS

TUT

POL

KEN

PEPPER

MIDGE

TOBIT

AIRMANS BROWNE

SAM BROWNE

NEACHLEY

AIRMANS

KINMOUNT JACK

JOSE

MUSTARD

BUSTLE

BEN MUSTARD

KY

POL

JACK DAW

SCAMP

FRERE